JN441426

Managing Transnational Flows in East Asia

Edited by

Shirlena Huang
Mike Hayes
Sang Kook Lee

Jimoondang
Seoul

Jimoondang
85 Gwanginsa-gil, Paju-si, Gyeonggi-do, 413-756, Korea
82 Donhwamun-ro, Jongno-gu, Seoul, 110-360, Korea
Phone: 82-2-743-3096 E-mail: edit@jimoon.co.kr
82-2-743-3192~3 E-mail: sale@jimoon.co.kr
Fax: 82-2-743-0227, 82-2-742-4657
Homepage: www.jimoon.co.kr

The National Library of Korea Cataloging-in-Publication (CIP)
Managing Transnational Flows in East Asia
Edited by Shirlena Huang, Mike Hayes and Sang Kook Lee
Paju: Jimoondang, 2012
ISBN 978-89-6297-151-4 93300 309.11-KDC5 950-DDC21 CIP2012005193

Printed in Korea

Acknowledgements

This volume is an outcome of the Korea-ASEAN Academic Conference on "Revisiting Transnationalism in East Asia: Emerging Issues, Evolving Concepts," held on 9-12 February 2011 in Bali, Indonesia, jointly organised by the ASEAN University Network (AUN) and Korean Association of Southeast Asian Studies (KASEAS). On behalf of AUN and KASEAS, we express our gratitude to the ASEAN Secretariat and the Ministry of Foreign Affairs and Trade, Republic of Korea for their generous support to organise the conference and make this volume possible. Special thanks also go to Professor Nantana Gajaseni, Executive Director of AUN; Naparat Phirawattanakul, Senior Programme Officer of AUN; Professor Jinpyo Yoon, former President of KASEAS; and Dong Yeob Kim, former Secretary of KASEAS.

We thank the contributors of the various papers in this volume for their patience and commitment to the project, and Rica Agnes Castaneda for her assistance in copyediting this book. We would also like to note that other papers from the Bali conference appear in a special issue on "Transnational Migration in East Asia" published in 2012 in *Asian and Pacific Migration Journal*, Vol. 21 (2).

Shirlena Huang, Mike Hayes and Sang Kook Lee
August 2012

Notes on the Editors and Contributors

Chantana Banpasirichote (PhD, University of Waterloo, Canada) is an Associate Professor, and serves as the Head of the Department of Government, Faculty of Political Science, Chulalongkorn University. Her training background was in Regional Planning and Resources Development. Her recent research interest is on non-conventional politics, focusing on development issues, democracy, human security and conflict resolutions.

Byong-Hee Cho (PhD, Sociology, University of Wisconsin-Madison, USA) is a Sociologist with special interest in health, illness and medicine. His research topics span from the study of Korean doctors and their profession (post 2000), to understanding medicalised everyday life. His current topic of interest is risk/trust, health promotion/community capacity, and alternative medicine, closely looking at the notion of trust in the relationship and risk perception related to HIV/AIDS and other communicable diseases such as Variant Creutzfeldt-Jakob disease (vCJD) and Avian flu. He has also conducted research on community health, health promotion and social networks of community organisations.

Mike Hayes (PhD, History and Communication Cultural Studies, University of Wollongong, Australia) is currently the Director of the Masters in Human Rights Programme at the Institute for Human Rights and Peace Studies, Mahidol University's Salaya Campus. He also teaches in a number of university programmes and professional courses throughout Southeast Asia, mainly in the areas of human rights and development. He is also involved in research in non-citizen rights, the media, and capacity development.

Shirlena Huang (PhD, Geography, University of Toronto, Canada) is an Associate Professor of Geography and a Vice Dean of the Faculty of Arts and Social Sciences at the National University of Singapore. Her research focuses on issues at the intersection of migration and gender (particularly labour migration and transnational families within the Asia-Pacific region), as well as urban redevelopment and conservation. Her publications include over 70 international journal articles, book chapters and encyclopedia entries, and the co-edited volumes, *Gender Politics in the Asia Pacific Region* (Routledge, 2002), *Asian Women as Transnational Domestic Workers* (Marshall Cavendish, 2005) and *The Cultural Politics of Talent Migration in East Asia* (Routledge, 2012).

Jaehyon Lee (PhD, Politics, Murdoch University, Australia) is a Visiting Professor at the Institute of Foreign Affairs and National Security (IFANS), Korean National Diplomatic Academy. He received his BA and MA from Yonsei University, Korea. He has published many articles and book chapters both in English and Korean. Selected publications include "Prospect for Korea-Southeast Asia Relations" in *Regional Outlook: Southeast Asia 2010-2011* and "Political crises after democratization in South Korea and Thailand" in *Korea Observer*, 2008. His research interests include Southeast Asian politics and international relations, ASEAN, Korea-ASEAN relations, and East Asian regional cooperation.

Sang Kook Lee (PhD, Anthropology, National University of Singapore) is an Assistant Professor at the Institute for East Asian Studies, Sogang University, Seoul, Korea. He has done research on refugees, cross-border movements and frontier societies in Southeast Asia. His publications include "Scattered but Connected: Karen Refugees' Networking in and beyond the Thailand-Burma Borderland," "Borderland Dynamics in Mae Sot, Thailand and the Pursuit of the Bangkok Dream and Resettlement" and "White Saviors and the Karen: A Karen Myth Becoming Reality."

Morshidi Sirat (PhD, Geography, Southampton University, United Kingdom) is a Professor of Urban Geography, School of Humanities, Universiti Sains Malaysia, Penang and the current Deputy Director-General, Department of Higher Education (Public Sector), Ministry of Higher Education in Malaysia. Morshidi has published several books and journal articles on topics related to higher education. He is also active in international research collaboration with organisations such as OECD/IMHE, the World Bank, UNESCO, the ADB, SEAMEO-RIHED and International Institute for Educational Planning in Paris. Presently, Morshidi is working on issues relating to international student experiences in Malaysia, specifically looking at policies to integrate students with the local communities.

Kwang Woo Noh (PhD, Mass Communication and Media Arts, Southern Illinois University, USA) is currently a Researcher at the Research Institute for Information and Culture, Korea University. He has published articles in the *Journal of the Korea Contents Association*, and Asian Cinema, to name a few. He previously organised New York's first festival on Korean cinema.

Inosentius Samsul (LL.D. Law, University of Indonesia) is a graduate of Constitutional Law from the Gadjah Mada University in Yogyakarta, and a Master of Law in International Trade Law from the Tarumanagara University in Jakarta. He is a senior researcher and has been a legislative drafter in the House of Representatives of the Republic of Indonesia for since 1990. He is also Lecturer in the University of Indonesia and University of Pancasila, and the Academic Director of the Law Postgraduate Program in University of Mahendradatta, Denpasar, Bali, Indonesia.

Jakkrit Sangkhamanee (PhD, Anthropology, The Australian National University) is a Lecturer at the Department of Sociology and Anthropology, Faculty of Political Science, Chulalongkorn University, Thailand. His areas of research interest include political ecology, anthropology of development, sociology of knowledge and cross-border studies.

Doobo Shim (PhD, Journalism and Mass Communication, University of Wisconsin-Madison, USA) is a Professor in the Department of Media and Communications at Sungshin Women's University, Seoul, Korea. He does research on media within critical, cultural and historical perspectives. His recent research focuses on the rise of Korean popular culture in Asia. Shim was previously an Assistant Professor at the National University of Singapore. His publications include *Pop Culture Formations across East Asia* (Jimoondang: Seoul, 2010), and many articles in international academic journals including *Asian Journal of Women's Studies, Media, Culture and Society, Acta Koreana, and Prometheus.*

Tran Kien (LLM Law, University of Glasgow, United Kingdom) is currently doing his PhD in Law at the University of Glasgow, the United Kingdom. He earned his Bachelors in Law (with Distinction) from Vietnam National University, Hanoi in 2007. His main interests lie in private law including but not limited to property (including intellectual property), contract, and corporation. He has also been involved in a number of projects concerning comparative law, human rights, and constitutional law studies.

Vu Cong Giao (PhD, Human Rights and Peace Studies, Mahidol University, Thailand) is one of several experienced human rights experts in Vietnam. He earned his first LLM degree on constitutional law from the Institute of State and Law in Vietnam in 2002 and his second LLM degree on International Human Rights Law from Raul Wallenberg Institute, Lund University, Sweden in 2005. He previously worked for the Research Institute of Human Rights under the Ho Chi Minh National Political Academy, Vietnam (1996-2005), Vietnam Lawyers' Association (2006-2009). He is currently teaching Constitutional and Human rights, as well as responsible for the International Relations and Human Rights Education Programmes of the School of Law, Vietnam National University Hanoi.

Contents

Part 2 Flows of Phenomena: Disease, Disaster and Crime

Part 3 Flows of Practices: Advocacy, Knowledge and Culture

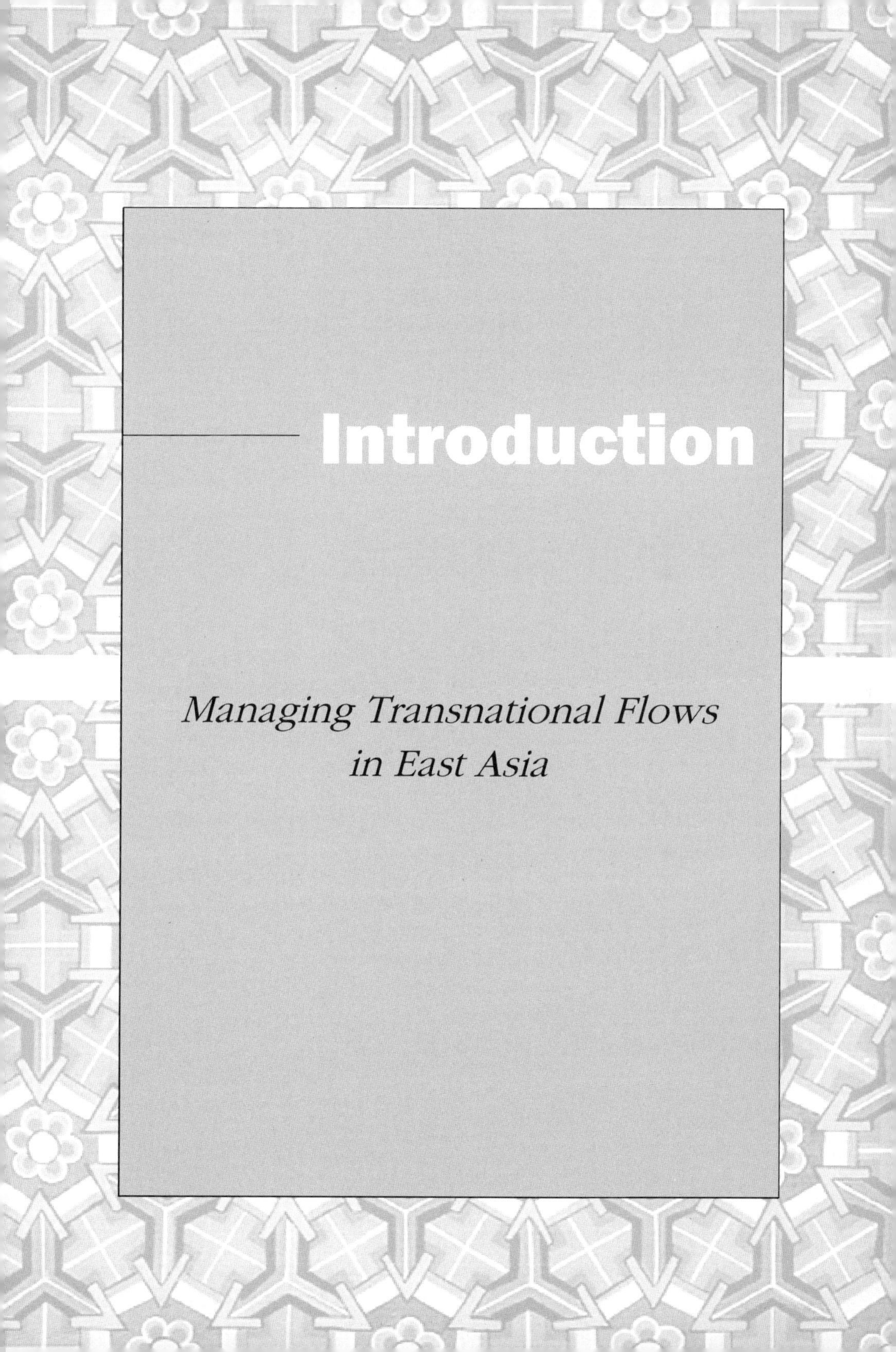

Introduction

Managing Transnational Flows in East Asia

Managing Transnational Flows in East Asia

Shirlena Huang
Mike Hayes
Sang Kook Lee

1. Introduction

This volume is about the connectivities of social, cultural, economic, political and other realms across national boundaries today brought about by the phenomenon that has come to be known as globalisation, or "the intensification of worldwide social relations which link distant localities in such a way that local happenings are shaped by events occurring many miles away and vice versa" (Giddens 1990, p. 64). Indeed, today, we recognise that this intensification of worldwide relations is better described by the term "transnational" in recognition of the condition of sustained and multiple interconnectedness and constant cross-border mobility of all kinds of bodies, phenomena, ideas and practices, both legally and illegally, across geographical space and social fields located in two or more nation-states. While some transnational flows are welcome (for example, valuable ideas, good practices and useful technologies), others (such as undesirable values, diseases and environmental problems) are less so. Whether wanted or unwanted, transborder movements often present challenges to the authority, integrity and security of nation-states, and may even give rise to political tensions (and even apparent tit-for-tat politics) between source and destination countries; however, they also present opportunities for regional and international cooperation between governments to manage the effects of the flows and diffuse potential political flashpoints.

Indeed, the currency of such transnational flows in East Asia, by which we mean Southeast Asia and Northeast Asia, is obvious from just a quick glance at the media. In the months that we were finalising this volume in the first half of 2012, news reports of all the above-mentioned transnational phenomena could be found in the media. For example, in March 2012, Malaysia's *New Straits Times* (4 March 2012) reported that a newly-signed (in July 2011) Memorandum of Understanding (MoU) between Malaysia and Indonesia was in jeopardy after reports of "two maids [being] physically abused by a senior government official and his wife" were received and the Indonesian embassy in Malaysia had advised the Indonesian Government "to suspend the sending of maids to Malaysia indefinitely." A couple of months later, the *Jakarta Globe* (19 May 2012) reported that the Malaysian Government had deported 81 Indonesian migrant workers (61 males and 15 females) after they had been held for three months at a detention centre; they had been arrested for not having their passports. In June 2012, the ASEAN (Association of Southeast Asian Nations) region experienced a recurrence of transboundary haze pollution caused by land and forest fires in Indonesia. As noted by *The New York Times* (23 June 2012) the haze "has become a recurring summer blight, engulfing parts of Malaysia, Thailand, Brunei and Singapore, and leaving a litany of health and economic costs in its wake." Since 1997/98, when the region faced some of its most severe episodes of haze arising from the forest fires, ASEAN nations have pledged to work together to combat the issue. Also in June 2012, the Food and Agriculture Organization's (FAO) Regional Office for Asia and the Pacific reported a rise of bovine foot-and-mouth disease in the agricultural economies of Southeast Asia and that Korea, because of its experience and expertise in handling such outbreaks, would be funding efforts to combat this "cross-border cattle disease" as well as sharing its knowledge to countries like Cambodia, Lao PDR and Vietnam (FAO, 27 June 2012). Around the same time, with Korean popular culture (K-Pop) having diffused to the shores of Singapore for the past year or two, fans of the Hallyu wave prepared to welcome Korean pop groups and performers (such as SHINee, B1A4, Teen Top, Jay Park and 7.9.4.2) to the country for a concert in June 2012 (*Channel News Asia*, 19 June 2012).

These cases, drawn from a short span of a few months in 2012, exemplify the range and diversity of issues in the contemporary politics of transnational flows in East Asia. While transnationalism is most often associated with migration, the examples above suggest that all transnational processes take place within a framework of interests and obligations that link countries of origin and destination. The papers in this collection cover three broad categories of transnational flows and their implications for source and destination countries: the international movements of labour; cross-border flows of threatening phenomena (such as disasters and diseases) and the transnational diffusion of ideas and cultures. International migrants, especially the unskilled and less skilled contract workers, who move in and out of East Asia are often caught between the "hegemonic dynamics"—to use Piper's (2011) term—of the policies of sending and receiving countries on the one hand, and the politics of international migration which often entails bilateral agreements and multi-organisation negotiations regarding the rights of the sending nation's citizens in host destinations on the other. At times, there is a disruption of relations between states when the rights of the sending nation's citizens are seen to be ignored. Many countries in East Asia are also facing new sources of transnational threats that transcend their borders. These include diseases, natural disasters and crimes. While these transnational challenges push individual countries of the region to come up with at times non-conventional measures, the responses are more often than not state centric, reflecting that defense of sovereignty and territory (rather than multi-dimensional cooperation with other partners and countries) continues to be key concerns for countries in East Asia. Another consequence of a more transnational world is the greater flow of information and culture in and out of states. This is an area where the state is only one arbiter in the space of flows, and it is clear that in an age of technology, the management of transnational flows of knowledge and practices—whether of formalised ideas, or of folk or popular culture—does not fall within the state's regulatory capacity but sits to different degrees within the scope of private institutions and individuals.

Overall, the ability of states to combat transnational challenges which already transcend the scope of bounded nations varies, depending on the particular phenomenon. While it would seem logical that transnational challenges would encourage countries to band together to deal with the problems and issues in concert, it would appear that for East Asia, transnational challenges have not overpowered the nationalistic voices of individual countries in the making of regional coping schemes, and many of the cases highlighted in the chapters of the book illustrate clearly that the state of regional cooperation in East Asia is still determined by state-centrism. However, the management of transnational flows should not be the purview of only the state. Other partners such as international organisations (e.g. International Organization of Migration, ASEAN), Non-Governmental Organisations (NGOs) and grassroots organisations also have key roles in helping to develop mechanisms for cooperation between nations. Furthermore, individuals and groups directly involved in or impacted by transnational flows, should also have their say in the regulation of flows through policy formulation. As Castles (2011, p. 236) has cautioned, management should not be a top-down process as such an approach "cannot resolve the crucial issues at stake"; instead, he notes that in the context of migration, "management should be understood as a cooperative process in which all participants have a voice, including the governments and civil societies of the sending countries, the receiving populations and above all the migrants themselves. To be effective, policies need to be fair and to be perceived as fair by all the groups involved." To what extent has this approach been applied at national, regional and global levels by countries in East Asia to manage the challenges arising from transnational flows of people (in the form of skilled and unskilled migration), phenomena (such as crime, disease, and disaster) as well as ideas and practices (including formal knowledge, folk beliefs and popular culture)?

2. People: Labour Migration

The study of international migration is often framed by transnationalism and the accompanying notion of globalisation. Research has suggested that the underlying factors behind migration can be modeled, conceptualised and often attributed to broader structural issues associated with global economic transformations. Indeed, the academic literature is replete with statements that note how the contemporary movements of people for work, particularly the migration of female labour, has been a response to the imbalances in wealth and resource distribution between the global North and South, and that globalisation has impacted the volume, direction and characteristics of international migration today. However, much less attention has been paid to theorising differential migrant movements in different regions of the world and how and why policy makers act (or fail to act) to protect their citizens in motion, or the migrant workers in their midst. Additionally, there is a relative absence of global governance with regard to international migration (Castles 2011, p. 233). Internationally available conventions and legal norms regulating migrant rights exist and could protect migrant workers, especially the less skilled and the women, but "rarely do any of the countries receiving migrant workers sign, let alone implement, such conventions" (Piper 2011, p. 260). As such, many states in Southeast Asia are complicit in perpetuating migration regimes that deprive migrant workers of employment and even basic human rights (Elias 2010, p. 78); however, the situation appears better in the host societies of Northeast Asia.

The chapters by **Vu Cong Giao** and **Tran Kien** and **Inosentius Samsul** make it clear that because of the lack of ratifications of international agreements such as the International Convention on the Protection of the Rights of All Migrant Workers and Members of their Families, otherwise known as the Migrant Workers Convention (MWC), unskilled workers from Vietnam and Indonesia are often accorded rights by the receiving countries that are much more limited than those they enjoy at home. Vu Cong and Tran note how, in the general absence of ASEAN countries' ratification of international treaties to protect migrant workers from abuse (no predominantly receiving country in ASEAN has signed the MWC), regional agreements are key in coordinating efforts among the member nations to protect workers. Given that the two principal migration corridors in Southeast Asia—first, the archipelagic ASEAN corridor with Malaysia, Singapore and Brunei as the major destination countries of migrant workers from Indonesia and the Philippines; and second, the Mekong sub-regional corridor with Thailand as the main destination country for migrant workers from Burma, Cambodia, Lao PDR and Vietnam (Kaur 2010)—involve all its member states, such regional agreements are needed to reinforce individual state's efforts to ensure workers receive fair treatment overseas. With respect to the latter, Vu Cong and Tran also highlight how the state authorities in Vietnam have been able to better perform their role in ensuring the provisions for the protection of its overseas workers when from 1990 onwards, it began to devolve its role of recruiting, contracting and marketing Vietnamese workers for export (and profit) to private enterprises, and concentrated instead on policy making and state management functions. This has allowed the Vietnamese government to put in place laws and regulations to monitor the rights and obligations of the labour export agencies as well as those of the workers. Hence, for example, the laws and regulations prohibit workers from being sent to work in industries and occupations that are deemed to have inhumane working conditions on the one hand, while requiring pre-departure training and cultural orientation on the other.

Vu Cong and Tran recognise, however, that these aforementioned mechanisms are inadequate and a long list of problems arising from abuse, unfair treatment, fraud and the lack of support continues to characterise the lives of overseas contract workers from Vietnam and other Asian countries. In particular, they highlight the patriarchal traditions and institutions that impact the patterns of women's international migration (usually in a narrow band of service occupations and under precarious conditions) in Asian societies such as Vietnam, and result in the very different experiences as compared to those of men, particularly in terms of women's higher levels of vulnerability and abuse (see also Geddes 2011; Piper 2011). They end their chapter with a series of proposed measures that governments of sending countries such as Vietnam should put in place to ensure more effective protection of their citizens working overseas. They draw attention to the importance of "go[ing] beyond the tendency to turn out 'one size fits all' pieces of legislation" (p. 51) and move towards measures that recognise the gendered nature of international migration. This is significant because, to date, an indifference to migrants' gender-specific activities, practices and concerns has led to gender-blind policies and management of migrant workers, and hence to a failure to protect the most vulnerable group of migrant workers in both countries of origin and destination.

The difference that strong legal structures, policy frameworks and bilateral agreements make to the protection of migrant workers is unmistakable in Samsul's chapter on Indonesian migrant workers (IMWs) and their divergent experiences in Malaysia and Korea; despite sharing cultural similarities with Malaysia, the country ranks the highest in terms of rights violations to Indonesian migrant workers (IMWs) while Korea, which is culturally more different, is perceived as the most favourable destination for IMWs. Unlike Vietnam where the state has moved on to focus on the management of its overseas workers, Indonesia's policy of sending workers abroad as an economic strategy without legal protection since 1988, reduces each worker to little more than "a trading commodity" (p. 58) and hence vulnerable to maltreatment and all forms of human rights violations. Perhaps Indonesia's slowness in formalising an MoU with Malaysia with regard to Indonesian domestic workers in Malaysia is unsurprising given that it is only now discussing the issue of establishing legislation to protect domestic workers within Indonesia. In contrast, Indonesia's cooperative agreement with Korea gives rise to benefits at the level of the worker (e.g. pre-departure training, better wages and working conditions) as well as the sending country (e.g. reduction of unemployment) and the host nation (e.g. labour supply, decline in illegal IMWs).

As Samsul points out, however, signing bilateral agreements with receiving countries is insufficient. Such agreements must be supported by "a well-managed system of sending migrant workers" (p. 69) if Indonesia is to provide "comprehensive and a high standard of protection for IMWs" (p. 69). Beyond ensuring that national standards meet with those of international conventions, Samsul argues that a key component of a better managed system of labour export is the translation of broad laws into detailed stipulations that can be operationalised on the ground. We would argue that a "well-managed system" of transnational flows of migrant labour also requires receiving nations to do their part. As observers such as Kaur (2010, p. 13) have pointed out in the context of Malaysia:

> …the state's weak governance structures have resulted in the marginalization and vulnerability of low-skilled migrant workers. … A major flaw is the large number of ministries and government agencies involved in the recruitment process and also the labyrinth of jurisdictions and poor inter-ministerial and departmental coordination that make it almost impossible for workers to seek redress and justice. … Employers retain their workers' passports, making them vulnerable to being caught by Malaysia's voluntary neighbourhood corps, RELA, and detained in detention camps.

Additionally, Malaysia's system of licensing firms to source migrant workers effectively transforms them into labour brokering firms and the contract workers they recruit into "bonded labour" (Kaur 2010, p. 13). Others, such as Piper (2011) and Elias (2010), have noted how NGOs that agitate for migrant workers' rights "still meet considerable barriers … from governments in the East and Southeast Asia region. … [T]he appropriation of rights talk by activist groups is clearly limited by the significant role that states in the region play in shaping and constraining civil activism" (Elias 2010, p. 78). As argued earlier, effective management of transnational migration must be an inclusive and cooperative process involving all levels of the system, from international organisations and governments, to civil society and individual migrants.

While transnational labour flows of migrants from the less well-off nations of Southeast Asia moving to the more well-off countries for less skilled contract work are often discussed in the literature, flows of skilled labour have been given much less attention. It is clear from the discussion of skilled worker migration to and from Malaysia by **Morshidi Sirat** that the politics of high skilled migration are quite different from those related to low-skilled migration. Unlike low-skilled migrants whose "export" is often treated like that of a commodity, sending states like Malaysia may endow their citizens who have moved to work abroad as skilled migrants with special rights and recognitions, in the hope of ensuring their long-term return (see also Nyberg-Sorenson et al. 2011). Like many countries that are pushing towards a knowledge-based economy (KBE), the Malaysian government is extremely concerned about the mobility of transnational skilled workers, from the perspective of Malaysia both as a source and host country. To ensure that it does not lose out in the fierce competition for talent in East Asia, the Malaysian government set up a Talent Corporation specifically to manage the transnational flow of world class talent, including Malaysian emigrants, to (and from) Malaysia so as to build its base of skilled human capital. Because the highly skilled are much more mobile and can move relatively freely among states (at least compared to lower-skilled workers), Morshidi highlights how Malaysia has found it as "tricky" to attract top talent to its shores as it is to attract skilled Malaysians home. Recognising that it is much easier for countries like Australia, Canada, the United Kingdom and the United States of America to draw skilled migrants, including Malaysians (particularly the "student-turned-migrant"), he flags the need for Malaysia's immigration process to be simplified in terms of a relaxation of entry criteria and enhanced in terms of the offering of better incentives to global talent. More specifically, he argues for a rethinking of Malaysia's current policy discourse focusing on getting its overseas diaspora to return home, which he contends is an "uphill task" given that this group of Malaysians are likely to be disgruntled with the state's policies on ethnic relations, its bureaucracy and the country's wider political landscape. Instead, he forwards a proposal much in the spirit of transnationalism: "Within the country's context, emigration must be considered within a framework of migration for the purpose of nation-building which includes the mode of 'contribution from a distance'" (p. 84). Thus, rather than viewing Malaysians overseas as scarce human capital plundered by richer countries of the west, he advocates that the government would be better off managing the process by strengthening the transnational practices of Malaysians abroad, both in terms of their reliance on their homeland as well as enabling them to "contribute from a distance."

In sum, then, the national and transnational contexts of labour migration are constantly shifting—laws are changed to impede or facilitate cross-border movements, international conventions are drawn up, bilateral agreements are negotiated and MoUs may or may not be signed, societal and cultural norms shift, and governments may decide to take more, or less, of an active role in promoting the outward flow of its citizens as overseas workers for economic reasons, or bringing home its skilled diaspora for development at home, and so on. Under the forces of globalisation, people will continue to move internationally for work. For effective management of such transnational flows of migrants, state policies for any country must continue to remain agile and move away from a "top down" state centrist approach and aim to include all participants of the process, including other countries from which it attracts migrant workers and to which its citizens move to work.

3. Phenomena: Disease, Disaster and Crime

The chapters in the Part 2 of the book highlight how a statist approach has also been problematic in tackling phenomena such as diseases, natural disasters and crime that transcend national boundaries and thus require a transnational scope. However, states in East Asia deal with these cross-border issues from a conventional stance where national sovereignty is the most crucial concern. As with the issue of labour migration, such a state-centric approach dismisses collaborations with other players such as NGOs and the people themselves who have transnational connections and capabilities to contribute to the tackling of these non-traditional security problems. The chapters elaborate on how these transnational threats are easily exploited by the state to build up statecraft. The state makes use of them to strengthen its regulatory capacity, consequently destabilising the lives of vulnerable non-citizens. While revealing the irresistible transnational processes that the state in East Asia cannot avoid in today's globalising world, the state's strong appeal to the traditional norms of state security also exposes the immaturity of the state in responding to transnational issues. East Asia is at the moment facing tension between transnational processes and nationalistic responses. The chapters suggest that we need to go beyond "methodological nationalism" (see Beck 2000; Glick Schiller 2009) if we are to understand how transnationalism shapes the statecraft of individual countries as well as the regional cooperation schemes of East Asia.

Byong-Hee Cho compares the statist and the global approaches through a focus on transnational diseases. While the former deals with transnational diseases as an internal affair with a national security perspective, the latter approaches it from a human rights stance, cooperating with partners such as NGOs and paying special attention to the fundamental causes of a disease, for instance, poverty, illiteracy and inequality. Drawing on the cases of China, Australia and Korea, Cho demonstrates how each approach produces different outcomes in response to transnational health threats. He identifies one of the main reasons for the worldwide outbreak of SARS (Severe Acute Respiratory Syndrome) from November 2002 to August 2003—the failure of the Chinese government to disclose the SARS information because the government was more preoccupied with the issue of national security and hence reluctant to cooperate with international organisations and with other countries. It was only when the situation became critical that the government had to disclose the occurrence of SARS and rely on global collaboration to combat it as a transnational issue. The case demonstrates how China's statist tactics in trying to manage the disease ironically made it even more of an international matter rather than allowing it to be successfully combatted in an effective way.

Shifting his attention to the case of AIDS (acquired immune deficiency syndrome), Cho then compares the responses of Australia and Korea to this health problem. Australia took a community-based approach and cooperated with other partners including homosexuals themselves. The government chose an AIDS prevention strategy, defining the fundamental cause of the disease as a lifestyle rather than as a virus, and promoting homosexuals' role in developing health education and practising safer sex. This resulted in the successful decrease of HIV infections. In contrast, the Korean government adopted a more statist approach to managing the problem of AIDS. While it successfully tackled the disease, it neglected to protect the rights and welfare of the infected. Instead, the latter were regarded merely as criminals and enemies in Korean society. Based on the Korean case, Cho identifies the limitations of the statist approach. For instance, mandatory testing imposed by the government turned out to be inefficient and did not bring about the hoped-for behavioral changes because the state failed to take advantage of the transnational connections and resources of the community-based organisations, NGOs and international organisations in their midst.

In a similar vein, **Jaehyon Lee** critiques the detrimental impact of state centrism on regional cooperation with regard to transnational natural disasters and environment issues in East Asia. The economic growth of countries in East Asia has allowed the countries of the region to turn to these issues, and regional cooperation to address these transborder issues has been growing in the region over the years. Lee provides an expanded scope to deal with Southeast Asia and Northeast Asia in an integrated framework concerning these transnational issues. His main argument is that state centrism is deeply associated with regional cooperation on these transnational issues in East Asia. He traces the historical development of this state centrism and suggests that "state building" has been a key project in colonial and post-colonial periods in East Asia. He identifies three symptoms that result from a state centric approach in managing transnational issues: mutual suspicion and a concern with relative gain; regional cooperation driven by developmentalism; and the exclusion of civil society.

Lee also observes that because transnational disasters such as tsunamis, earthquakes, cyclones, the haze and yellow sand phenomenon affect so many countries, they have become the bases to bringing individual countries together to cope with the problems. Although some schemes were established in earlier days in particular within ASEAN, it was only when the 2004 tsunami occurred that substantial progress towards managing the issues in a regional context became visible. As the main mechanism of East Asian cooperation, ASEAN+3 has been holding various levels of meetings to discuss natural disasters and environmental problems. Lee, however, contends that cooperation on these phenomena within East Asia is still underdeveloped in comparison to ASEAN. Even so, he goes on to argue that the cooperation schemes of ASEAN have also been inefficient. In response to his own provocative question of what went wrong with East Asia, he shows that the answer lies in the long history of state centrism in the region. If state centrism still characterises ASEAN despite its long history of over 40 years, what else can be expected of ASEAN+3 and the East Asian Summit, both of which have a relative short history? Individual member countries have been suspicious of other member countries in the same organisation and conscious about the relative gains of each country in the alliance. This mutual mistrust has made it difficult for individual countries to set aside sovereignty when it comes to regional matters. Indeed, as Lee reasons, state centrism has propelled them to pursue the maximisation of national interest rather than regional common good. Above all, it has dismissed the roles of partners such as NGOs, civil society and grassroots organisations which could contribute to the solving of the transnational problems. Lee suggests that these non-traditional security problems cannot be resolved in an efficient way without the participation of all these organisations that have developed transnational networks to engage in the issues. Like Cho, Lee appreciates their potential in tackling transnational phenomena.

Moving away from natural disasters and environmental problems, **Mike Hayes** reveals, through convincing evidence, the weak association between transnational migrants and crime. However, attempts to connect them persist, leading him to examine the multiple ways in which the myth of transnational migrants as criminals has come about in Southeast Asia and the consequences of such myth-making. He explores the role of the media in associating the transnational with crime, subsequently destabilising their lives and leading to their arrest and deportation. Indeed, widespread movements across porous borders in Asia and the expansion of transnational networks are exploited by transnational criminal organisations. Although this does not imply transnational migrants are more involved in crime, transnational communities can be easily stigmatised by the media and the state. Like Cho and Lee, Hayes displays a critical stance to the state. The state reacts to international crime from the security of the state, not from that of human beings. The strengthening of state capacity to cope with the crime often results in the persecution of transnational migrants. The state is still trapped in the traditional security framework where the defense of sovereignty and national borders is the key concern even though non-traditional security issues require a different approach (as with Lee). Hayes provocatively suggests that the transnational criminal is a ubiquitous figure not because transnational migrants are universally prone to crime but because criminal laws the state makes seek them out as easy targets. Thus, the basic rights of the migrants are ignored in the name of national security against transnational crime.

Hayes contends that globalisation does not weaken or mean the end of the state but instead, strengthens its capacity to police transnational crimes and fortify security policies. More importantly, the emergence of transnational organised crime has led to the development of international laws; a notable example is the United Nations Convention against Transnational Organized Crime. These laws enable the state to play a much stronger role and ensure that the state can prosecute international crime. However, Hayes states that although this move may contribute to lessening international crime, the state might misuse its power and violate human rights of migrants. His attention, then, moves to what aspects of transnational migration are linked to crime and invite state intervention. Here, smuggling and trafficking activities that take place with relative ease across porous borders in East Asia have been associated with transnational communities. On the one hand, their presence creates a significant incentive for people to risk being smuggled; on the other hand, it often provides an incentive for the state to strengthen security systems to eliminate these crimes. Smuggling and trafficking are to a great degree mediated and accelerated through transnational networks. Because these networks are persistent structures that can withstand significant damage, the response of the state through policing and arrest will have little impact. Hayes suggests that the responses must be multi-dimensional, the source of the problem addressed and the market for the problem reduced. All in all, he suggests that the state's increasing capacity to combat the phenomenon of transnational crime does not result in the protection of the rights of transnational migrants. Too often, transnational migrants lie outside the protection of the state and rather than being the perpetrators of the crimes, easily become instead, the scapegoats of feared transnational crimes.

In the region, nation-building involving the protection of sovereignty and borders is still an important task and transnational phenomena (such as diseases, disasters and crime) which present threats to national integrity are of great concern to the state. The continued prevalence of state centrism in East Asia poses a great obstacle to transnational cooperation in the regional context. Indeed, the pursuit of national interests has prevented even regional schemes that have been established from operating in an efficient and cooperative manner. As discussed next, such fortification, however, is even more difficult and hence less successful in the management of transnational flows of ideas and practices.

4. Practices: Advocacy, Knowledge and Culture

A consequence of a more transnational world is the greater flow of the intangible, in and out of states, in the form of ideas, beliefs, knowledge, information, customs, value systems and so on, and the range of practices associated with them. Some of these tend to be more institutionally bound within nation states, and others less so, but we need to ask what the relationship of these ideas and practices is to state power in the transnational context, when borders, cultures, and social understandings are traversed and even transgressed? The chapters in Part 3 of this collection address this question. Each paper is concerned with how ideas and practices—related to security, grassroots knowledge and popular and youth culture (music)—become formulated, distributed and potentially controlled. What is clear is that the state is only one arbiter of these flows of abstract phenomena. Indeed, the transnationalised context of their flows reveals that the state must cooperate or compete with a wide variety of institutions and individuals as their ideas and practices are challenged. In some areas like security, the states' views of what constitutes security is in competition with ideas from civil society organisations, while in the area of diseases, the state must learn to work together with them. Yet for other areas, like pop music which operates almost wholly within a corporate field, the state is almost absent.

Chantana Banpasirichote demonstrates how the state's desire to control ideas of security, in particular national security, is being challenged and overturned by civil society organisations which criticise the notion that the state should be the centre of security. They argue rather, that security should be "human centric," in that the focus of protection should be people and not the state. Banpasirichote explores how the turn to human security (also labeled non-traditional security within the ASEAN region) has come about. For some, the change was initiated by the state in response to the many regional disasters, such as tsunamis or the transboundary haze. However, as Banpasirichote shows, the pressure on the state to change ideas of security arises from other sources. The facts on the ground, in terms of what threatens people's lives, shows that armed conflict has been significantly reduced as a threat. Also, a more expansive definition of threat, which includes threats to health or food sources, asks states to consider protection in these normally non-security sectors. Finally, the incentive to transform has been influenced and assisted by NGOs through their advocacy.

All of these pressures change the way a state sees the utility of its security apparatus, for the military does not have the means to respond to many of these non-traditional security threats. Indeed, as Banpasirichote highlights, it is the state security apparatus that has been seen as the security threat in some Southeast Asian countries.

Banpasirichote details how civil society has been active in the transformation of security. Her paper shows how transnational networks of civil society organisations have been advocating for peoples' security agenda. In what has been termed "alternative regionalism," these networks respond to the policy agendas set by ASEAN and other inter-governmental regional organisations. Banpasirichote shows that there are several advantages of advocating at the regional level: the challenges to traditional security can be more specific and focused on issues most relevant in the region; regionalism calls for states to be regionally responsive and not just consider security as a concern within their territory; and finally, thinking of security at this level "transcends the dichotomy of state versus human security" (p. 168), so that security must consider how national security and human security are interrelated. Like many other papers in this collection, a key finding is the importance of civil society in managing concerns arising from globalisation. While quick to point out that civil society is not the magic solution for this sector, for there are inherent problems within civil society such as funding, Banpasirichote argues for greater linkages between civil society and the state in the form of "soft cooperation," or non-formal coordination in responding to issues of transnational social protection. What can be learned from Banpasirichote's paper is that the state can no longer monopolise issues such as security because the development of civil society has indelibly changed the system; this is shown by mapping out the transition from a state-centric and state-controlled response to security, to a transnational and civil society sympathetic response. This mapping of the historical transformation is also covered in the next paper by Sangkamanee, who examines changing responses to the environment around the Mekong River.

By outlining the historical context to the production of knowledge on the Mekong, **Jakkrit Sangkhamanee** shows how knowledge moved from traditional institutional centres, like the university, to more advocacy-based local knowledge at the level of the village. The diversity of knowledge on this river pre-existed the advent of nationalism. As Sangkamanee's historical analysis reveals, the river became a subject of colonial knowledge gathering as part of the civilising mission of French colonialism, and ultimately for commercial and political reasons. Yet, as Sangkamanee notes, even during these early colonial endeavours there existed an idea of a parallel realm of knowledge and ideas, or a local knowledge, which worked both in competition and cooperation with the knowledge produced by the colonial powers. However, these local perspectives were low in priority compared to the political agenda of controlling the river as a "strategic space," in the greater strategy for the occupation and control of territory between the colonial powers at the time.

Sangkamanee outlines how this production and control of knowledge moved from colonial institutes to academic institutions in post-World-War-Two Southeast Asia, ending up in practices of grassroots research and village level advocacy around issues of resource management and the environment by the 1980s. In the period immediately after World War Two, which coincided with the period of more scientific-orientated theories of development, the programmes focused primarily around making the river the subject of scientific studies. During the era, which emphasised the Modernisation theory in development, maximising resource use was prioritised. In the case of the Mekong, this appeared as damming the river for hydroelectricity or flood control, and increasing the amount of irrigated land. Knowledge here was directed at benefitting the national economy, although a border river like the Mekong made this problematic as resources are shared across different nation states. Hence, at this stage, the transnationalisation of knowledge was simply that of knowledge shared between nation states. It was not until the concept of "local knowledge" became prevalent in the study of the Mekong Basin that nation state-based understandings were challenged, and the emergence of what could be called a more transnational knowledge came to the fore. This transnational knowledge is knowledge not produced for the national economy, nor intended to emphasise national security, but knowledge that is either predominantly local (at the village level), or regional (knowledge for transnational advocacy around the environment). With protests from villagers and farmers against the impact of bad development (as in the case of the Pak Mun Dam), we see that knowledge operates on many levels: there is respect for knowledge created within the village; there is the use of this knowledge to bolster transnational activism through NGOs challenging unjust state-based development plans; and there is a diverse "transnational ecology" which Sangkamanee's argues leads to a contestation over the rights and control of resources.

While much attention has been devoted to how modern information and communication technologies allow for greater networking, monitoring, and advocacy in political arenas, relatively less has been done on knowledge flows in popular and youth cultures, especially within East Asia. The chapter by **Doobo Shim and Kwang Woo Noh** on fandom through YouTube in relation to Korean girl pop bands exposes the online culture, fandom, and the youth-managed discourse of information around the band Girls' Generation. Shim and Noh used "netnography" to study the community of fans online. Netnography is a research methodology for the study of online communities that essentially recognises online communication as a valid form of social interaction which may be understood through traditional anthropological methodology. By examining comments made online by these fans, Shim and Noh outline a number of socially significant points of both knowledge management, and of community participation. The management of online knowledge has interesting transnational consequences, for many fans see Korean pop music as a way to introduce Korean culture to the rest of the world. For example, this can be by detailing how Koreans count a person's age (starting from age one and not zero, like the west), or by giving basic language and vocabulary lessons so people can understand the lyrics. It is interesting that these forms of knowledge management conscript the fans in regimes of taste and behaviour as the practice of being a fan also demands certain norms, such as requests made to the fans that "I shall promote the girls to friends," or fans should "respect other groups" and not be involved in flaming wars with fans of other Korean pop music groups. The online community thus develops an etiquette for being an online fan.

Online communities like this are almost purely non-state. The national identity of the users can be unclear and the audience of viewers is global, as Shim and Noh point out. These online communities are hyper transnational in a sense, for they are only faintly grounded by a sense of nation (and in this case just the nationality of the pop group) and are more identified by the corporate structure of the Korean music industry and the media technology companies who make these online spaces available. This is not to say, as Shim and Noh argue, that the fans are merely a tool of the corporation. Rather there are still important affinities which provide a sense of community here, in terms of the affective ties and emotional investment of the fans to both the group and their fellow fans. The understanding which Shim and Noh provide here is in some ways quite similar to many studies of transnational or migrant communities, yet also radically different. More traditional studies will detail how aspects of a culture are transplanted from one situation to another, and how transnationals then construct a new culture away from their homes. With online communities, however, we are dealing with a deterritorialised space, as Shim and Noh contend, which cannot be transplanted, but is invented new. Hence, as the paper details, there is much time devoted to adumbrating rules, marking territory, and classifying values and ideas so as to manage the transnational flows of ideas and knowledge in and out of this space.

Overall, then, each of the papers in this final part of the book demonstrates the challenges to the power of the state in controlling the flows of ideas and practices across transnational borders, and how different groups—ranging from advocacy groups like NGOs, to local communities and even unseen online communities—produce a counter discourse to the state's management of the flows. The counter discourse does not operate within a uniform strategy across the different transnational passages of knowledge. The responses of NGOs to security or to environmental concerns (which are highlighted the papers by Banpasirichote and Sangkhamanee respectively) are similar in the sense that they demand that responses to threats must be seen not only from the state viewpoint alone, but also from the local and regional perspectives, a view made in a number of papers in this collection. For Shim and Noh, the opposition is not between state and civil society. Although the online fan groups they research are not grounded in the same territorial reality, challenges to state-centric knowledge exist in the very absence of the state from discussions of national identity in Korean pop music groups, as the authors have explored in their article.

5. Conclusion

The cross-border flows of people, phenomena, ideas and practices discussed in this collection (and summarised above) will continue to present challenges to states and societies in East Asia. In the region, the protection of sovereignty and borders is still an important task and in that sense, transnational issues which might unsettle it present great concern to the state. States need to acknowledge, where relevant, past policy failures in terms of state-centrist attempts to manage the issues. The scale, intensity and spread of these transnational issues requires a move towards a management regime that involves the constructive engagement of parties across the region and at all levels, from governments to civil society groups, to local communities (real or virtual) and the individual on the ground (whether citizen or migrant). While some of these transnational flows, especially those of ideas and practices, do better with less involvement from the state, other flows, such as the transnational movements of people and adverse phenomena, are at a scale and impact that require more state commitment (at regional and country level) to implementing effective policies and measures that will work on the ground. As such, transnationalism will continue to act as a barometer of regional cooperation in East Asia in the future.

References

Beck, U. (2000). "The Cosmopolitan Perspective: Sociology of the Second Age of Modernity." *British Journal of Sociology*, 51, 1, 79-105.

Castles, S. (2011). "The Factors that Make and Unmake Migration Policies." In A. Geddes, ed. *International Migration, Vol. 2*. London: Sage.

Channel News Asia (2012). "A night out with the K-Pop Boys" (19 June). Accessed on 18 August 2012 from http://www.channelnewsasia.com/stories/entertainmentfeatures/view/1208570/1/.html.

Elias, J. (2010). "Gendered Political Economy and the Politics of Migrant Worker Rights: The View from South-East Asia." *Australian Journal of International Affairs*, 64, 1, 70-85.

Food and Agriculture Organization (FAO) of the United Nations (2012). "FAO and Republic of Korea helping Southeast Asia fight a cross-border cattle disease" (12 June). Accessed on 18 August from www.fao.org/asiapacific/rap/home/news/detail/en/?no_cache=1&news_uid=148782.

Geddes, A. (2011). "Editor's Introduction." In A. Geddes, ed. *International Migration*, Vol. 1. London: Sage.

Giddens, A. (1990). *The Consequences of Modernity*. Stanford: Stanford University Press.

Glick Schiller, N. (2009). "A Global Perspective on Transnational Migration: Theorizing Migration without Methodological Nationalism." *Working Paper*, No. 67. Centre on Migration, Policy and Society (COMPAS), University of Oxford.

Jakarta Globe (2012). "Malaysia Deports 81 Indonesian Migrant Workers" (19 May). Accessed on 18 August 2012 from http://www.thejakartaglobe.com/home/malaysia-deports-81-indonesian-migrant-workers/518785.

Kaur, A. (2010). "Labour Migration in Southeast Asia: Migration Policies, Labour Exploitation and Regulation." *Journal of the Asia Pacific Economy*, 15, 1, 6-19.

New Straits Times (2012). "Fresh Maid Abuse Claims Hit Malaysia" (4 March). Accessed on 18 August 2012 from http://www.asiaone.com/News/AsiaOne+News/Malaysia/Story/A1Story20120304-331491.html.

The New York Times (2012). "Malaysia Haze Points to a Regional Problem" (23 June). Accessed on 18 August 2012 from http://www.nytimes.com/2012/06/24/world/asia/smoky-haze-over-malaysia-signals-a-regional-problem.html.

Nyberg-Sorenson, N., Van Hear, N. and Engberg-Pederson, P. (2002). "The Migration-Development Nexus Evidence and Policy Options: State-of-the-Art Overview." *International Migration*, 40, 5, 3-43.

Piper, N. (2011). "Feminization of Labor Migration as Violence against Women: International, Regional, and Local Nongovernmental Organization Responses in Asia." In A. Geddes, ed. *International Migration, Vol. 3*. London: Sage.

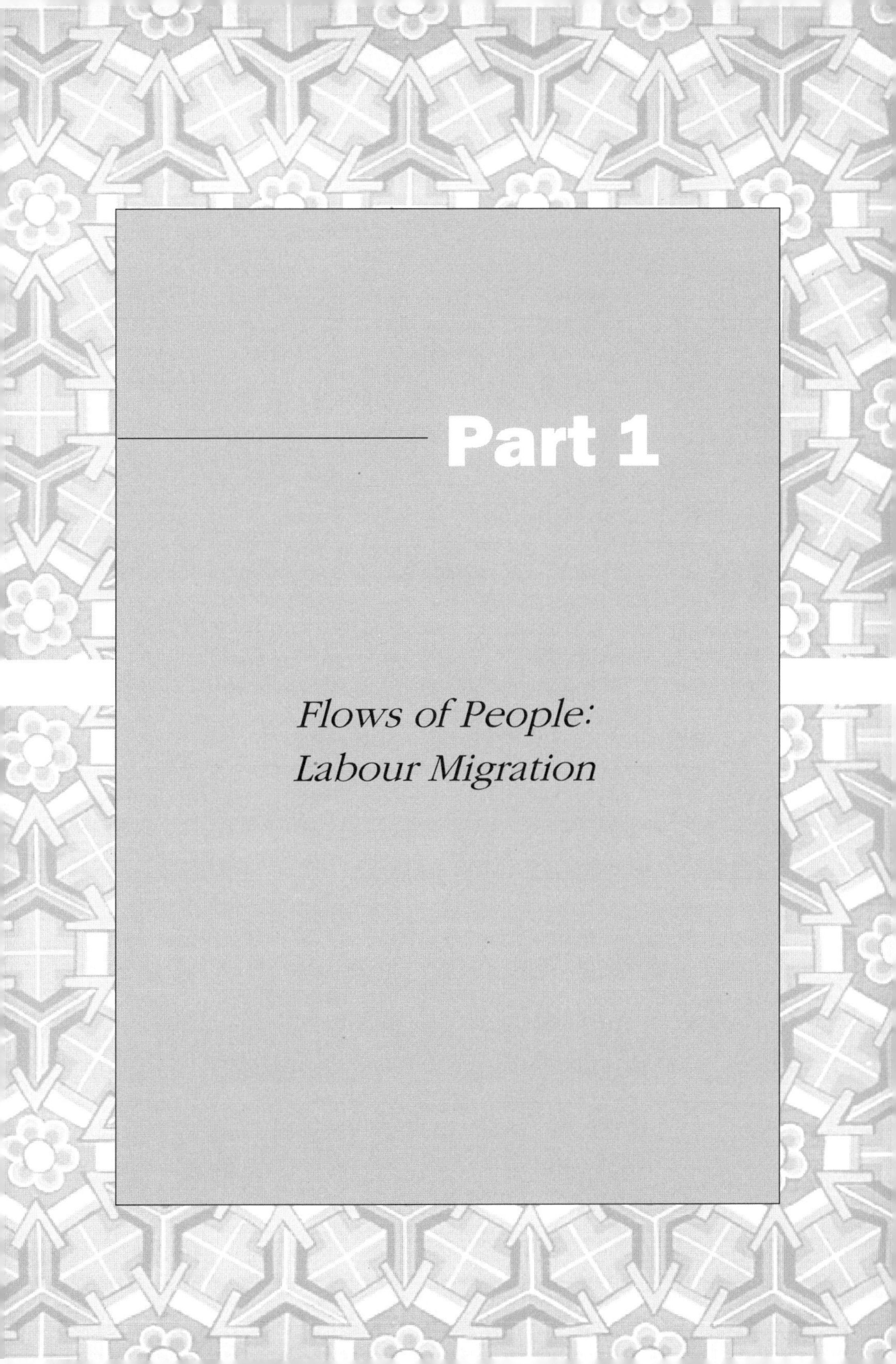

Part 1

Flows of People: Labour Migration

Protection of Overseas Vietnamese Labourers: Situation and Policy Challenges

Vu Cong Giao
Tran Kien

1. Overview

In this paper, the term "overseas Vietnamese labourers" is understood in a narrow sense, referring only to Vietnamese documented migrant workers in other countries under the contracts signed between local recruitment agencies and foreign partners; they, presumably, will return to Vietnam at the end of their contracts. In Vietnam, such migrants are called "export workers" or *lao dong xuat khau*. These workers are part of but do not include all Vietnamese documented migrant workers, which comprise both temporary and permanent migrant workers, in national statistical figures. For example, there are many other Vietnamese documented migrant workers who themselves go abroad to work under direct contracts; furthermore, there are also Vietnamese undocumented migrant workers working in many countries around the world, but their numbers are unknown. Due to the lack of data, these groups of migrant workers will not be discussed in this paper.

However, it is possible to confirm that "export workers" account for the highest number of Vietnamese labourers working abroad. Currently, it is estimated that there are about 500,000 documented Vietnamese workers working in 40 different countries in the world. Among these major receiving countries are Malaysia (34 per cent), Taiwan (27 per cent), Korea (14 per cent), Qatar (7 per cent) and Japan (5 per cent) (Dang 2011, pp. 79-80). The Government of Vietnam is expected to increase the number of overseas workers being deployed by up to 1.5

million by the end of 2015 (Vu & La 2011, p. 34).

Due to their large numbers, the money remitted by this group of workers makes the largest contribution to the total amount remitted home by all Vietnamese migrant workers (about USD1.6-2 billion each year) (Lao Dong Online 2010). This amount has significantly supported the financial situations of these workers' households, greatly improved the living conditions of their families, as well as met other essential needs, such as education (International Labour Migration Vietnam 2009). Beyond the economic benefits, the protection of the rights of these overseas workers has also been a significant challenge for the Government of Vietnam.

Hence, this paper will also examine the current legal framework of Vietnamese overseas workers, and analyse the main challenges presented to the Vietnamese government in protecting them. We also suggest a number of measures to promote the effective protection of the rights of this group against violations and wrongdoings brought about by local recruitment agencies, brokers and foreign employers. Before going into in-depth discussion, the following brief description will identify and describe who these Vietnamese overseas workers are within the broader international context.

The number of international migrants has increased dramatically, standing at 175 million at the dawn of the 21st century (Oishi 2005, p. 1). Conventionally, international migration has been perceived as a male dominated phenomenon. International migratory movements, especially those which are labour-related, are caused by demand-driven factors such as high unemployment, low wages and poverty. Labourers move from countries where poverty is visible, wages are relatively low and unemployment is at a level at which they cannot find a suitable job to support themselves or their families. Thus they are pushed to emigrate to foreign countries to work. A number of theories have been put forward to support the explanation of male-dominated international migration—ranging from neoclassical theory to structuralism and world systems theory. However, as Oishi (2005) pointed out in her work, these theories often focus on macro-level analyses which neglect the micro-level factors. Such theoretical gaps render these macro theories unable to provide a full account of international migrant movement in different regions in the world. In particular, they cannot help us understand the increase of women—48.6 per cent of the world's migrant workers in 2000 (Oishi 2005, p. 2)—within the number of international migrants. In Asia, for example, more and more women are participating in working overseas, most of them as temporary rather than permanent migrants. The majority of them work in other neighbouring countries in Asia, instead of going far away from home. These variables and corresponding analyses usually cannot be found in the abovementioned macro theories.

Within the Southeast Asian region, the growing figures of migrant workers seem to confirm both findings of conventional studies and of Oishi. ASEAN constituted nine per cent of the world's migrant workers in 2010. Low wages and high unemployment are the main reasons for international migration. The number is predicted to continue to increase as there are more than 148 million workers earning less than USD2 a day in ASEAN, while one out of ten earns less than USD1 a day (Vu & La 2011, p. 60). Such circumstances inevitably encourage labourers to emigrate for better jobs. However, no country in the region can be considered as a purely receiving or sending country of migrant workers any more. There is a growing trend of migrant workers of ASEAN countries migrating within the region, especially as temporary migrants. For instance, Thailand and Malaysia have each received 35 per cent of the ASEAN migrants coming to work in their countries, while also sending their workers to other countries to work (Vu & La 2011, p. 61).

The number of female migrant workers has also risen significantly. The so-called feminisation of migratory populations is considered one of six important changes and characteristic of international immigration in the 1990s (Vu & La 2011, p. 13). Not only do women account for nearly 50 per cent of the world's migrants, it is also reported that 40 per cent of Vietnam's overseas workers are women (International Labour Migration Vietnam 2009, p. 17). In the case of Vietnam, the scenario of women immigrating to either work or marry has given rise to tensions and fierce debate between Vietnam and receiving countries, in terms of national security, nationalism and human trafficking (International Labour Migration Vietnam 2009, p. 13). While the feminisation of migratory populations is increasing, much is still needed to be done in terms of research and study to comprehend its causes. Oishi (2005, pp. 2-3) pointed out a number of possible reasons to explain why migrant women are in high demand, the main cause being the restructuring of the global economy, with the global manufacturing sector requiring a large demand for female migrant labour; additionally, welfare states have failed to provide sufficient and effective welfare services to meet the actual needs of their citizens.

More specifically, the feminisation of international migration is seen as brought about by a combination of different factors working at different scales, ranging from the level of the supra state (globalisation and the international legal framework), to the macro level (the role of the state), the micro level (individual autonomy), as well as macro-micro links (social legitimacy) (Oishi 2005, pp. 10-14). Globalisation is surely a main push behind the drastic increase in the number of migrant workers (Vu & Pham 2011, p. 12). Factors such as the boom of the global economy, the ease of travel, and better connectivity between countries, enable workers, both male and female, to move around with ease to find jobs. These, however, are general arguments. To help us better understand the specific situations in Asia and particularly ASEAN, we need to consider the following issues.

First, international movements greatly depend on the state policies of both sending and receiving countries. Different countries raise different conditions to restrict or encourage certain types of migrant workers immigrating to their countries. In Asia, Taiwan favors female housekeepers and caregivers while Japan attracts "female entertainers." Bangladesh does not encourage their women to work overseas because of its religious and social perceptions. All in all, state policies exert significant influence on international migration.

Second, apart from the traditional causes noted above, research has also highlighted the decision making power of households, and the changes of social attitude toward female migrants as new determinant factors. It is easier for women in societies where they have more voice in their families to migrate for work abroad. For example, in Vietnam, only 23 per cent of overseas workers, both male and female, upon deciding to work abroad were met with protestations by their families (Vu & Pham 2011, p. 21). Understanding that migration is based on a household's collective decision, rather than on individual autonomy in Vietnam helps us understand why increasing numbers of Vietnamese women intend to emigrate to work overseas, especially in countries like Taiwan, Japan or Korea, all of which are favorite Vietnamese destinations (Vu & Pham 2011, p. 21).

While it is vital to understand the push factors of international immigration and the associated problems, resolving problems on the ground level should be given more emphasis. Within ASEAN, the most serious labour migration problems lie with the abuse of migrant workers by foreign employers. ASEAN has not been successful in adopting regional binding standards towards better working conditions for migrant workers. Many ASEAN countries have not ratified or joined the international treaties of the protection of migrant workers. For instance, only four countries—Indonesia, Cambodia, the Philippines and Timor Leste—are members of the International Convention on the Protection of the Rights of All Migrant workers and Members of their Families. Furthermore, the majority of ASEAN countries does not have an effective social welfare to protect and support all types of workers irrespective of work location (migrant or domestic). This deficiency, along with the absence of effective civil society organisations such as trade unions, makes the protection of migrant workers more difficult. Lastly, the differences in terms of working skills and experiences between domestic and migrant workers in the receiving country also trigger discrimination and abuse of these migrant workers by their foreign employers (Vu & La 2011, pp. 65-66).

To address these problems, ASEAN adopted the ASEAN Declaration on the Protection and Promotion of the Rights of Migrant Workers in 2007. This Declaration does not only sketch a principal framework with main goals for the protection of migrant workers, it also identifies key measures to achieve set goals. In addition, it sets a number of obligations that sending countries must fulfill to protect their emigrating workers. Along with other activities such as bilateral agreements, and regional forums on the protection of the migrant workers, it is hoped that the situation of ASEAN migrant workers will improve soon. However, as a global matter, international immigration and the protection of migrant workers, especially women, need global efforts to push through. One country (and region) alone will face difficulties in dealing with the issue. It needs globally coordinated efforts to resolve the occurring problem and better protect the legitimate rights of migrant workers (Vu & Pham 2011, pp. 14-22).

2. Legal Framework of Vietnam Regarding the Protection of Overseas Workers

Of the estimated 500,000 documented Vietnamese overseas workers, about 90 per cent are working in Asia at the moment (Dang 2011, pp. 79-80). The profile of a Vietnamese overseas worker is quite varied, depending largely on

Table 1 Characteristics of Vietnamese Migrant Workers by Migration Path

Migrants' characteristics		Returned home before contract completion (%)	Completed contract and returned home (%)	Stayed after contract completion (%)	Total (%)
Sex	Male	35.7	49.3	15	100
	Female	24.2	69.6	6.2	100
Destination country	Taiwan	29.7	63.9	6.4	100
	South Korea	11.9	52.0	36.1	100
	Japan	14.3	61.9	23.8	100
	Malaysia	40.7	55.6	3.7	100
Province (within Vietnam)	Ha Tay	29.4	56.7	13.9	100
	Thai Binh	25.9	65.3	8.8	100
	Ha Tinh	38.2	53.9	7.9	100
Type of job abroad	Factory worker	25.5	58.0	16.5	100
	Domestic worker	27.9	68.6	3.5	100
	Construction worker	53.3	42.3	4.4	100
	Worker/ agriculture or fishery	38.7	45.1	16.2	100
	Worker/ service sector	18.8	75.3	5.9	100
All migrants		30.0	59.4	10.6	100

Source: ILAMI Vietnam 2009 Survey.

individual reports and geographical regions. According to a recent survey of International Labour Migration (ILAMI) Vietnam that was conducted in the three northern provinces of the country in 2009, approximately 60 per cent of Vietnamese overseas workers are men, while 40 per cent are women. Among the women migrants, 61.0 per cent immigrated to Taiwan; 41.6 per cent went to Japan, and 35.9 per cent and 9.6 per cent went to Japan and Korea, respectively (Table 1).

In terms of their usual jobs in their host countries, about 60 per cent of these workers are employed in factories; 18.7 per cent are domestic workers or caregivers, 7.0 per cent work as construction workers, 12.0 per cent are in the farming and fishing sector and 3.5 per cent work in the service industry. Half of these Vietnamese women work in households, while the other half work in factories. Almost all male migrants work in factories. Most of the domestic workers and caregivers work in Taiwan, while factory/agricultural/fishing labourers go to Korea or Malaysia. This means that a large part of women migrants are working in Taiwan now.

Most migrant workers are quite young: 85 per cent of these workers are aged 20-39 at the time of their return (of these, 25.5 per cent are aged 25-29, while 22.9 per cent are 30-34 year olds). Two-thirds of the migrant workers are married; of these, 55.8 per cent are male and the rest are female. Of the unmarried workers, 74.8 per cent are male and 25.2 per cent are women. It should also be noted that among the 3 per cent of divorced workers in the said population, 85 per cent are women (ILAMI 2009, p. 17).

The ILAMI survey also found that the main motivation for immigrating to work abroad are financially-related, *viz*, to earn more money (the main reason), pay the family's debt, "know more about the world as well as pay tuition fees," acquire land, refurbish houses and pay for living maintenance and medical treatment, learn new skills and other reasons (p. 17). Japan has the largest number of Vietnamese workers migrating there based on the motivation to know more about the world (18 per cent) (p. 24). In terms of gender, the main reason for women's migration is to pay the families' debts as well as their children's education and healthcare, while for men, "house building" is a main push factor (p. 20).

The above figures confirm the trend of the feminisation of migrant workers in Vietnam. They also provide a clearer understanding of who these overseas workers are—in terms of their demographic characteristics, destination countries, and reasons to immigrate. However, it is difficult to identify these migrant workers in terms of occupation and education levels. It can be predicted that a large part of these overseas workers do not have a college degree and/or did not work in white-collar jobs before migrating, as most of them are from the rural areas. One statistic estimates that around 80 per cent of these workers come from rural areas, with 67.5 per cent having attended secondary or just primary education. Nearly 60 per cent of these migrant workers did not attend necessary training courses before departure, contributing to major difficulties experienced overseas, such as the early termination of contracts, wage decreases, and/or transfer of jobs (Nguyen 2009, p. 3).

Sending labourers to work overseas is not a new policy in Vietnam. Since the early 1980s, under the agreements signed with the former Soviet Union and other East European socialist countries, Vietnam had sent thousands of workers to work in factories and enterprises of the said countries. After the collapse of the Soviet Union and the Eastern European socialist countries in the early 1990s, most of these workers were repatriated (however, thousands still remain, working under different industries, some as undocumented migrant workers). Vietnam then resumed sending labourers to work in countries which did not belong to the former Soviet bloc. In the first phase of this period (before the first Gulf War), Vietnam sent thousands of workers to selected African countries, including Libya, Iraq and Kuwait. As mentioned earlier, these overseas workers are currently concentrated in countries in Asia and the Middle East. For each period of migration, Vietnam has set different goals and issued different legal documents to regulate labour export activities.

2.1 The 1980s

In the 1980s, the main goal was to build a relationship of friendship and co-operation with countries in the Socialist system in the Soviet Union and Eastern Europe; another goal was to resolve unemployment and improve professional skills among labourers in the country. The economic objective of labour export in this period was not emphasised. In order to carry out the policy of exporting labourers, the Government of Vietnam signed agreements and protocols with the governments of the said socialist countries, and assigned state agencies to do the recruitment, training, sending, managing workers during their time living abroad, as well as the repatriation of the workers upon the completion of their contracts.

The major legal documents with respect to Vietnam's labour export policy in this period include the following:[1]

a) Decision 46/CP dated 11 February 1980 of the Government Council, in respect of sending technical labourers to work within a time limit and for

[1] For the full text of these documents (in Vietnamese), please refer to http://vietlaw.gov.vn/LAWNET.

skills training in the Socialist countries;

b) Resolution 362/CP dated 20 November 1980 of the Government Council, with respect to the two goals in labour co-operation with the Soviet Union and Eastern Europe;

c) Decision 263/CT dated 24 July 1984 of the President of Council of Ministers, in respect of sending medical, educational and agricultural experts to help the developing countries in the Middle East and Africa;

d) Decision 398/QD dated 26 December 1987 of the President of the Council of Ministers assigning to the Ministry of Construction to preside over the labour co-operation of construction techniques, with a view to sending workers in the construction industry to receive contracts abroad (e.g. in Iraq, Kuwait); and

e) Directive 108/HDBT dated 30 June 1988 of the Council of Ministers (currently referred to as the Government) providing for the extension of labour co-operation with foreign experts directly between enterprise and enterprise, industry and industry.

Determined by the international cooperation that is characteristic of immigration policy in this period and also of the initial implementation of sending workers overseas, there were several legislations adopted by the state to regulate the matter. All five mentioned above are of a secondary source, which means that they were issued by the Government, which is the executive branch of Vietnam. There was no law from the National Assembly, the legislative body. Laws made in the 1980s considered the role of regulating and protecting migrant workers as a matter of a centrally planned economy bearing administrative and government management responsibilities. Thus they mainly aimed to provide a very general framework. What were mostly created were the conditions to recruit workers, terms of labour, and other administrative management issues such as overseas employment management.

As such it is not difficult to imagine that the laws of this period contained a number of shortcomings ranging from the mechanisms of protection, channels to settle disputes arising out of overseas employment and recruitment fees, and so on. Even within the issues regulated, a great number of shortcomings were pointed out: a lack of understanding of international agreement terms on migrant workers, ineffective management of workers overseas, and bad behaviour demonstrated by some of the migrant workers, just to name a few (Bui,

2010). However, this period of immigration is at times considered a success, as thousands of migrant workers were sent overseas, owing to the high respect of foreign employers towards Vietnamese migrants. It was also viewed as a success because of the significant economic contribution these migrants made to their families in Vietnam (Nguyen 2010).

2.2 The 1990s onwards

Unlike the previous period, from 1990 to the present, the economic goals of labour export have been greatly emphasised. The actors engaged in this activity are more extensive, not just limited to state agencies, but also include the private sector. The number of overseas workers also expanded and their working destinations became more diversified, which highlighted the need to amend and supplement the legal system in place. The undertaking of sending labourers to work overseas is no longer considered as a simple matter of a centrally planned economy having government management concerns. Instead, it became an issue of a newly reformed market economy which should be governed by contracts, agreements and laws, rather than administrative mechanism and decisions. Therefore, much legislation has been gradually adopted to create a new market framework for exporting migrant workers. Of the most important legislations, the Labour Code 1994 and the Law on Sending Vietnamese Workers to Work Abroad under a Contract 2006 are two key documents.[2]

The underlying spirit of the Labour Code is a primary concern for the protection of the employee in an employment relationship. Employees are often considered the weaker party in the relationship with his/her employer. However, employees are also a valuable capital source of the nation, including migrant workers. Migrant workers are seen as a particularly vulnerable group of employees because they have to live and work far from their families, their nation, and domestic legal protection (Le 2011). It is thus not surprising that the labour code has provided many favorable provisions for the protection of employees. However, the governing scope of the labour code is wide, and

[2] Full texts of these documents (in Vietnamese) can be accessed through: http://vietlaw.gov.vn/LAWNET/. Detailed titles of other legal documents can be found in the reference section of this paper.

principally targets a domestic rather than overseas employment environment. Due to the complexity as well as the foreign elements concerned, a new law focusing on sending Vietnamese workers to work abroad under contract was adopted in 2006. The promulgation of this law can be considered as a major step in the legislation process. As a result of this law, important issues have been more specifically stated and addressed, in comparison to the previous period of the 1980s. To implement the two key documents, a number of regulations and guiding documents have been issued by executive authorities in the form of circulars, decisions, decrees, etc.

Generally speaking, the current legal framework of Vietnam regarding labour export has two objectives: (i) creating a favorable environment for labour export; and (ii) better protection of the rights and interests of overseas workers. These are to be achieved through a wide range of methods.

First, it distinguishes the state management function of public authorities from the business and service function of enterprises. In other words, state authorities now focus mainly on policy making and management rather than doing business as a corporate entity, as it used to in the past. Private companies will take over the business of marketing, negotiating, contracting and sending workers overseas through settlements with corresponding foreign parties. The types of enterprise organisations deploying these workers abroad include: a) service enterprises; b) bid-winning enterprises and contractors in foreign countries; c) organisations and individuals making investment abroad; and d) enterprises sending workers to work overseas in the form of work practice, to improve professional skills and the non-productive organisation of the State. They are all profit making entities independent of state organs, which see exporting workers overseas as a form of business—a conditioned business line. In other words, they are not state organs assigned with the task of exporting workers, subjected to a centrally planned mechanism not aimed at making a profit.

Second, the channels through which workers are sent overseas have also expanded. Now they can emigrate through private companies (as listed in the previous paragraph) or via individual contracts. The expansion of these channels has accounted for the growing number of migrant worker populations.

Third, it clearly provides for checks and balances in terms of the rights and obligations for each type of enterprise and labour export agency, as well as establishes corresponding rights and obligations of these workers abroad. It sets out conditions that enterprises need to meet, if they want to be licensed by the relevant government authorities to function as labour export agencies. It prescribes conditions, dossiers, and regulation procedures for the registration of the labour supply contracts with state agencies of foreign partners, before the workers are sent overseas. Finally, it sets a cap for the fees and other service charges which an enterprise is allowed to collect from its workers, laying the financial responsibility upon the enterprise via security deposits towards the implementation of obligations, such as contributing to the Overseas Employment Support Fund. It does not only aim at restraining the high service fee irregularly imposed by labour export agencies, but also tries to reduce the expense of emigrating to work abroad, making the option to work overseas more accessible to the people.

It must be emphasised that the main contribution of the laws lie on their provisions at preventing abusive behaviours toward and the abandonment of the workers. They do so via three mechanisms. First, they stipulate what the prohibited acts are (for example, granting licenses for enterprises which are not qualified; taking unfair advantage of sending Vietnamese workers abroad simply to benefit from the collection of recruitment, training and fees from the workers; and sending workers abroad without initially registering a labour supply contract with the relevant state authorities).

Second, they stipulate the areas, industries and jobs which are prohibited (these include areas with inhumane working conditions and real/impending threats of violence; areas affected by radioactivity, infections and epidemic diseases that are particularly dangerous; occupations where work is extremely hard, harmful and dangerous, and which are inconsistent with the Vietnamese people's habits). As there are areas where abuse may easily take place, such prohibitions can then be seen as a rational and necessary mean to protect overseas workers rights, even when they are still at home. These laws also stipulate supplementary occupational training, providing the necessary foreign language skills and orientation for workers before sending them to work abroad. As some reports show, sending unskilled workers who lack pre-departure training has led to very difficult situations abroad. The lack of knowledge exposes them to vulnerable circumstances such as abuse, a decrease of wages, or even terminations of contracts (International Labour Migration Vietnam 2009, pp. 10-

11). The requirement of occupational, language and cultural training will better prepare migrants to adapt quickly to their new working and living environments, thereby reducing potentially abusive and exploitative situations. Thus, these legislations have been key components toward the protection of overseas workers.

Third, it is required that every labour export agency must have at least one representative in the receiving country where the workers are being deployed to. The representative does not only act as a staff of the agency, but also as a form of safeguard for the migrant labourers. He (or she) has to promptly get involved in resolving problems that concern these overseas workers. In extraordinary circumstances, he has to report the problems immediately to his agency or the relevant Vietnamese authorities to find a solution. Aside from that, this representative should also coordinate with the enterprises, should the worker need return home prior to the deadline.

In addition to the substantive provisions provided for in the said legislations, the Government of Vietnam also adopts various remedies to redress violations, wrongdoings as well as disputes related to the issue. Currently, disputes arising out of service contracts between workers and labour export agencies can be tried in the Labour Court, following a civil procedure. The Labour Court is entitled to apply civil remedies provided in the Civil Code 2005 or Labour Code 1994, to the disputes before it. Violations of laws can be imposed with administrative sanctions, applying procedures prescribed through the Ordinance on Handling Administrative Violations. The sanctions can in turn be tried before the administrative court using the Law on Administrative Procedure. Above all, Vietnam's criminal law can be applied to certain cases involving the export of workers (such as when fraud or rape is committed).

All in all, the aforementioned provisions and mechanisms have made significant contributions to the protection of the lawful rights and interests of the Vietnamese overseas workers, especially when compared to the earlier period of the 1980s with its limited number of secondary legislation. Table 2 summarises the tasks that overseas workers, labour agencies and state authorities have to fulfill in the course of exporting workers to work abroad, in accordance with Vietnamese laws.

Table 2 Tasks to be Undertaken in order to Send Workers Overseas

Sequence of tasks	Prospective Workers	Labour Agencies	State Authorities
1		Apply for license to operate as an export agency.	Issue license to qualified applicants.
2		Seek partners, market, negotiate, and directly sign agreements with foreign partners (Labour export agencies can sign contracts with either brokers or foreign employers).	
3		Register contracts with the Department of Overseas Labour Management (DOLAB), which is under the Ministry of Labour, Invalids and Social Affairs.	After evaluation, DOLAB issues an official letter of certification for contract performance.
4		Give notice on labour recruitment and recruit local workers.	
5		Provide training and orientation services for employees.	
6	Sign contract with labour export agencies.	Labour export agencies sign contract with local workers.	
7	Workers get to work abroad.	Manage migrant workers by agency's representative abroad.	
8	Sign labour contract with foreign employer.		
9	Return to their home country and liquidate contract with labour export agency involved.	Settle contract liquidation with migrant workers.	

10		Labour export agencies report to DOLAB in respect of labour recruitment for export on an annual and six monthly basic.	Collect labour export agencies report to DOLAB in respect of labour recruitment for export on an annual and six monthly basis.
11		Labour export agencies report its operations to the Ministry of Labour, Invalids and Social Affairs on an annual and extraordinary requirement basis.	Collect labour export agencies report on its operations to the Ministry of Labour, Invalids and Social Affairs on an annual and extraordinary requirement basis.

Source: Compiled by authors.

3. Situations and Difficulties: Challenges in Protecting the Rights of Vietnamese Overseas Workers

Vietnamese overseas workers are not an exception to these difficulties faced by migrant workers from countries all over Asia. Figure 1 shows the common problems faced by all migrant workers in Asia as stipulated in the *Consultation Statement*,[3] a policy paper concerning the protection of migrant workers adopted by local civil society organisations in Hanoi on March 2008. These problems include:

a) weak and limited protection of the rights of migrant workers;

b) non-payment of salaries, or workers being paid significantly less than specified by the written contract;

c) unsafe working conditions, resulting in frequent injuries, and unhygienic living conditions;

d) harassment and abuse specifically directed at women migrant workers;

e) high recruitment fees in both the sending and receiving countries, leaving

[3] *Consultation Statement*, Vietnam National Consultation Workshop on the Protection and Promotion of the Rights of Migrant Workers, 3-4 March 2008, Hanoi, Vietnam. The English version can be found in: http://www.workersconnection.org/articles.php?more=92.

Figure 1 Vietnamese Overseas Workers Who Reported Negative Experiences in the Workplace

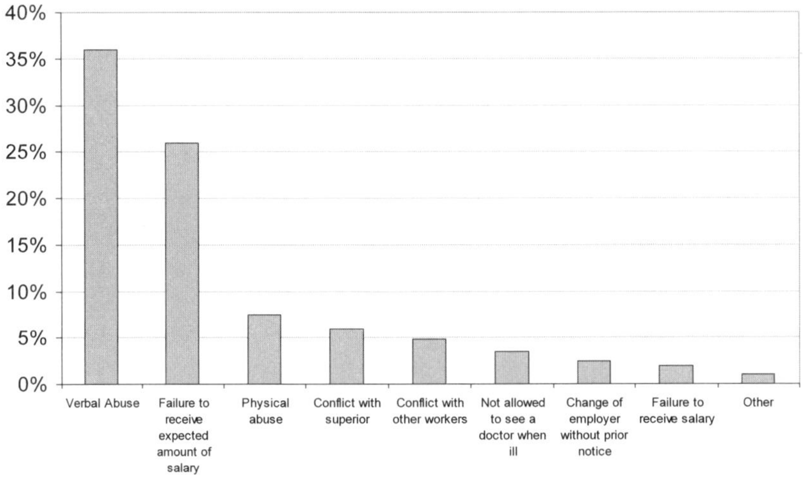

40%
35%
30%
25%
20%
15%
10%
5%
0%

Verbal Abuse
Failure to receive expected amount of salary
Physical abuse
Conflict with superior
Conflict with other workers
Not allowed to see a doctor when ill
Change of employer without prior notice
Failure to receive salary
Other

Source: ILAMI Vietnam 2009 Survey, in Belanger et al. (2010).

workers with significant debts and impoverishing their families because migrant workers cannot send home sufficient remittances;

f) cases of labour contracts being unilaterally changed by the final employer in the country of destination, yet the workers must pay the recruitment agency high compensation fees or face an alleged "breach of the labour contract" if they choose to leave the job;

g) frequent seizure of worker's passport and personal documents by employers or agents; and

h) desperate workers forced to become undocumented workers, leaving them more vulnerable to becoming victims of trafficking.

Aside from the abuse and unfair treatment that these workers face overseas, the ILAMI report also identified these workers as suffering from pre-departure problems, even while participating in the recruitment process at home. Figure 2 reveals that female workers seem to suffer more than male workers in every criterion, except for living conditions. While the results hardly explain the causes of such problems, they do confirm that female overseas workers are a more vulnerable

Figure 2 Types of Problems Experienced by Vietnamese Overseas Workers with Pre-departure Training

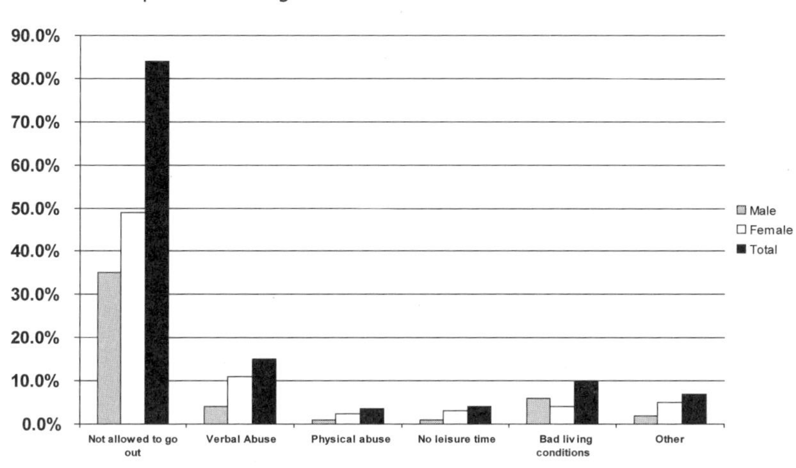

Source: ILAMI Vietnam 2009 Survey, in Belanger et al. (2010).

group, therefore needing further protective measures within and outside the country. The situation of Vietnamese overseas workers and the challenges facing them are discussed more specifically below.

3.1 Appointing labour export agencies' representative in receiving countries

As noted earlier, according to the Law on Sending Vietnamese Workers to Work Abroad under a Contract 2006, the main responsibility of protecting Vietnamese overseas workers belongs to labour export agencies and the practice of exporting workers is now considered a business done by private enterprises. As these agencies are in charge of establishing contracts with foreign partners, as well as the recruitment and deployment of workers, they have better information and resources to effectively manage and protect these overseas workers. They are also responsible for appointing a permanent representative in the receiving countries to promptly settle problems arising between the workers and their foreign employers. However, some receiving countries have disapproved of the appointment of such representatives, and not approved their visa applications. There are also internal difficulties experienced by a number of enterprises, for example, when they cannot afford to appoint permanent representatives to all the markets where they sent workers to work.

In order to solve the aforementioned difficulties, some labour export agencies have proposed that the Government of Vietnam amend the related law to allow them to implement other protective measures without sending their representatives abroad. However, local civil society organisations believe that the government should keep this stipulation to ensure that the responsibility of these labour export agencies towards the overseas workers is maintained, and that labour export agencies that are unable to send their representative to the receiving countries must have their license, together with those of their overseas workers, withdrawn. In addition, the Vietnamese government needs to work with the relevant bodies of the governments in each receiving country to facilitate visa issuance for the representatives of these labour export agencies.

3.2 Fraud, brokerage, and illegal collection of money from overseas workers

Fraud, brokerage, and the illegal collection of money from overseas workers occur in all sending countries including Vietnam. According to a newspaper report in 2010, from 2007 to 2010, there were 137 cases related to fraud which were investigated with 5,490 victims; 186 people were prosecuted (Nguyen 2010). To solve this, the Government of Vietnam tried to establish relationships between labour export agencies and state agencies from central to local levels. These relationships between the different actors under the current law can be generalised as follows:

a) With the management agency at central level, labour export agencies have to:
   i. report on the establishment of local branches (no more than three branches);
   ii. facilitate the registration of labour supply contract and execute it only after approval by the state management agency;
   iii. regularly and irregularly report on the activity of sending workers working abroad;

iv. be subjected to regular and irregular examination and inspection; and

v. be subjected to paying administrative fines, if having violated the provisions of the law.

b) With overseas Vietnamese representative missions (under DOLAP), labour export agencies have to:

i. report on the list of workers working in foreign countries to the Vietnamese representative mission in such country;

ii. deal with cases related to workers as required by the mission; and

iii. solve cases together with a representative mission, which are beyond the capability of the enterprise.

c) With labour agencies at municipal and provincial level, labour export agencies are expected to:

i. report on the establishment of a branch;

ii. be subject to the examination and inspection over the activities of the branch;

iii. notify the Department of Labour, Invalids and Social Affairs upon recruitment of local workers; and

iv. report on the result of recruitment and number of local workers that have been sent to work overseas to the Department of Labour, Invalids and Social Affairs on an annual and semi-annual basis.

d) With the district authorities, labour export agencies have to:

i. specifically notify the conditions of labour recruitment (number, occupation, age, gender and other specific requirement);

ii. coordinate with the representatives of the communities, to inform them of the conditions of recruitment, and terms and conditions of labour supply contracts for the industries;

iii. verify the necessary documents from branches of banks located in the districts, to provide loans for workers; and

iv. be subject to the supervision of the district administration in the entire recruitment activities in the local area.

e) With the commune authorities, labour export agencies have to:

i. co-coordinately hold direct counseling for workers in respect of conditions of contract to work abroad and receive registration forms made by workers for working abroad;

ii. instruct workers completing dossiers and procedures relating to health examination, loans, country exit, etc.; and

iii. coordinate with commune authorities and workers' families, in the process of resolving specific incidents involving workers.

The above-mentioned provisions have enhanced the management of recruitment of overseas workers, significantly reducing experiences that lead to deceptiveness, brokerage, and illegal collection of money, while at the same time helping labour export agencies recruit qualified labourers. However, a recent (2010) survey[4] shows that deceptiveness and the illegal collection of money from workers still take place—caused by some organisations and individuals that are not authorised to send workers overseas. Mostly, such cases are due to the lack of employment information in foreign countries. According to the mentioned survey, most people have acquired recruitment information from personal contacts/friends. Recruitment information gathered through personal contact/friends ranks high among the population intending to work overseas (41.5 per cent on average, with the highest 55.7 per cent for workers bound for Taiwan).

3.3 Labour contracts

According to the current law in Vietnam, there are three types of contracts which need to be signed in the process:

a) Labour supply contract: the contract signed between local labour export agencies and foreign partners (the brokers or employers). This contract must conform to Vietnamese laws, the law of each receiving country and international law. The contents of the contract include the general terms and conditions in respect of work, contract duration, number of employees to be recruited; occupations and jobs to do; place of work; working conditions and environment, working and rest time, safety and labour protection; salary, wage and bonus (if any), overtime pay; conditions of accommodations and meals; medical care; social insurance; condition of contract termination prior to the period of the contract, and responsibility for indemnity of damage; responsibility for payment of travel costs from Vietnam to the workplace and vice versa; brokerage

---

[4] *Survey of local recruitment agencies in Vietnam*, conducted by the Vietnam Lawyers' Association and Oxfam Quebec, Draft Report of Findings, June 2010.

fee (if any); responsibility borne by the respective parties on the event a worker passes away while working abroad; dispute settlement; and the responsibility of helping the remit money to their families. The approval of such contracts by a relevant state competent authority is necessary before it can be executed by the enterprises.

b) Contract on sending workers abroad: the contract signed between labour export agencies and overseas workers.

c) Labour contract: the contract signed between the overseas worker and foreign employers.

In addition, under the current laws of Vietnam, labour export agencies will have to negotiate with the parties so that the last two types of contracts (contract on sending workers abroad and the labour contract) shall contain specific and consistent contents with the former (labour supply contract). The provisions concerning the brokerage fee, service charge, and deposit amount of the workers must be included in the contract on sending workers to work abroad. This contract must clearly define the following: contract duration, occupations and jobs to do; working places; working condition and environment, working and rest time, safety and labour protection; salary, wage and bonus (if any), overtime pay, conditions of accommodation, meal; medical care; social insurance; condition of contract termination prior to the time limit and responsibility for indemnity of damage; responsibility for payment of travel cost from Vietnam to the workplace and vice versa; brokerage fee (if any); responsibility of the parties when the employee passes away while working abroad; dispute settlement; responsibility for helping the workers wire money to their families. This contract must also clearly define the general terms and conditions with respect to work, contract duration, and so on as stated for the first contract (on labour supply).

However, the contents of the third contract have not been specifically stipulated in the law of Vietnam, despite the fact that this type of contract is the most direct and crucial in terms of protecting the rights of overseas workers. In addition, overseas workers in many cases are not carefully consulted before signing the contract, as they often have to sign at the last minute, just before deployment. As a result, many overseas workers tend to be disadvantaged. According to the above mentioned survey, some Vietnamese overseas workers who returned home from Malaysia said that they were given low salaries, and had little or no work to do, while some had to return home before their contract expiry, and others did not have enough food, causing them to flee from their work places. Ironically, these cases were covered by labour contracts which were supposed to protect them from such exploitation.

3.4 Fees and deposit

Fees and deposit schedules applied for Vietnamese overseas workers are specifically stated in Decision No. 61/2008/QD-BLDTBXH, dated 12 August 2008 by the Ministry of Labour, Invalids and Social Affairs. However, in practice, many labour export agencies collect fees higher than the ceiling stipulated in that Decision, especially from those who want to work in high income markets such as Korea, Japan and Taiwan (Figure 3). In addition, such fees and charges vary across different localities, and among overseas workers.

In this regard, the above mentioned survey shows that many overseas workers face extreme difficulties due to the high cost of working abroad. Some of them have to sell all their assets and property to finance their travel. Many others borrow from relatives and friends to shoulder these costs. Thus, in order to clear debts more quickly, many Vietnamese overseas workers, upon settling in their host countries, tend to move to other companies that offer higher wages. Vietnamese overseas workers have gained notoriety for this.

Figure 3 Comparison between Official Fees and Actual Costs Applied to Vietnamese Overseas Workers (in USD), 2008

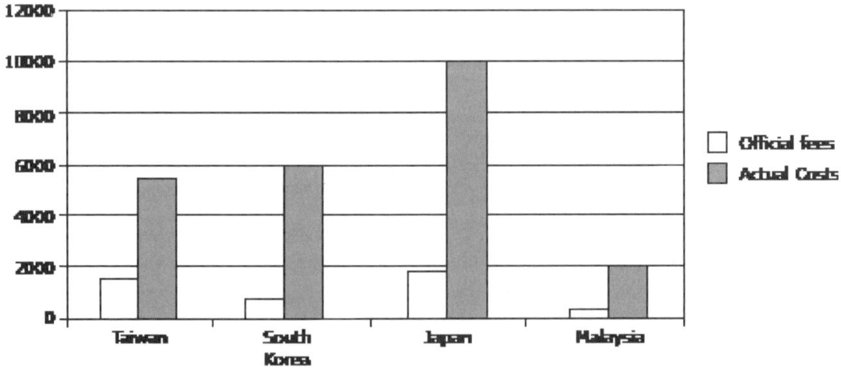

Sources: Decision 61/2008 QD-LDTBXH (for official fees); ILAMI 2009 Survey, in Belanger et al. (2010) (for actual costs).

In terms of collecting fees and deposit from workers, sometimes higher than the ceiling stipulated by law, some labour export agencies argue that they have to do so because the ceiling is too low anyway, and higher deposits act as security bonds to keep overseas workers from evading their contracts. However, as revealed by the same survey, the "anti-evasion deposit" is not always returned to these overseas workers by labour export agencies upon termination of their respective contracts.

3.5 Support before departure

The provision for training, foreign language learning and other support with regards to knowledge and information for workers before going abroad is a mandatory obligation of labour export companies. However, the above-mentioned survey found that the time and efficiency of orientations and training provided by labour export companies vary. Some companies do not comply, while some resort to short cuts in pre-departure training. According to the current laws of Vietnam, the minimum time for orientation, training and education, and foreign language learning should be 2-3 months. The fact is, it is normally held by labour export companies within a mere 2-3 weeks. Indeed, the survey revealed that in reality, only about 60 per cent of these overseas workers went through the essential orientation and introduction to living and working abroad.

3.6 Support while working abroad

According to current Vietnamese law, overseas workers can get help from the Vietnamese representative missions in their respective receiving countries (usually located in the Embassy of Vietnam), over and above the representative of the labour export agency that deployed them abroad. Again, the survey shows that only 29.95 per cent of these overseas workers received help from the representative missions, of which 27.4 per cent are male workers, and 31.3 per cent being female workers. As for the workers who have been sent by labour export companies, the rate is 44.7 per cent, with the percentage of male workers receiving help higher than their female counterparts (46.6 per cent against 43.8 per cent).

The above survey also shows that the level of support received by these overseas varies, according to their host country. Some overseas worker-returnees from Malaysia and Taiwan, for example, stated that their interests have been seriously infringed by their employers, yet they have not received any form of support, from neither overseas Vietnamese representative missions nor representative of labour export agencies (survey report conducted in Thai Binh, Hau Giang and Soc Trang provinces).

4. Proposed Measures to Promote the Effective Protection of Rights

From the above analyses, it is possible to propose to the Government of Vietnam the following measures for the protection of Vietnamese overseas workers.

4.1 Recruitment activity and local recruitment agencies

While maintaining the existing mechanism and procedures of recruitment, it is necessary to specifically clarify responsibilities of government agencies at all local levels in relation to preventing activities of deceptive recruiting, brokering, and tampering with the stipulated ceiling amount for fee and deposit collection from overseas workers. In this regard, the process of granting labour recruitment licenses must be serious and strictly managed. There should be continuous monitoring of the activities of migrant recruitment agencies, and prompt action to withdraw licenses of those who violate the law, including maintaining and continually updating a list of agencies involved in deceiving and cheating workers, prohibiting those agencies to be involved in any way in labour recruitment.

In addition, the government should ensure that information on recruitment (including associated procedures), recruitment fees and deposit allowed to be charged, and other related information is widely publicised. Furthermore, information on the legal status of labour recruitment agencies, including their mandate, responsibilities and authority should also be publicly known. In the long run, the government should implement the "one stop service center" approach (through a consolidation of the procedures and services related to the registration and administration of migrant workers in one service center, where representatives of all relevant government agencies are present), in order to reduce the time and cut down the risk of workers being taken advantage of.

4.2 Labour contracts

The government should ensure that all overseas workers receive and agree to a written contract with the foreign employer, and that the contract should be in both Vietnamese and the language of the receiving country. The recruitment agency should be required to provide a copy of all workers' contracts to the Department of Overseas Labour Management (DOLAB), and the contracts shall be verified by DOLAB. The government should also ensure that all contracts must be not only strictly in conformity with both the laws of Vietnam and the laws of the receiving country, but also in accordance with the core labour standards of the International Labor Organization (ILO).

4.3 Policies and support for overseas workers

The government should ensure that all overseas workers are provided with pre-departure training at no cost and an information package before departure. The training should be fully conducted within the time stipulated by law. The training and information package should include at least the following: (i) information about all relevant laws and regulations of the receiving country; (ii) information about the cultural and social customs of the receiving country; (iii) contact information of the focal points/complaints desks where migrant workers can file a complaint and receive assistance; (iv) information about basic knowledge and skills required in emergency situations; and (v) other information, as deemed necessary.

The government should be aware of the vulnerability of female migrant workers in jobs known to have a high level of potential exploitation and sexual harassment, such as service sector jobs and domestic work. Special measures should be taken to protect women who choose to enter such employment. In addition, the Government should set up a system of effective legal aid to assist these migrant workers when they lodge complaints about ill treatment and violations of the law.

4.4 Protection and support for Vietnamese overseas workers in receiving countries

The government should put significant pressure on local recruitment agencies regarding the protection of overseas workers in receiving countries, forcing them to send representatives to the receiving country for the very function of assisting and protecting their workers. The government should also mandate that the Vietnamese Embassies in each receiving countries should build effective collaboration with recruitment agencies to provide prompt protection measures for workers in their respective locales. In this regard, officials at Vietnamese Embassies and Consulates in each receiving countries should be trained and provided with clear policy guidance on protecting the rights of overseas workers with outmost importance. In addition, the government should establish a system enabling the posting of Vietnamese trade union representatives overseas in embassies, to help further the rights of these overseas workers. Finally, the government should continually request that the host country government implement provisions to protect the rights of the migrant workers whom they have committed to protect.

4.5 National laws and regulations

The Law on Sending Vietnamese Workers to Work Abroad should be revised to further clarify responsibilities of local recruitment agencies and state units regarding the protection of overseas workers, as well as to harmonise this law with ILO's core labour standards. In addition, this law should be also further concretised by regulations, which should specify measures on the protection of overseas workers.

In addition, the government should conduct a study on the feasibility and desirability of ratifying the UN Convention on the Protection of the Rights of All Migrant Workers and Members of their Families in order to strengthen capacity and explore international mechanism for the protection of these overseas workers.

5. Conclusion

This chapter has highlighted the trend of an increasing number of overseas workers from Vietnam to other countries, mostly in Asia. Not only is the country growing its worker population overseas, it can also be noted that more women are joining the trend. This feminisation phenomenon is actually in line with the general situation of the world today, in terms of labour migration. It is reported that while female workers divide quite equally between different job sectors, with half working in the household and another half joining factories, almost all male overseas workers are concentrated in factory jobs.

While the statistics regarding these overseas workers are quite clear and help us to understand their increasing numbers, the causes of the trends are still much debated and need further research. Conventional theories such as neoclassical, network or structuralism theories are not able to fully explain the push factors behind the increase of overseas female workers, even though the feminisation of the migrant workforce is one of six prominent characteristics of international immigration today. State policies, individual autonomy and even social perceptions all play their part in this notable increase of female migrant figures. However, it still needs further empirical survey for us to fully understand the trend.

This increasing number of (women) overseas workers presents serious problems and calls for the development of policies and legislation to better protect the legitimate interests of workers overseas. Along with a number of benefits gained, especially financial benefits, these overseas workers also face and suffer various abuses and unfair treatment while working abroad. Even worse, these workers—especially the females—suffer unfair treatment even before they leave home. Other forms of maltreatment, such as verbal abuses, physical abuses, and the confiscation of their passports, often occur abroad.

To address these problems, the government of Vietnam has gradually adopted a number of statutes and regulations to better enhance the protection of the Vietnamese overseas worker. Such measures range from the enactment of new, substantive and stricter rules to the adoption of new legal remedies such as civil, administrative, and criminal law to redress wrongdoings. Moving forward, we would argue that the next step is for the Vietnamese government to go beyond the current tendency to turn out "one size fits all" pieces of legislation deemed applicable to both genders. Instead, they must pay specific attention to the different conditions of both female and male overseas workers, their varied destinations as well as their desire to work abroad, if they are ensure the effective protection of the increasing numbers of Vietnamese, both men and women, who migrate overseas to work.

Further efforts are required to further improve the situation and response to the challenges posed. The chapter has proposed some recommendations to improve the effectiveness of existing protective measures. They range from pre-departure measures to real work time suggestions, to return mechanisms. It is hoped that this paper can catalyse further discussions about the appropriate policies needed.

References

Bélanger, D., Le, B. D., Tran, G. L. and Khuat, G. H. (2010). "International labour migration from Vietnam to Asian countries: Process, Experiences and Impact." Report presented at the International workshop 'Labour Migration from Vietnam to Asian Countries: Sharing research findings and NGO's experiences'. 15 March. Hanoi. Accessed 6 August 2012 from http://www.sociology.uwo.ca/CRCpopulation/ILAMIper cent20Report.pdf.

Bui, N. T. (2010). "Hợp tác quốc tế về lao động: Tình hình xưa, bài học nay." *Tạp chí cộng sản điện tử*. Accessed 6 August 2012 from http://www.tapchicongsan.org.vn/Home/Nghiencuu-Traodoi/2010/1213/Hop-tac-quoc-te-ve-lao-dong-tinh-hinh-xua-bai-hoc.aspx.

Dang, N. A. (2011). "Xuất khảo lao động—Một số vấn đề chính sách và thực tiễn" in Vu, C. G. et al. (eds), *Lao động di trú trong pháp luật quốc tế và Việt Nam*. Hanoi. Nhà xuất bản Lao động Xã hội. pp. 76-96.

Dao, C. H. (2008). Head of Bureau for Overseas Workers under Ministry of Labour, War Invalid and Social Affairs of Vietnam. "Exporting labourers of Vietnam." Paper presented at the workshop on migrant workers' rights organised by Vietnam Lawyers Association in March 2008.

ILAMI Vietnam (2009 Survey). Impact of Migration. Household Members' Assessment of Impact of Migration. Lao Dong Online. 19 September 2010. Accessed http://www.laodong.com.vn/Tin-Tuc/Nhat-tri-ban-hanh-nghi-quyet-chuyen-de-ve-xuat-khau-laodong/12957.

Le, T. H. T. (2011). "Pháp luật hiện hành về bảo vệ người lao động Việt Nam đi làm việc ở nước ngoài." in Vu, C. G. et al. (eds.), *Lao động di trú trong pháp luật quốc tế và Việt Nam*. Hanoi. Nhà xuất bản Lao động Xã hội. pp. 112-168.

Nguyen, T. D. (2009). "Một số giải pháp tăng cường quản lý lao động Việt Nam làm việc ở nước ngoài." *Tạp chí phát triển kinh tế*, 211, 3. Accessed 6 August 2012 from http://tcptkt.ueh.edu.vn.

Nguyen, T. M. (2010). "Bao ve nguoi lao dong o nuoc ngoai la danh du quoc gia." Accessed on 12 june 2012, from www.cand.com.vn.

Oishi, N. (2005). *Women in Motion: Globalization, State Policies, and Labour Migration in Asia*. Stanford: Stanford University Press.

Vietnam National Consultation on the Protection and Promotion of the Rights of Migrant Workers (2008). "Consultation Statement." 3-4 March. Hanoi, Vietnam. English version accessed 06 August 2012 from http://www.workersconnection.org/downloads.php?RCID=3.

Vu, C. G. and La, K. T. (2011). "Bảo vệ người lao động di trú ở khu vực Đông Nam Á." In C.G. Vu, et al., eds. *Lao động di trú trong pháp luật quốc tế và Việt Nam*. Hanoi. Nhà xuất bản Lao động Xã hội. pp. 13-76.

Vu, C. G and Pham, H. T. (2011). "Lao động di trú: Một xu hướng toàn cầu, một nỗ lực toàn cầu." in C. G. Vu, et al., eds. *Lao động di trú trong pháp luật quốc tế và Việt Nam*. Hanoi. Nhà xuất bản Lao động Xã hội. pp. 9-24.

Legal documents

Decision 46/CP dated 11 February 1980 of the Government Council in respect of sending a part of technical labourers to work under a time limit and skill training in the Socialist countries.

Decision 263/CT dated 24 July 1984 of the President of Council of Ministers in respect of sending medical, educational and agricultural experts to help the developing countries in the Middle East and Africa.

Decision 398/QD dated 26 December 1987 of the President of the Council of Ministers assigning to the Ministry of Construction to preside over labour co-operation of construction technique with a view to sending workers in the construction industry to receive contracts abroad (Iraq, Kuwait, etc).

Directive 108/HDBT dated 30 June 1988 of the Council of Ministers (referred as the Government now) providing extension of labour co-operation with foreign experts in the direct form between enterprise and enterprise, industry and industry.

Labour Code 1994 (amended and supplemented in 2002), of which providing some provisions on sending workers to work abroad.

Resolution 362/CP dated 20 November 1980 of the Government Council providing determination of the two goals in labour co-operation with the Soviet Union and Eastern Europe.

Indonesian Migrant Workers (IMWs):
Legal and Policy Perspectives

Inosentius Samsul

1. Introduction

The International Labor Organization (ILO) has estimated that there are over 80 million workers worldwide, of whom 27 per cent are in Asia; every year, about 2 million of these workers leave their home countries for overseas contract work within and outside the region (Mackenzie 2005, p. 9). Indonesia is highly concerned about the issue of migrant workers for several reasons. First, the *number* of Indonesian Migrant Workers (IMWs), particularly women, has been on the rise. Female migrant workers increased from 89.0 per cent of all registered IMWs in 1992, to 91.5 per cent in 2001. Although the percentage of female migrant workers dropped to 82.8 per cent in 2004, their absolute number is still much higher compared to the number of male migrant workers. In 2011, of the 581,081 IMWs sent abroad, 64.0 per cent (374,373) were females (National Agency for Placement and Protection of IMWs 2012, p. 1). These workers are spread across different destination countries, with the top ten (ranked consecutively) being Saudi Arabia, Malaysia, Taiwan, Hong Kong, Singapore, United Arab Emirates (UAE), Qatar, United State Of America (USA), South Korea and Brunei Darussalam (National Agency for Placement and Protection of IMWs, 2012).

Second, the country benefits economically from sending IMWs abroad. In quantity, IMWs have contributed substantially towards the national economy. Their remittance reached USD8.24 billion in 2008 (National Agency for Placement and Protection of IMWs 2012, p. 1), producing the highest revenue for the service sector, and second largest national revenue after oil and gas. IMWs' remittance has also contributed to enhancing the wellbeing of their families, an effect transcending almost 16 million people. This enormous contribution has caused IMWs to be often referred to as the "heroes of national income."

Third, the working conditions and treatment of IMWs are considerably poor, with the provision of the legal protection to the interests of IMWs being below the national and international convention standards, as well as the principles of human rights.

As Oishi (2002, p. 4) has argued, existing migration theories (including the neo-classical economic, structuralist, household, and the network theory) cannot explain the patterns of international female migration in Indonesia. Neo-classical economic theory, for instance, attributes the patterns of international migration to economic factors such as labour demand and supply, and wage differentials; however, Gross Domestic Product (GDP) and unemployment rates are not related to the patterns of international female migration. As Oishi (2002) demonstrated, major "sending countries" of migrant women (Philipines, Sri Lanka, and Indonesia) have higher GDP per capita than "non sending countries" (Bangladesh, India, and Pakistan).

Given the limitation of existing theories, Oishi proposed an "integrative approach" to explain international female migration. The integrative approach adopts three levels of analysis: (1) macro-level (the state), (2) micro-level (individuals), and (3) meso-level (society) (Oishi 2002, p. 8). It can be noted that the value dimension of emigration policies does not necessarily represent religious values alone. Islam as a religion does not always lead to restrictive policies for female migration. In fact, Indonesia, a Muslim country, is a major source of female migrant labour. Such issues embedded in most emigration policies lie in the perceptions of policy makers and elites who tend to disregard women and their role in economic development (Oishi 2005, p. 98).

There are two major gaps found in most of the current policies in Asia in terms of the laws and bilateral agreements: first, a migrant is seen as an economic tool and not as a social being; and second, no recognition is given to migrants' families (Coordination of Action Research on Aids and Mobility ASIA 2005, p. 2). It is well known that the national instruments designed to provide protection for migrant workers and their families are insufficient. They are easily amended without the workers' knowledge, thus denying the basic right of the workers to an adequate standard of living. At another level, agreements made between sending and receiving countries are kept away from migrant workers and those advocating on their behalf (for their protection and promotion of their rights). Because sending countries within the region have become dependent on the remittances from abroad, policy makers have arguably closed their eyes to the issue of protection of rights of migrant workers. The laws are written in such a way that they fail to provide a strong legal framework to punish those who abuse the system. Insufficient regard is also given to how migration is affecting the migrant workers' families who are highly tied in to the migration process. Not only has there been extensive disintegration of families in all the sending countries, including an increase in single parent families, but there has also been an increased incidence of poverty as family land and other resources and assets are sold to cover migration costs.

This paper has several aims. It will first explain the pattern of sending IMWs to foreign countries and the general conditions of protection for IMWs. Second, it will shed light on the differences between the conditions and problems of the IMWs in Malaysia and Korea, as case studies underlining the problems associated with policy implementation of sending IMWs. Malaysia and Korea have been selected as examples because of several important differences between the two countries making for interesting comparisons. Finally, the paper will describe the existing legal challenges of the current policies tied to migrant workers.

Due to the limitation of the research methodology, this paper does not aim to examine Indonesia's policy with regard to its migrant workers using international migration theory. This paper is based on secondary data and legal documents on sending IMWs, covering female and male migrant workers in general.

2. Indonesia's Policy of Exporting Migrant Workers

The policy of sending Indonesian migrant workers overseas can be traced back to the colonial government of the Dutch East Indies. During the colonial period (at the beginning of the 20th century), many of the policies, including emigration from the main island of Java to the neighboring islands (the so-called "outer islands") were aimed at raising agricultural productivity outside Java and to protect their status quo (for example, to decrease social and political tensions, and to structure commerce to serve the state's economic and security purposes) (CARAM Indonesia 2006).

Migration continued to play an important role in the next era. Ten years after the declaration of independence, the Indonesian Government described internal migration as an instrument for reducing population pressure in Java, as well as to provide labour in sparsely populated provinces, support military strategy, and accelerate the process of assimilation, thereby fast tracking the national integration process (CARAM Indonesia 2006).

During the New Order regime (1966-1998), Indonesia entered the global economy: the sending of migrant workers no longer took place only internally (inter-island), but took a step towards the global market. Aside from being founded on conventional issues such as domestic unemployment and population-density, the process of sending IMWs overseas became a response to the issues of international trading promotion. For example, in 1983, when drastic oil pricing was taking place, the Indonesian government promoted the country as a provider of the lowest labour-wage rate globally to attract foreign investors. At the time, work as IMWs was considered more prestigious and such workers received higher wages than their domestic counterparts. This led to problems of extensive corruption, with manipulative government officials collaborating with irresponsible business people, as they saw the sending of IMWs abroad as purely a profitable business (in a parasitic way). This common practice continued until the "Era of Reformation" began in 1988, when IMWs were treated as a trading commodity, without the consideration and provision of legal protection. The fact that an estimated 400,000 IMWs have left Indonesia each year since 1988 to

Table 1 Remittance of IMWs, 2003-2008

YEAR	USD (millions)
2003	1.67
2004	188
2005	2.93
2006	3.42
2007	5.84
2008	2.23 (until April)

Source: Republic of Indonesia, National Agency for Placement and Protection of IMW (2010).

work legally abroad (World Bank 2006, p. 1) reflects the government's policy of sending IMWs abroad as an economic strategy, i.e., to absorb the workforce as the national economy is unable to do so (for example, in 2009, out of a workforce 113.73 million people, 9.26 million people remained unemployed). As Table 1 shows, remittances from IMWs' income whilst working abroad grew steadily from USD1.67 million in 2003 to 5.84 million in 2007.

However, IMWs lack protection and are vulnerable to maltreatment that endangers both their health and lives. They are subjected to numerous rights violations including torture, death, arbitrary loss, confinement, unpaid wages, overtime work, prohibition and sabotage of communication (with their families), forced prostitution, imprisonment without due process of law, unwanted pregnancies after being raped by their employer or the family members of their employer, being trafficked, low wages, deportation (that is carried out every year), death due to falling from a high-rise building, prohibition from practicing their religion, major salary deductions by their agency, torture by employer, and the imposition of a death sentence (International NGO Forum on Indonesian Development 2006, p. 1).

Malaysia ranked the highest in rights violations related to IMWs; Saudi Arabia placed second, while Jordan was in third place, followed consecutively

Figure 1 Amount of IMW's Rights Violations in Several Destination Countries, 2009

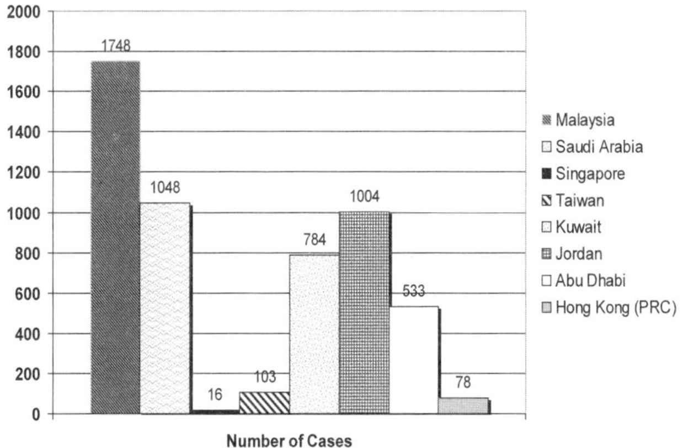

Source: Database Migrant CARE (2009), in Mahfiz (2010).

by Kuwait, Abu Dhabi, Taiwan, Hong Kong, and finally, Singapore (Figure 1). Mahfiz (2010, p. 6) argues that the lack of protection towards IMWs abroad could have been instigated by several factors, viz, the governmental-institutional aspect, budget and bureaucracy politics, and the overlap of authority.

The institutional aspect that is most highlighted is the lack of governmental effectiveness. Based on the Governmental Effectiveness Index (GEI) that measures the quality of policy formulations relative to its implementation, as well as a government's credibility in terms of its commitment to the policies, Indonesia ranks lower than five other ASEAN countries: Singapore, Malaysia, Brunei, Thailand, and the Philippines (Mahfiz 2010, p. 7). In terms of budgets and bureaucracy, the issues concerning IMWs are tackled by at least seven governmental institutions. Consequently, the task of managing financial resources is shared between these government institutions.[1] IMWs bear the consequences of these problems, facing various difficulties as a result of the many malpractices related to their departing illegally; this makes them easily subject to indecent treatment, and poses a problem for municipal governmental offices in registering and obtaining data of Indonesians working abroad.

3. IMWs in Malaysia: An Unfinished Solution

Malaysia currently receives the highest number of IMWs (Table 2). The increase in number of IMWs being sent is congruent with the frequent number of cases of violence and exploitation towards IMWs. These issues even affect other political issues between the two countries. For example, in mid-2010, the tension over the way IMWs were treated in Malaysia spilled over into the border dispute between the governments of these two countries: when Indonesian officers

[1] The following ministries are accorded with the authority of managing IMWs: Ministry of Manpower and Transmigration (Binapenta General Directorate); National Body for Placement and Protection of IMWs (Badan Nasional Penempatan dan Perlindungan Tenaga Kerja Indonesia BNP2TKI); Ministry of Social Welfare (Director of Social Aid for Victims of Violence and Migrant Workers/General Directorate of Social Aid and Social Security-Guarantees); State Ministry of Women Empowerment and Child Protection; Coordinating Ministry of Social Welfare; Ministry of Foreign Affairs; and the Police Department. A related issue is the overlapping of authority between the Ministry of Manpower and Transmigration and BNP2TKI, as mandated by Law No. 39 of the Year 2004 on the Placement and Protection of IMWs.

Table 2 Number of IMWs in Malaysia by Sector and Type of Occupation, 2006-2010

SECTOR	OCCUPATION	2006*	2007*	2008*	2009*	2010**
Formal	Construction	216,898	211,016	207,623	196,929	192,789
	Un-irrigated agricultural field	316,832	290,484	287,781	260,232	202,156
	Mining/Factory	213,108	206,780	199,784	167,155	198,643
	Service	40,993	41,012	41,021	38,684	38,684
	Agriculture	92,003	103,974	105,485	98,799	82,435
Informal	Domestic Worker	294,115	294,784	279,134	230,141	203,225
Total		1,174,013	1,148,050	1,120,828	991,940	917,932

* Counted from July of the previous year to July of that year.
** Until May 2010.
Source: Bachtiar (2010).

detained several Malaysian fishermen for fishing illegally in Indonesian waters, the Malaysian Marine Police in turn arrested the Indonesian government officers. The case of IMWs in Malaysia can also be utilised as a significant issue to resolve political tensions between two countries. For instance, border disputes between the two governments (such as over the Ambalat stretch of the Celebes Sea) were reconciled amicably by the efforts of the two countries as they also worked to resolve the legal issue of more than 300 IMWs in Malaysia who were being charged for offences that could lead to the death penalty (Republika Newspaper 2010).

Sidel (2007, p. 19) looked into the different conditions often faced by IMWs in Malaysia, for example, being forced to surrender their passports either to the recruitment agencies' representatives or to their employers. Thus, workers are left without legal travel documents to prove their official status in the country and facilitate the extension of their work permits, making them more vulnerable to exploitation and abuse from their employers and recruitment agency. A similar condition was observed by Warren (2004, cited in Sidel 2007, p. 20) with regard to illegal migrant workers in Malaysia; their larger numbers make their situation even more problematic. In the absence of proper documentation, such workers are in a very weak position as far as the negotiation of wages and working conditions is concerned. In the absence of legal status, formal contracts, and other

Table 3 Types of IMW Rights Violations in Malaysia, 2006-2009

Type of Cases	2006	2007	2008	2009
Unpaid salary/wage	310	231	209	211
Inappropriate working conditions/ Scamming (victim of fraud)	328	300	287	380
Sexual harassment	31	29	23	53
Torture	141	106	93	114
Neglected (abandoned)/Illegal	14	17	82	177
Trafficking victim/Underage	20	19	57	56
Others (Unfit)	73	42	103	179
Total Number of Cases	917	744	854	1,170

Source: Bachtiar (2010).

forms of protection, illegal migrant workers face a variety of difficulties, including unpaid wages, long working hours, poor health and safety conditions, restrictions on movement, and intimidation and violence at the hands of employers and labour brokers. There is also a pattern of human trafficking, with thousands of Indonesian women being brought to Malaysia to work as prostitutes and subjected to harsh sexual abuse and exploitation (Sidel 2007, p. 20).

In fact, all categories of rights violations experienced by IMWs in Malaysia have increased over the years; the one exception is the number of trafficked victims (Table 3). The most significant increases are with regard to sexual harrasment and inappropriate working conditions.

There are two important policies recently undertaken to resolve the long-standing problems of IMWs in Malaysia. One is the formulation of a moratorium for sending informally, IMWs to Malaysia. The other policy involves the establishment of a Joint Commitee between the Republic of Indonesia and the Malaysian Diraja Government.

During the 2010 discussion of the MoU for IMWs working in the domestic sector as housemaids, Indonesia was driven by the interest to have their migrant workers able to retain their own passports; this, however, is not compatible with the long-standing tradition of Malaysian employers holding their respective charge's passports as a form of "assurance" that the latter will not run away. On the opposite side, the Malaysian Union of Foreign Workers Agencies (PAPA) persisted with their demands that IMWs' passports and saving-books should be in the temporary possession of their employers as a guarantee that IMWs will stay on with and obey their employers (Kompas Newspaper 2010). Other points in negotiation included the setting of minimum wages and a more standardised expense structure for placement.

While the issues of passport "safekeeping" and day offs have been agreed upon, the Indonesian and Malaysian Governments have yet to reach an agreement over the overall contents of the Memorandum of Understanding (MoU) for IMWs working as domestic workers. Indonesia's efforts are intended to protect the estimated 400,000 (at the very least) IMWs working in Malaysia as domestic workers (Kompas 2010). However, the Malaysian counter-argument to the issue is that Indonesia has not yet issued such regulations internally. This has driven Indonesia to propose a law on The Protection of Domestic Workers or Housemaids, currently being discussed in Indonesia's House of Representatives.

4. IMWs in Korea: A Success Story

Compared to their counterparts in Malaysia, IMWs in Korea generally experience better treatment. The most obvious difference is highlighted in the cooperation framework contained within the MoU between the governments of both countries, and the types of occupations available for IMWs, as well as the education levels of IMWs, sent to Korea.

Manpower relations between Indonesia and Korea began in 1994 through an industrial training programme, and continued in 2004 through an MoU of IMWs sent out based on the Employment Permit System (EPS). Because the EPS is a system whereby businesses unable to employ suitable Korean workers can hire foreigners instead, this system requires an effective management of foreign workers by the Korean Government. In 2008, the MoU was renewed for the second time, and was last updated in 2010. Korea is the most favorable destination country for IMWs, with the number of IMWs in the country ranking fourth after the Vietnamese, Thais and Filipinos.

Table 4 Tally of Participants, Selection Test to Korea in 2009

	Participants	Attendance Rate	Graduated	Did not graduate
Males	37,610	36,647 (97.4%)	N.A.	30,853
Females	4,146	3,994 (96.3%)	N.A.	3,248
Total	41,756	40,641 (97.3%)	6,540 (16.1%)	34,101

Source: BNP2TKI /HRDS Korea (2009). Accessed from www.bnp2tki.go.id.

Table 5 Data on IMWs Deployed to Korea

Year	No. of Persons
2004	360
2005	4,376
2006	1,214
2007	4,294

Source: BNP2TKI News (2008).

In order to comply with the requirements of the EPS, the Indonesian Government has been conducting several activities, such as training programmes, for IMWs prior to their departure to Korea. The training is intended to enhance each IMW candidate's mastery of the Korean language, culture and legal system, so as to adequately equip the IMWs for adaptation and communication during their work in Korea. In 2008, as many as 6,540 participants of the Korean Language Test (KLT) were declared graduates by the Human Resources Development Service President of Korea.[2] Table 4 shows a strong participation figure, and the result of the selection in 2009.

IMWs' interest in working in Korea has increased noticeably because of the relatively high wages, which is more than IDR8.5 million (USD900) monthly

[2] These 6,540 participants were part of the 41,996 individuals who undertook the KLT on 9-10 May 2009. The selection test was carried out within six universities throughout Indonesia: Pancasila University in Jakarta, Islamic Education Higher Learning in Cirebon, August 17th University in Surabaya, Hasanuddin University in Makasar, and Mataram Teaching School. Out of the 41,756 participants, there were 37,610 males and the rest were females. Meanwhile, participants who failed the test numbered as many as 34,101; of these, 47 individuals were declared unable to graduate due to cheating (BNP2TKI News 2009).

(Table 5). This surge of interest has benefited the Koreans, in terms of reducing the number of illegal IMWs, fulfilling the demand for labour, enhancing the semi-skilled workforce in Korea, as well as fostering economic growth and better understanding of another nation's culture. According to the Head of the National Agency on Indonesian Migrant Worker, Indonesia had the highest numbers of sending migrant workers in Korea for the period January-August 2009 (The Role Model of Education Institution 2010, p. 1). Better cooperation efforts can be observed from numerous activities carried out in the form of meetings between representatives of both countries in order to formulate strategies for highly qualified IMWs send-outs to Korea, such as the improvement of the recruitment process.[3]

In 2008, 9,500 Indonesians were targeted to be sent for work in Korea. However, at the end of 2008, the Korean Government issued a policy to not generate E-9 visas for foreign workers until February 2009. The policy created a huge impact on the number of IMWs sent to Korea. The policy was taken because the quota of 7,000 foreign workers had been filled up in 2008. By December, Indonesia had placed 11,890 IMWs from the target quota for 9,500 persons. This is an increase of 1,000 per cent compared to 2006 (BNP2TKI News 2009).

There are considerable success stories, where after three years or more working in Korea, some IMWs are able to establish enterprises with Koreans after their return home. Some of them have even started schools to teach Korean language courses. It is evident that the cooperation between Indonesia and Korea has benefited both countries. Indonesia has gained an advantage of unemployment reduction and the ability to absorb Korean industrial abilities, as well as the benefit of knowing the culture of another nation. However, it must also be admitted that several issues still need to be addressed, such as the wage disparity in the workforce between Koreans and non-Koreans. Many IMWs have also experienced abuse in their workplaces, undergoing poor working conditions, and not having freedom or off-days.

[3] These meetings, titled "Improvement of the Recruitment and Preparation of Migrant Workers to Korea," took place in Jakarta on 29-30 March 2008, and in Hanoi on 1-2 April, 2008 (International Labor Organization 2008).

5. Current Legal Framework and Problems

The fundamental and inalienable rights of all migrants, as human beings, have been universally acknowledged in international law instruments. Such instruments are based on the Universal Declaration of Human Rights, adopted by the United Nations General Assembly in 1948, the International Covenant on Economic, Social and Cultural Rights (ICESCR), and the International Covenant on Civil and Political Rights (ICCPR).

One of the major institutional accomplishments in relation to the protection of migrant workers rights is UN's adoption of the International Convention on The Protection of the Rights of All Migrants Workers and Members of Their Families which took effect on 1 July 2003. The implementation of this convention materialised through the establishment of several national policies within each assignatory country. They are first, to ensure the compatibility of migration policies, procedures and national legal systems with the international standards of human rights through the ratification of related covenants, and to address the issue of these international measures being adopted into laws or by the generation of national regulations. Second, to establish nationwide laws that are substantially concordant to international convention standards through the creation and management of manpower laws, penal codes and other national laws. Third, to set social policies that take the interests of the migrant workers in terms of education, housing and health into account. Fourth, to establish anti-discrimination laws. And fifth, to explain the laws in concrete and practical guides, understandable by ordinary people, particularly candidates of migrant workers (IOM and CMS 2010, p. 2).

The Indonesian Constitution currently provides adequate standards of protection, harmonising with the standards of international laws on the rights of workers.[4] However, the basic legal norms in the Constitution need to be

[4] Several measures within the Constitution of 1945 of the Republic of Indonesia ensure and protect civil rights in terms of manpower. These are: the right for an occupation and decent living in humanity (Article 27 Clause 2); the right for recognition, assurance, protection and fairly balanced certainty, as well as equal treatment before the law; and the right to work and receive wages/fees and fare and decent treatment within working relations; the right of citizenship (Article 28 D Clause 1, 2, and 4); the right to education and the choice of form of teaching, to choose domicile in a country and abandon it, as well as the right to return; the right to gather and establish unions, and the right of expression of opinion (Article 28 E Clause 1 and 3); the right to self protection and freedom from torture and other humanity-degrading treatments

translated into more detailed stipulation and operationalised in subordinate laws and regulations.

On 13 October 2010, the Indonesian government issued new policies intended to provide better protection towards the interests of IMWs. These policies cover aspects such as the requirement for any company involved in sending outs of IMWs to possess a permit for deploying IMWs, the importance of working contracts between IMWs and their employers, pre-departure training programmes for IMWs, the provision of an identification card that indicates the holder as having a "working abroad" status, the coordination of home-returns and the protection of IMWs in their regions.

However, the policies cover only limited aspects and Indonesia is still facing several fundamental legal problems in protecting its migrant workers. First, the protection of IMWs is still based on general articles derived from the Constitution. The protection guaranteed by the Constitution in this context may be regarded as similar to those stated in international standards and ILO conventions. Ratifications to the 1990 ILO Convention on the Protection of the Rights of All Migrant Workers and Members of their Families[5] should be adopted and integrated within the principles of legal and human rights protection for IMWs in national legal systems. From the perspective of receiving countries, this would be a good starting point for the advancement of legal and policy standards towards the fair management and treatment of IMWs.

---

as well as to acquire political asylum from other countries (Article 28 G), and the right to receive an education (Article 31).

[5] The Government of Indonesia recently ratified the 1990 Convention, co-enacted by the House of Representatives of the Republic of Indonesia and the President. The 1990 Convention supports the related national laws and regulations, including the following: (a) Law No. 13 Year 2003 on Manpower governs manpower or industrial relations, emphasising the rights and obligations of workers in the country, as well as the placement of workers internally and internationally. For workers that are stationed abroad, this law mandates that the issue must be governed in a specialised law; (b) Law No. 39 Year 2004 on the Placement and Protection of Indonesian Workers was generated from the mandate given by the Law on Manpower that specifically governs the placement and protection of IMWs. This law substituted for an earlier law, a legacy from the Dutch Colonial Government, which covered the directing of manpower abroad (Staatsblad 1887 Number 8 and Staatsblad 1936 No. 650 jo. Staatsblad 1938 No. 3888); (c) Law No. 48 Year 2000 on Anti-discrimination guarantees equality of rights in various forms between citizens, including terms of acquiring an occupation; and (d) Law No. 12 Year 2006 on Citizenship recognises the rights of Indonesian citizens concerning their citizenship status, including IMWs. (e) The Regulation of Manpower and Trans-migration Ministry through Number 14/Men/X0/2010 on the Conducts of Placement and Protection of IMWs Abroad.

Second, IMW placements abroad is conducted through MoUs between the Indonesian government and the government of destination countries (Tedja 2010). In 2007, Indonesia's target was to establish 17 MoUs with various receiving countries, but only 5 MoUs were ratified by the end of 2009; these were with Malaysia, Taiwan, Korea, Kuwait and Jordan. However, MoUs are insufficient in providing maximum protection, as they do not give Indonesia the authority to intervene with a destination country's policies.

Third, there is a conflict of jurisdiction among government institutions involved in the placement of IMWs abroad. This issue arose because of loopholes in a 2004 legislation (Law No. 39) regarding the procedures of IMWs send-outs (Hidayah 2010). The overlap in jurisdiction further affects the already lengthy bureaucratic processes involved in the placement of IMWs placement abroad.[6]

Given these legal problems, the Government of Indonesia should take into account the following policies. First, The Indonesian government needs to continuously ensure that it establishes MoUs with new destination countries that IMWs are sent to. For countries with existing MoUs on IMWs, effort needs to be made in improving the standard of protection. One positive example is the revision of the existing MoU with Korea. In contrast, the MoU with Malaysia is yet to reach an agreement to provide better protection of IMWs' rights. Second, the Indonesian government needs to ensure legal certainty by revising Law No. 39 Year 2004 on the Placement and Protection of IMWs. It needs to not only specifically clarify and clearly stipulate the tasks, functions and authorities of the related institutions in the placement and the standard of protection of IMWs, the management of the insurance for workers, but also strengthen the standard procedures prior, during and after their placement, as well as upon their return home to Indonesia. Finally, Indonesia needs to enact a law on the Protection of Housemaids. This law is required as a point of reference for IMWs' destination countries, to recognise housemaids as workers.

---

[6] Article 10 governs the conduct of the placement of IMWs abroad, which is carried out by the government and private sector, while Article 94 governs the establishment of the National Body for the Placement and Protection of IMWs (BNP2TKI 2010). This has created the issue of overlapping in terms of authority with the Ministry of Manpower and Transmigration, since the ministry is still given (and practicing) the authority to manage placement and protection of IMWs. In addition, the institution carrying out placements should be state-owned instead of directly "by the state."

6. Conclusion

The Indonesian policy of sending migrants workers abroad can be traced to its roots in colonial times. While international migration theories can explain the policy of sending Indonesian workers abroad, the most relevant issue and the focus of this paper is that Indonesia has not been able to create a sending policy that can provide comprehensive and a high standard of protection for IMWs.

While IMWs contribute to the economic benefit of the nation, on other side, these workers, particularly the unskilled female IMWs, face unfair treatment even prior to their reaching their receiving countries, as well as upon their return home. A well-managed system of sending migrant workers supported by bilateral agreements will be in line with providing better protection and security of IMWs.

Indonesia has a weak legal standard and there is a lack of legal certainty regarding the protection of IMWs. To its credit, the country has just ratified the UN Convention on Migrant Workers 1990, which has required the government to adopt the Convention into the national laws. This new standard of legal protection should ensure better security and protection for Indonesia's migrant workers prior to, during and when they return home. To get a more comprehensive and deeper understanding of how effective this will be in reality in terms of protecting IMWs will require further research, including fieldwork, in receiving countries.

References

Bachtiar, D. (2010). "Problem of Indonesian Migrant Workers in Malaysia." Paper presented in the Public Hearing of Committee IX, the Indonesian House of the Republic of Indonesia. 19 August. Jakarta.

Coordination of Action Research on Aids and Mobility (CARAM) Asia (2005). "Migrant Workers in Asia: Issues and Concerns." Paper presented on One Day General Discussion on Migrant Worker. Organised by the UN High Commissioner for Human Rights. 15 December.

Coordination of Action Research on Aids and Mobility (CARAM) Indonesia (Indonesian National Commission on Violence Against Women and Solidaritas Perempuan) (2006). *Indonesian Migrant Workers: Systematic Abuse at Home and Abroad.* Indonesian Country Report to the UN Special Rapporteur on the Human Rights of Migrants. Kuala Lumpur.

Hidayah, A. (2010). "Government Treats Migrant Worker as Export Commodities." *Jakarta Post*. 11 June. Jakarta. Accessed on 23 August 2010 from https://www.thejakartapost.com/news/2010/06/11/discourse-government-treats-migrant-workers-export-commodities.html.

International Labor Organization (2008). Press Release: Situation of Indonesian, Vietnamese Wokers in Korea to be discussed at ILO Meeting. *ILO News*. 28 March. Bangkok.

International NGO Forum on Indonesian Development (2006). "Indonesian Migrant Workers, a Never Ending Suffering." Written Statement on Migrant Workers. Jakarta. Accessed on 18 August 2012 from http://www.kontras.org/data/Item%2014a,%20Migrant%20Workers.pdf.

International Organization for Migration and Center for Migration Studies (2010). "Legal Aspect Pertaining to Irregular Migration." Paper presented at the conference on Irregular Migration: Legal & Policy Perspectives. 21-22 January. Millenium UN Plaza, New York.

Kompas Newspaper (2010). "Indonesia Harus Tegas Soal Paspor" (Indonesia should be strict on passport matter). 26 August. Accessed on 27 August 2010 from http://internasional.kompas.com/read/2010/08/26/21373092/Indonesia.Harus.Tegas.soal.Paspor.

Mahfiz, I. C. (2010). "The Protection of the IMWs Abroad: A Mandate of the Independence Declaration of the Republic of Indonesia." Paper presented in the Public Hearing of Committee IX, the Indonesian House of the Republic of Indonesia. 19 August. Jakarta.

Mackenzie, C. (2005). (ed.) *Labor Migration in Asia, Protection of Migrant Workers, Support Services and Enhancing Development Benefits*. International Organization for Migration. Geneva, Switzerland.

Oishi, N. (2002). *Gender and Migration: An Integrative Studies*. Working Paper. The Center for Comparative Studies, University of California: San Diego.

Oishi, N. (2005). *Women in Motion: Globalization, State Policies, and Labor Migration in Asia*. Stanford University Press.

Republic of Indonesia, National Agency for Placement and Protection of IMWs. "Statistics of Indonesian Migrant Workers." Accessed on 10 November 2010 from www.bnp2tki.go.id.

Republika Newspaper. "Border Dispute Between Indonesia and Malaysia." Accessed on 10 September 2010 from http://www.republica.co.id.

Role Model of Education Institution (2010). "Indonesian Migrant Worker is the Highest Number in Korea." Accessed on 6 August 2012 from http./teladancourse.wordpress.com.

Sidel, J. T. (2007). "Indonesia: Minorities, Migrant Workers, Refugees, and the New Citizenship Law." Writenet Report, commissioned by United Nations High Commissioner for Refugees, Status Determination and Protection Information Section (DIPS). Accessed on 27 July 2012 from http://www.ecoi.net/file_upload/432_1176282950_2007-03-writenet-indonesia.pdf.

Tedja, H. (2010). "Annual Review in Indonesian Migrant Workers." ANTARA. Republic of Indonesia News. 23 August.

World Bank, Female Migrant Workers Research Team (2006). Migration, Remittance and Female Migrant Workers Fact Sheet. Accessed on from http://siteresources.worldbank.org/INTINDONESIA/Resources/fact_sheet-migrant_workers_en_jan06.pdf.

Transnationalism and Skilled Worker Migration in an Innovation-led Economy: The Case of Malaysia

Morshidi Sirat

1. Introduction and Context

At the outset, this chapter acknowledges the assertion that transnational migration studies form a highly fragmented field, quite often ambiguous and that is in search of a well-defined theoretical framework (Portes et al. 1999; Smith & Guarnizo 1998) but significant progress has been made since the late-1990s (Levitt & Jaworsky 2007). It is also pertinent to note that in this chapter, transnationalism is approached from the angle of transnational migration within the discipline of geography. From this perspective, transnationalism is understood as a set of processes and their elements can be studied or explained in relation to influencing factors at the micro (family and individual) and macro (national and international) levels. Primarily, our interest is on the pattern and implications of migration flows of highly skilled workers to and from Malaysia—a country that is actively seeking talent and highly skilled workers in order to achieve national socioeconomic development objectives. Since the mid-2000s, Malaysia has laid out a plan to shift towards a knowledge-based economy (KBE) to achieve national development objectives (Malaysia 2006; 2010). Notably, to achieve these objectives, the Malaysian Government established a Talent Corporation (TalentCorp) under the Prime Minister's Department in 2011. This entity is mandated "to attract, motivate and retain the talent needed for a high income economy" (Malaysia 2010, p. 239). Within its terms of reference, TalentCorp has three key roles: (1) to develop and drive specific catalytic and innovative talent management initiatives to attract and develop world class talent in collaboration with both the public and private sectors; (2) to facilitate industry and private sector efforts in creating, motivating and retaining a skilled workforce; and (3) to be responsible for ensuring the delivery of major national initiatives on talent across the human capital development pipeline in line with Malaysia's economic transformation plan (Malaysia 2010, p. 240). To date, TalentCorp has outlined its programme-managing and tracking plans in its TalentCorp Road Map.

Malaysia's blueprint for creating, retaining and engaging talents as embodied in the activities of TalentCorp must be considered in the context of the Malaysian economy which is going through a transformation phase—from one which is production-based to one which is based on knowledge and innovation. There are many definitions of a KBE, all revolving around the notion of an economy based on the production, distribution and utilisation of knowledge. These activities constitute the primary engine of growth and wealth creation in the KBE (Organization for Economic Co-operation and Development 1996). Along this line, Malaysia's push towards a knowledge economy is based on the assertion that the economy will be driven by knowledge, creativity and innovation which will generate and sustain growth. It is argued that in a knowledge- (in contrast to a production-) based economy, educated and skilled human capital is the most valuable asset. As a matter of fact, Malaysia's journey towards becoming a KBE began when Vision 2020 was launched in February 1991. From the perspective of the Malaysian government, the KBE will provide the platform to sustain a rapid rate of economic growth and enhance international competitiveness via Malaysia's capability and capacity to innovate; adapt and create indigenous technology; and design, develop and market new products, thereby providing the foundation for endogenously-driven growth. More importantly, a KBE will complement and accelerate the change from an input-driven to a productivity driven growth strategy (Institute for Strategic and International Studies 2002).

It is now widely recognised that a highly skilled workforce is a prerequisite for sustaining economic growth in modern knowledge-based economies where research and innovation drive economic expansion (Tremblay 2004). However, due to the lack of resources and/or effective human capital development systems, many countries on their own are unable to produce, in adequate number, a highly skilled workforce. Among such countries, rapid rates of economic development based on high technology industrialisation but declining rates of growth in the indigenous labour force, fuel a demand for imported skilled labour (Skeldon 2005). Furthermore, globalisation and efficient communication and transportation systems have expanded opportunities for high skilled workers to migrate across nation-states.

Admittedly, some countries experiencing intense skilled emigration may gradually lose their capacity to develop in the medium to longer term if this trend is not compensated by the domestic production of a skilled workforce. The migration of skilled workers to the developed world, from countries that can ill afford to lose valuable human capital, is a major issue in migration literature. Some developing countries exhibit brain drain rates frequently higher than 50 per cent (which is typically the case for Sub-Saharan African countries) or even 80 per cent (in countries such as Jamaica and Guyana) (Docquier et al. 2009 as cited in Docquier & Rapoport 2009, p. 3). In the final analysis, discourse on the migration of skilled workers, from nations in the developing south to the developed north, will invoke issues such as brain drain (Wickramasekara 2002). At this juncture it is sufficient to refer to the term "brain drain" as the international transfer of resources in the form of human capital, mainly applying to the migration of highly educated individuals from developing to developed countries (Docquire & Rapoport 2006). However increasingly, as noted by Vertovec (2002), with the recognition of networks of skilled-worker circulation, many social scientists and national policymakers have tended to shift from a discourse of "brain drain" to a more positive notion of the globalisation of human capital: "brain exchange," "brain circulation" and the creation of a global mobile workforce.

Even though the existing literature on the brain drain suggests that skilled emigration may induce positive feedback effects for sending countries (e.g., increased remittances, trade, transfer of knowledge and behavioural modes), these tend to be dominated by the direct effect of brain drain on the stock of human capital (Docquier & Schiff 2009). Interestingly in this regard, sending countries of the South recently began to view this brain drain problem positively, given that in the medium- to longer-term, such "brain circulation" and "brain gain" will benefit them (Malaysia 2010; Beine et al. 2008).

Before proceeding further, it is important to highlight the difficulty in examining transnational skilled-worker migration so that we are aware of the limitations of the resultant analysis. Skeldon (2005), among others, has pointed out that this difficulty can be attributed to several factors. First, there is the intricate problem of defining precisely who are normally regarded as highly skilled workers. Cerna (2010) and Beine et al. (2007) allude to the fact that the literature includes a wide variety of definitions for highly skilled immigrants. However, while definitions vary according to country, organisations and disciplinary focus of studies, there are some common elements in the literature as to what skilled workers or immigrants refer to. Vertovec (2002, p. 2), for instance, defines skilled migrants as "those in possession of a tertiary degree or extensive specialized work experience." Skilled workers, according to Vertovec, include architects, accountants and financial experts, engineers, technicians, researchers, scientists, chefs, teachers, health professionals and increasingly—specialists in information technology (e.g., computing professionals, computing engineers, managers and sales representatives) (p. 2). Having a "university degree or extensive/equivalent experience in a given field" is another commonly cited criterion (Iredale 2001, p. 8; Salt 1997, p. 5, as cited in Cerna, 2010, p. 1). While not adequate in itself, at a general level, a highly skilled migrant can arguably be defined as someone who has either tertiary education qualifications (after completing at least two years of study) or work experience that provides that person with the equivalent skills. Interestingly, in the current emerging focus on the knowledge economy, the International Organization for Migration (IOM) has refined the definition of highly skilled workers by suggesting that these are persons with high value-added and high productivity activities that are essential to the global knowledge society (International Organization for Migration 2008).

Another intractable problem relates to the availability of data that may assist us in relating the skills set to international migration. Adding to all of the above-mentioned constraints is the fact that, as Skeldon (2005) and Lowell and Findlay (2002) have noted, source countries of international migration rarely keep records of those who leave in a systematic way, and data usually have to be compiled from countries of destination, and mostly from population censuses, to provide stock estimates. Apparently, there are serious limitations in data on skilled migration even in developed economies (Carrington & Detragiache 1998, as cited in Wickramasekara 2002). Consequently, despite the existence of a great deal of literature on transnational migration, it is impossible to draw a systematic global quantitative picture of migration of the highly skilled (Dunnewijk 2008).

All of the above problems are pertinent to our analysis of highly skilled migration in Malaysia. However specifically, and these need to be made clear at this juncture—data collection activities of the Malaysian government are focused more on recording immigration rather than emigration (Kanapathy 2008). Data collection is also based on the type of visa or work permit issued to foreigners. Notably in this regard, two categories of highly skilled workers are recorded, namely, expatriates and foreign skilled workers. The former category refers to all professional and technical migrant workers who earn a monthly salary of not less than RM3,000 (or USD945). These expatriates are issued with an "Employment Pass" if the employment contract is for at least two years. The foreign skilled workers category on the other hand, includes all professional and technical migrant workers on short-term contracts of less than a year and they are issued a "Visit Pass for Professional Employment." Another point to note is that the Malaysian government has not been closely monitoring the emigration of highly skilled Malaysians.

2. The Issues

In 2000, World Bank data indicated that emigration of the tertiary-educated population in Malaysia was at 10.4 per cent, a level relatively low compared to many other ASEAN countries such as Vietnam (39.0 per cent), Brunei (21.0 per cent), Singapore (15.2 per cent) and the Philippines (14.8 per cent) (Docquier & Marfouk 2007, cited in Fong 2010, p. 3). For Malaysia, about 30 per cent of the "17-24 age-group" cohort was enrolled in tertiary higher education in the mid-2000s; the high gross enrolment ratio of this cohort made emigration of the tertiary-educated population less of a problem then. In fact, data have shown that the rate of skilled-worker emigration in Malaysia had fallen from 24.7 per cent in 1990 to 10.4 per cent in 2000 (Docquier & Marfouk 2007, cited in Fong 2010, p. 3).

2.1 Emigration flows out of Malaysia

Fong (2010, p. 24), citing United Nations (UN) (2010) data, summarised some of the important facts observed in emigration flows out of Malaysia: (1) the number of Malaysians residing in the United Kingdom, Australia and New Zealand (traditional emigration destinations for Malaysians) has increased substantially since the early 1980s; (2) Australia is a major destination for Malaysians, with 31,598 Malaysians emigrating in 1981 and increasing to 92,337 migrants in 2007; (3) the United Kingdom continues to attract Malaysians (45,430 migrants in 1981 to 61,000 migrants in 2007); and (4) closer to home, there were 120,104 Malaysians in Singapore in 1981, increasing to 303,828 Malaysians in 2001. However, the figures noted above relate to the emigration of Malaysians of all categories. A pertinent question to ask is "What is the situation in terms of emigration among highly skilled Malaysians?"

Based on data from The World Bank's (2007) Brain Drain Database (cited in Fong 2010, p. 24), the following can be observed. While Canada did not appear as a major destination for emigration among Malaysians, it attracted 12,170 Malaysians with tertiary education in 2000; assuming that tertiary-educated Malaysians are highly skilled workers, the emigration of Malaysians to Canada in 2000 represents an increase of 43.5 per cent from the 1990 figure of 8,480 migrants. Australia, the United States and the United Kingdom were typically the major destinations for tertiary-educated Malaysians in 2000. Australia has been especially successful in attracting Malaysians with tertiary education; in 1990, there were 34,716 tertiary-educated Malaysians in Australia, increasing to 39,601 (an increase of 14.1 per cent) by 2000. The United States, on the other hand, attracted almost 13,000 tertiary-educated Malaysians over the same 10-year period, with 24,695 tertiary-educated Malaysians resident there; in fact, the United States experienced a 100.5 per cent increase in the number of tertiary-educated Malaysians in from the period of 1990 to 2000 (Fong, 2010, p. 27).

More specifically then, the questions to be asked are "Who are these highly skilled emigrants from Malaysia?" and "Were they Malaysians who were educated overseas (in the United States of America, the United Kingdom and Australia) or educated locally but have made the decision to emigrate?" These questions cannot be answered factually as the relevant Malaysian Immigration does not collect information on emigration. However, the following provides us with a glimpse of emigration from Malaysia. Docquier and Rapoport (2009) reported that in 2003, there were 10,419 Science and Technology (S&T) researchers in Malaysia. Of great interest is the fact that in 2003, there were 7,955 S&T researchers from Malaysia residing in the United States, giving a ratio of 76.4:100 of Malaysian researchers in Malaysia to Malaysian researchers in the United States. This ratio for Malaysia is low in comparison to Vietnam (449.5:100) and Hong Kong (214.4:100) (Fong 2010, p. 3).

2.2 Immigration flows to Malaysia

The next issues are "Who are attracted to Malaysia?" and "Who appears on Malaysia's radar for highly skilled workers?" Based on UN (2010) data cited in Fong (2010, p. 2), which assumes that immigrants from Singapore (46,400), Japan (8,800), the United States (5,750), Australia (3,100) and New Zealand (1,250) are highly skilled workers, the numbers appear low in comparison to the total immigration figure for Malaysia in 2000. Notably, while there were huge numbers of immigrants from Indonesia (627,700), the Philippines (124,600) and immigrants from China, India and Bangladesh combined (no less than 150,000) (Fong 2010, p. 2), there is no way to determine the number of highly skilled workers among them migrating to Malaysia. We can arguably assume that the numbers of highly skilled workers migrating to Malaysia from Indonesia and China to be small given that worldwide, the overall emigration rate of the tertiary-educated population from these countries in 2000 was as low as 2.0 per cent for Indonesia and 4.2 per cent for China. However, even then, considering the total population of these two countries, those numbers could be huge. Furthermore, the main destinations for Chinese and Indonesian emigrants appear to be the Organisation for Economic Co-operation and Development (OECD) countries and the United States of America (Docquier & Marfouk 2007; Docquier & Rapoport 2009). Similar patterns are displayed by Indian and Bangladeshi highly skilled workers. Viewed from the angle of emigration of PhD holders, the estimated migration rate of PhD holders from China, Bangladesh and the Philippines to the United States were 22.8 per cent, 21.7 per cent and 10.2 per cent respectively (Docquier & Rapoport 2009, p. 6).

Not many studies on highly skilled worker migration to Malaysia have been conducted to understand this phenomenon. Studies that have been undertaken tend to focus on the migration of unskilled legal and illegal workers from Indonesia and the Philippines at the micro level (Azizah 2003; Azizah 2007; Morshidi & Suriati 2011). Untypically, Tan and Santhapparaj (2007) analysed the macroeconomic determinants of skilled migration into Malaysia from 39 countries during the 1998-2004 period. Tan and Santhapparaj's study provides important insights on the pattern of skilled worker migration and the reasons for immigration to Malaysia. The 39 countries listed by Tan and Santhapparaj as important sending countries were aggregated and presented in their analysis as regions rather than individual countries; in order of importance for skilled worker immigration to Malaysia are East Asia, South Asia and Southeast Asia (Table 1). It is reported that in 1998, 30.4 per cent of the total skilled immigrants to Malaysia were from East Asia, 22.5 per cent from Southeast Asia and 21.0 per cent from South Asia. In addition, skilled worker migration from the European Union at 15.3 per cent (or 10,885 migrants) in 1998 (Tan and Santhapparaj 2007, p. 3018), though not very considerable, was very important too. Arguably, the marked inflow of skilled immigration from East Asia to Malaysia in the late 1980s could be attributed to the setting up of large numbers of Japanese and

Table 1 Number and Percentage of Skilled Immigrants to Malaysia by Region/Country and Year, 1998-2004

Region/ Country	Number (% in parentheses)						
	1998	1999	2000	2001	2002	2003	2004
South East Asia (SEA)	15,960 (22.5)	14,048 (22.9)	15,119 (24.4)	13,320 (24.5)	11,439 (25.0)	7,882 (22.9)	7,155 (20.7)
South Asia (SA)	14,934 (21.0)	13,045 (21.2)	13,566 (21.9)	12,159 (22.4)	10,157 (23.0)	8,477 (24.6)	9,692 (28.1)
East Asia (EA)	21,608 (30.4)	18,694 (30.4)	18,443 (29.8)	16,326 (30.0)	13,690 (30.0)	10,883 (31.6)	11,101 (32.1)
Europe (EU)	10,885 (15.3)	9,161 (14.9)	8,582 (13.9)	7,266 (13.4)	5,780 (12.7)	4,162 (12.1)	3,469 (10.0)
Middle East (ME)	864 (1.2)	740 (1.2)	707 (1.1)	624 (1.2)	556 (1.2)	491 (1.4)	508 (1.5)
USA and Canada	3,359 (4.7)	2,853 (4.7)	2,642 (4.7)	2,216 (4.1)	1,652 (3.6)	1,170 (3.4)	1,238 (3.6)
Australia & New Zealand	3,367 (4.7)	2,888 (4.7)	2,889 (4.7)	2,467 (4.5)	2,042 (4.5)	1,382 (4.0)	1,383 (4.0)
Total	70,977 (100.0)	61,429 (100.0)	61,948 (100.0)	54,378 (100.0)	45,676 (100.0)	34,447 (100.0)	34,546 (100.0)

Source: Malaysia Immigration Department (2005), cited in Tan and Santhapparaj (2007, p. 3018).

Korean multinational corporations (electronic and electrical firms) in regional production centres such as Penang, Johor and the Klang Valley (Best 1999; Rasiah 2005; Rasiah 2007). Transnational enterprises have resulted in significant inflows of skilled migration to Malaysia since the early 1980s when global production systems within the electronic and electrical sector necessitated the relocation of major production activities in Malaysia. Admittedly, the recent proliferation of professional international intermediaries confirms the fact that globalisation of the highly skilled-labour market does not occur without massive network investments (Meyer 2001, as cited in Vertovec 2002). Apparently, besides recruiting skilled workers from their own home base countries, multinational corporations from the European Union and of other nationalities have a tendency to recruit skilled workers from countries in the ASEAN/Asian region. By 2004, skilled worker migration from East Asia remained high (32.1 per cent), followed by South Asia (28.1 per cent) and Southeast Asia at 20.7 per cent (Table 1). This, to some extent, led to the decline in the share of skilled worker immigration into Malaysia from the European Union—10.0 per cent in 2004. It is important to realise that while some regions maintained their share of skilled worker immigration to Malaysia, the total number of skilled worker immigration in fact decreased markedly between 1998 and 2004. Table 1 also shows that by 2004, skilled worker immigration to Malaysia stood at 34,546 migrants as compared to 70,977 migrants in 1998.

While Malaysia continues to produce graduates in science and technology, it is important that public universities produce graduates with the required skill competencies. As the future scenario for the attraction of talent and skilled workers remains highly competitive in the Asian region, Malaysia will continue to experience a steady decrease in skilled worker immigration and ultimately Malaysia has to depend on locally produced engineers and ICT workers to meet the demand of an economy undergoing a transformation phase.

In the absence of other research on the topic, the Tan and Santhapparaj (2007) study provides important evidence as to the macroeconomic determinants of skilled immigration to Malaysia and its policy implications. Arguably, while short-run changes in skilled immigration flows to Malaysia tend to be dominated by cyclical economic conditions, long-term trends are determined by income growth in Malaysia (Tan & Santhapparaj 2007). In other words, economic development in both sending and host countries, or more likely economic prosperity in Malaysia and economic difficulty in sending countries, play an important role in determining the volume and intensity of immigration flows. Foreign direct investment and the establishment of transnational enterprises in developing countries have been shown to have contributed significantly to the growth of skilled workers (Lowell & Findlay 2002). Policy-wise, such evidence suggests that two instruments may be introduced to increase skilled migration to Malaysia: entry relaxation in Malaysia, and the offering of attractive incentives to skilled immigrants (Fong 2010; Tan & Santhapparaj 2007). Fong (2010) has gone further in terms of policy directions, recommending that Malaysia should not only enhance skilled worker immigration to Malaysia but more importantly, implement strategies that will retain skilled workers in Malaysia. Attracting skilled workers to Malaysia has proved to be very tricky as other countries are simplifying their immigration procedures (Canadavisa.com 2008; Home Office 2006); more importantly, they are offering better employment opportunities for skilled migrants. In this connection, Malaysian student-turned-migrants in Australia, Canada, the United Kingdom and the United States are an important phenomenon that has accounted for substantial skilled emigration.

3. The Way Forward for Malaysia

As noted at the outset, there are many definitions for "transnationalism" and the related theoretical framework varies according to disciplinary focus and emphasis. In this regard, policy actions in response to transnationalism also vary tremendously among countries of the developed and developing world. In Malaysia, for professionals and highly skilled workers, there are no limitations imposed on source countries (with the exception of Israel and some African states) for such workers. Job contracts are normally confined to two years (with a maximum term of five years). There is a tendency for expatriates to be employed in multinational enterprises, although increasing numbers are employed in the computing, medical and engineering field as well as in the higher education and sports sector (Azizah 2005, as cited in Kaur 2008). The number employed in the information technology sector has quantum leaped with the establishment of the Multimedia Super Corridor. In view of the strategic importance of expatriate recruitment, policy regarding this sphere has always been under the jurisdiction of the Committee for Expatriate Workers which comprises government representatives from nine ministries, and approval for recruitment can come from a variety of agencies (Kaur 2008). Policy changes on expatriate and skilled-worker recruitment are instituted from time to time, depending on national and regional situations. For example, in April 2008, the Malaysian government announced that highly skilled migrants would be allowed to stay in Malaysia for a maximum of ten years (*New Straits Times*, 16 April 2008, as cited in Kaur 2008).

Recent activities and policy statements in pursuit of the potential benefits of transnationalism serve as clear indications on how the country views this phenomenon. TalentCorp's blueprint to retain and source talents worldwide should in the longer term provide the necessary human and intellectual capital to push Malaysia towards a high-income economy. It came to realise that a policy based on domestic production of skilled workers to support a knowledge-driven economy is untenable in the shorter to medium term (Morshidi 2010). Malaysia, as a host country for skilled immigration, has started to incorporate the transnational fields in order to achieve national development objectives and presently, it is on the radar for unskilled rather than highly skilled migrants. Much has been said about the steep increase in the numbers of official labour migrants in the country which reached a peak of 2,235,200 migrants in 2007, although it is estimated that there were also one million undocumented migrants (Badri 2008; Hugo 2009; Kaur 2008). Since Malaysia has been unable to attract significant numbers of highly skilled workers to contribute to national development objectives, it has to retain local talent and engage talented Malaysians abroad more aggressively. Current policy discourse emphasising on tapping the potential of overseas diaspora for home country development needs to be reviewed. This is because many talented Malaysians abroad continue to have an outdated view of the socio-political situation in Malaysia. Under both the Eighth and Ninth Malaysia Plan, the government announced an ambitious "reverse brain drain" project, especially in the key fields of information and communication technology, science and technology, manufacturing industries, finance, and medicine, to propel Malaysia to transform itself into a "K-economy and Information Society." Now, Malaysians expect the Talent Corporation to deliver the results in terms of talent development in the Tenth Malaysia Plan development period. With only 28 per cent of the total labour force considered as skilled workers, Malaysia certainly has a long way to go and will need to concentrate much efforts to catch up with a first-world skill and talent base by 2020 (Malaysia 2010). Inevitably, the country should not be over-focusing on just bringing home overseas Malaysian talent; it is worthwhile to explore strategies that would attract overseas talent in general. Focusing effort on such an undertaking would be an uphill task, as this group (overseas Malaysians) are more likely to question Malaysia's policies on inter-ethnic relations, the future political scenario, and bureaucracy. All these questions would unnecessarily put TalentCorp in a defensive mode and much time will be needed to address these questions. In the final analysis, in order to achieve national aspirations and development objectives Malaysia should attract global talent and this search should not be confined to Malaysians residing overseas. The search must be global in nature and the target must be talented workers who see Malaysia as a land of opportunity to realise their dreams.

The discussion in this chapter has highlighted one very important dimension of the approaches to the study and analysis of transnational migration. Malaysia is trying to achieve a substantial pool of talented and skilled workers encompassing brain-circulation and the sharing of these resources. Within the country's context, emigration must be considered within a framework of migration for the purpose of nation-building which includes the mode of "contributing from a distance." Within this framework, Malaysians who have emigrated should not be pressured into thinking that their lives are fragmented between two countries and this situation is not conducive to talent management in Malaysia. Instead, the country should facilitate these transnational practices to enable Malaysians abroad to rely on their homeland as well as their host countries to construct, in a meaningful manner, their "contribution from a distance" to nation-building.

References

Azizah, K. (2007). "Development and International Migration in Malaysia: Patterns, Policy and Human Rights." In A. Rahman, ed. *Social science and Malaysian National Development*. Kuala Lumpur: Malaysian Social Science Association & IKMAS.

_________ (2005). "Security and Social Implications of Cross-national Migration in Malaysia." In H. Mohamed Jawhar, ed. *Pacifying the Pacific: Confronting the Challenges*. Kuala Lumpur: ISIS Malaysia.

_________ (2003). "Trans-national Migration Within and Among the ASEAN Member Countries: Issues and Challenges for Malaysia." In A. O. Marja & D. Peters, eds. *ASEAN Universities Student Leaders Conference Proceedings*. Kota Kinabalu: Penerbit UMS.

Badri, M. (2008). "Malaysia: Labour Migration Management, Trends and Challenges." Paper presented at the regional conference on Labour Migration Management in the Process of Regional Integration (27-30 May). Bangkok, Thailand.

Beine, M., Docquier, F. and Rapoport, H. (2008). "Brain Drain and Human Capital Formation in Developing Countries: Winners and Losers." *Economic Journal*, 118, 631-652.

___________ (2007). "Measuring International Skilled Migration: New Estimates Controlling for Age of Entry." *World Bank Economic Review*, 21, 249-254. Accessed on 18 August 2012 from http://perso.uclouvain.be/frederic.docquier/filePDF/BDRageofentry.pdf.

Best, M. (1999). "Cluster Dynamics In Theory And Practice: Singapore/Johor And Penang Electronics." Accessed on 6 November 2010 from http://www.tci-network.org/media/asset_publics/resources/000/000/797/original/singapore_electronics_cluster-best.pdf .

Canadavisa.com (2008). "*Work Permit Now More Accessible to International Students in Canada*." Accessed on 11 November 2010 from http://www.canadavisa.com.

Carrington, W. J. & Detragiache, E. (1998). *How Big is the Brain Drain?* Working Paper: WP/98/102. Washington D.C.: IMF.

Cerna, L. (2010). "Policies and Practices of Highly Skilled Migration in Times of the Economic Crisis." *International Migration Papers* (99). International Migration Program, Geneva, ILO. Accessed on 6 November 2010 from www.ilo.org/ public/english/protection/migrant/.../ imp99.pdf.

Docquier, F. and Marfouk, A. (2007). *The Brain Data Base*. Washington DC: The World Bank.

Docquier, F., Lowell, B. L. and Marfouk, A. (2009). "A Gendered Assessment of the Brain Drain." *Population and Development Review*, 35 (2), 297-321.

Docquier, F. and Rapoport, H. (2009). "Documenting the Brain Drain of la crème de la crème: Three Case-studies on International Migration at the Upper Tail of the Education Distribution." *Journal of Economics and Statistics*, 229 (6), 679-705.

Docquier, F. and Schiff, M. (2009). *Measuring Skilled Migration Rates-The Case of Small States*. Policy Research Working Paper 4827. The World Bank, Development Research Group, Trade Team.

Dunnewijk, T. (2008). *Global Migration of the Highly Skilled: A Tentative and Quantitative Approach*. Working Paper Series, No. 2008-070, UNU-MERIT. Accessed on 26

October 2010 from http:// www.merit.unu.edu/ publications/wppdf/2008/ wp2008-070.pdf.

Fong, C. O. (2010). "Tracing the Brain Drain Trend—Many Ways to Attract Overseas Talent." *Sunday Star* (May 16), pp. 2-3, 24 and 27.

Home Office (2006). *Working in the UK*. Accessed on 11 November 2010 from http://www/workingintheuk.gov.uk.

Hugo, G. (2009). *Governance and Institutional Issues in Migration in Asia and the Pacific*. Draft Paper for East-West Centre Project on Cross-Border Governance. http://www.snap-undp.org/lepknowledgebank/Public%20Document%20Library/ Governance%20and%20Institutional%20Issues%20in%20Migration%20in%20Asia%20Pacific%202009.pdf.

Institute of Strategic and International Studies (2002). *Knowledge Base Economy Master Plan*. Ministry of Finance: Kuala Lumpur.

International Organization for Migration (2008). *World Migration 2008: Managing Labour Mobility in the Evolving Global Economy*. Geneva: International Organization for Migration.

Iredale, R. (2001). "The Migration of Professionals: Theories and Typologies." *International Migration*, 39 (5), 7-24.

Kanapathy, V. (2008). *Controlling Irregular Migration. The Malaysian Experience*. ILO Asian Regional Programme in Governance of Labour Migration. Working Paper No. 14. Geneva: ILO and EU. Accessed on 10 November 2010 from http://pstalker.com/ilo/resources/ WP14%20%20Malaysia%20Irregular%20Migration.pdf.

Kaur, A. (2008). "International Migration and Governance in Malaysia: Policy and Performance." *UNEAC Asia Papers*, No. 22. Accessed on 10 November 2010 from http://www.une.edu.au/asiacentre/PDF/No22.pdf.

Levitt, P. and Jaworsky, N. (2007). "Transnational Migration Studies: Past Developments and Future Trends." *Annual Review of Sociology*, Vol. 33, 129-156.

Lowell, L. and Findlay, A. (2002). "Migration of Highly Skilled Persons from Developing Countries: Impact and Policy Responses. A Synthesis Report." Geneva: ILO. Accessed on 10 November 2010 from http://www.ilo.org/public/english/protection/migrant/download/imp/imp44.pdf.

Malaysia (2010). *The Tenth Malaysia Plan, 2011-2015*. Kuala Lumpur: Percetakan Nasional Malaysia Berhad.

________ (2006). *The Ninth Malaysia Plan, 2006-2010*. Kuala Lumpur: Percetakan Nasional Malaysia Berhad.

Meyer, J. B. (2001). "Network Approach versus Brain Drain: Lessons from the Diaspora." *International Migration*, 39, 91-108.

Morshidi, S. (2010). "Education Transformation and Human/intellectual Capital Formation in Malaysia: Plans Aplenty but What Are the Outcomes?" Paper presented at the 14th UNESCO-APEID International Conference, Education for Human Resource Development. 21-23 October. Bangkok, Thailand.

Morshidi, S. and Suriati, G. (2011). "Migrant Labour, Residential Conflict and the City: The Case of Foreign Workers' Invasion of Residential Neighbourhoods in Penang, Malaysia." In T. C. Wong and J. Rigg, eds. *Asian Cities, Migrant Labour and Contested Spaces*. Routledge Contemporary Asia series. Abingdon, Oxon: Routledge.

Organisation for Economic Co-operation and Development (1996). The Knowledge-based Economy. Paris: OECD.

Portes, A., Guarnizo, L. E. and Landolt, P. (1999). "The Study of Transnationalism: Pitfalls and Promise of an Emergent Research Field. Introduction to a Special Issue." *Ethnic and Racial Studies*, 22 (2), 217-237.

Rasiah, R. (2007). "From Export Processing Zones to Clusters: Explaining Industrial Synergies in the Electronics Industry in Malaysia." In C. Ramachandriah, G. V. Westen and S. Prasad, eds. *High-tech Urban Spaces: Asian and European Perspectives*. New Delhi: Manohar Publishers.

_________ (2005). "Human Capital Development and Knowledge Flows: The Experience of the Electronics Industry in Penang and Klang Valley." In R. A. Nungsari, ed. *New Challengers Facing Rural Development and Poverty Alleviation*. Kuala Lumpur: Yayasan Tun Razak.

Skeldon, R. (2005). *Globalization, Skilled Migration and Poverty Alleviation: Brain Drains in Context*. Working Paper T15. Development Research Centre on Migration, Globalisation and Poverty, University of Sussex.

Salt, J. (1997). "International Movement of the Highly Skilled." *OECD Occasional Paper* 3. London: International Migration Unit.

Smith, M. P. and Guarnizo, L. E. (eds.) (1998). "Transnationalism from Below." *Comparative Urban and Community Research,* Vol. 6. News Brunswick, N.J.: Transaction Publishers.

Tan, C. H. and Santhapparaj, A. S. (2007). "Macroeconomic Determinants of Skilled Labour Migration: The Case of Malaysia." *J. Applied Sci*, (7), 3015-3022.

The World Bank (2007). *Malaysia and the Knowledge Economy: Building a World-class Higher Education System*. Washington: The World Bank. Accessed on 5 November 2010 from http://web.worldbank.org.

Tremblay, K. (2004). "Links between Academic Mobility and Immigration." Paper presented at the Symposium on International Labour and Academic Mobility: Emerging Trends and Implications for Public Policy. (22 October) Toronto.

United Nations (2010). *Global Migration Database.* New York: United Nations.

Vertovec, S. (2002). "*Transnational Networks and Skilled Labour Migration*." Accessed 5 November 2010 from http://www.transcomm.ox.ac.uk/.../WPTC-02-02%20Vertovec.pdf.

Wickramasekara, P. (2002). "Perspectives on Labour Migration. Policy Responses to Skilled Migration: Retention, Return and Circulation." Geneva, ILO. Accessed 10 November 2010 from http://www.ilo.org/public/english/protection/migrant/download/pom/pom5e.pdf.

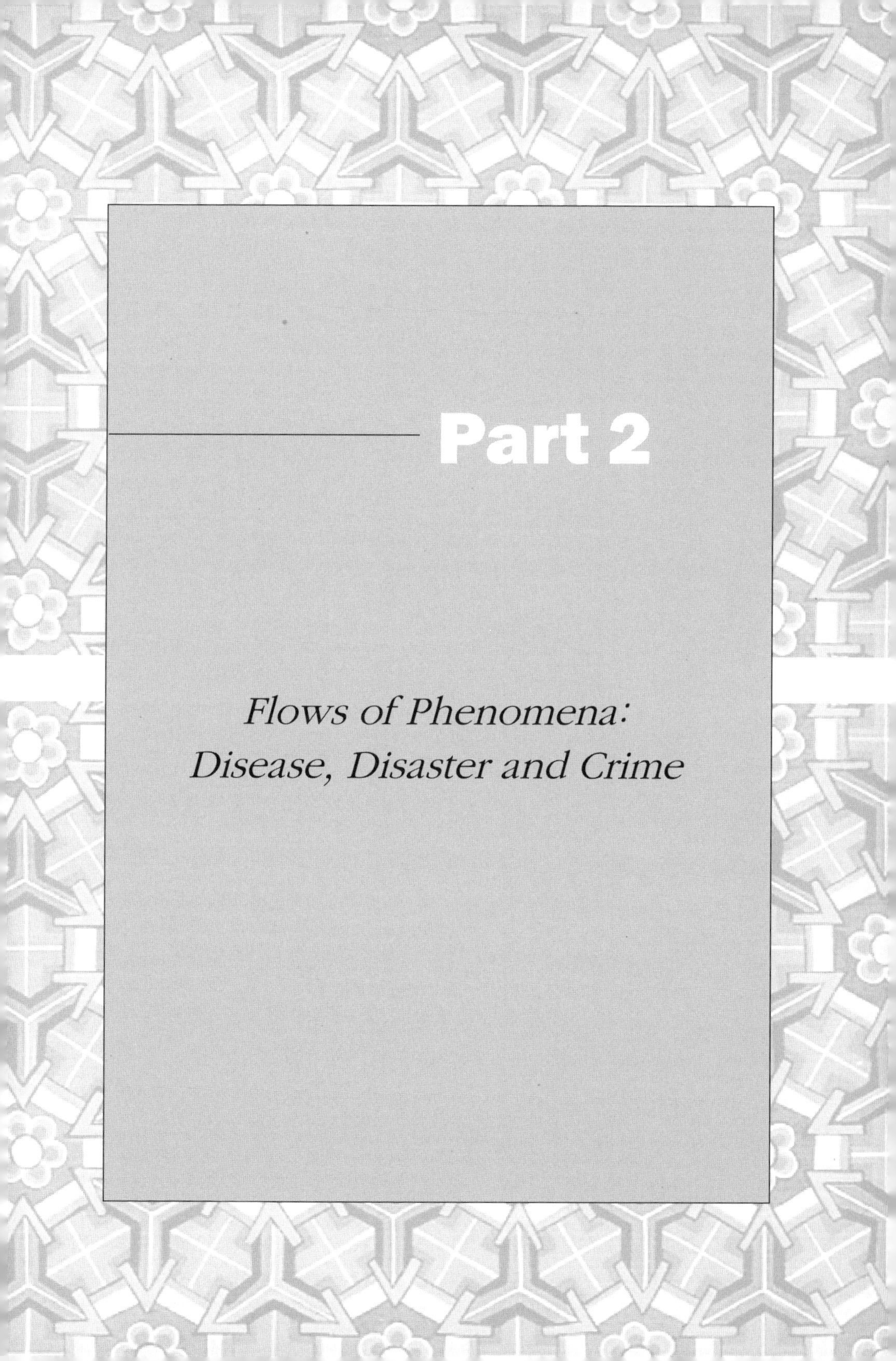

Part 2

Flows of Phenomena: Disease, Disaster and Crime

Globalisation of Diseases and the Limitations of the Statist Approach to Health Threats: A Review of the Korean AIDS Policy[1]

Byong-Hee Cho

1. The Statist and the Globalist Approach to Health Threats

Since the outbreak of HIV/AIDS in 1981, the optimism that infectious diseases have been long conquered has dissipated, and new fears have emerged. For more than 30 years, HIV/AIDS has been one of the most detrimental infectious diseases in the world, while other infectious diseases have frequently newly emerged or reemerged. An outbreak of plague was reported in India in 1994, followed by the Hong Kong Influenza in 1997, SARS (Severe Acute Respiratory Syndrome) and avian flu in 2003, and Influenza A in 2009. These incidences have resulted in huge socioeconomic losses for the countries affected, including a significant drop in foreign visitors,[2] as well as discrimination and hate crimes towards the victims of such diseases (Rider 2003). Thus, affected governments try to remain vigilant in order to prevent these diseases.

Prevention activities can be generally categorized into "the statist approach" and "the globalist approach" (Davies 2010). Traditionally, disease prevention and public health activities are government-driven. By utilising methods such as

[1] Work supported by the Korea Research Foundation Grant funded by the Korean Government (MEST) KRF-2011-330-B00120.

[2] The Economist (2003). Epidemics and Economics. 10 April. Accessed on 22 August 2012 from www.economist.com/node/1698814.

airport or seaport quarantines, the isolation of infected people, travel restrictions, vaccinations, and blocking the epicenter of disease, a government can further its objective to prevent the spread of infectious diseases and outbreaks of epidemic diseases (pandemics), thereby minimising the loss of social and economic burdens that can stem from such epidemics. The statist approach regards infectious diseases as a matter of national security, and sets the protection of the state system as the primary goal of policy. When national security is heightened, the rights of the individual tend to be neglected or restricted (d'Evie 2003). The statist approach strictly distinguishes "friend" from "foe" (Davies 2010, p. 18). The virus itself and the people carrying the virus are suddenly regarded as the enemy. If the state's national security concerns force all infected people to be segregated from society, the infected would then begin to hide their status, for fear of being quarantined. Thus, epidemic prevention protocols clumsily applied by the state might have adverse results.

It has been recently pointed out that the government-led approach to epidemics is not appropriate or applicable to the conditions inherent to the modern international environment. The epidemic prevention protocols of individual governments are predicated in the principles of "sovereignty" that were established in the mid-nineteenth century (Fiedler 2004). Epidemic prevention activities are regarded as "internal affairs," with which foreign countries cannot interfere. Every country has the duty to report the outbreaks of only three diseases, *viz*, plague, cholera and yellow fever. Thus, a government may deny the outbreak of an epidemic or scale down its impact, fearing the possible economic damages, even though such epidemics can readily spread across borders. For example, the Gabonese government concealed the outbreak of Ebola fever in 1996, and even the British government tried to minimise the significance of the BSE (Bovine Spongiform Encephalopathy, commonly known as mad-cow disease) affair (Aaltola 1999).

Increasingly, however, the frequent exchanges of people and goods between countries, as well as the Internet, email and Twitter, can render these governments' information lockout useless. For instance, when the SARS epidemic took place, the Chinese government attempted to hide its occurrence, underestimating the number of affected people. But advanced technologies in monitoring the outbreak of infectious disease worldwide made the Chinese government withdraw its concealment policy and release the information concerning the epidemic (Fiedler 2004).

The globalist approach, in contrast, focuses on the health and welfare of individual citizens. It is geared toward identifying the most vulnerable individuals in the epidemic, protecting them from threats. Additionally, in the course of policy implementation, cooperation and solidarity between the government and private organisations are emphasised. Non-governmental organisations (NGOs) can actively expand their roles in terms of ameliorating health problems by constructing a network comprising domestic and transnational organisations.

The globalist approach to disease management emphasises that the appropriate reference of public health should be human security and health equity, as opposed to national security (Davies 2010, p. 23). While the statist approach focuses on detecting virus among the risk groups most susceptible to an infectious disease, the globalist approach attempts to find individuals who are most vulnerable to the disease. Health is now regarded as a human rights issue; everybody in the world has the right to enjoy good health. United Nations (UN) Secretary-General Ban Ki Moon made the following speech at the opening ceremony of the international AIDS conference at Mexico in 2008:

> In most countries, discrimination remains legal against women, men who have sex with men, sex workers, drug users and ethnic minorities. This must change. I call on all countries to live up to their commitments to enact or enforce legislation outlawing discrimination against people living with HIV and members of vulnerable groups … In countries without laws to protect sex workers, drug users and men who have sex with men, only a fraction of the population have access to prevention. Conversely, in countries with legal protection and the commitment to the protection of human rights for these people, many more have access to services. As a result, there are fewer infections, less demand for antiretroviral treatment and fewer deaths. Not only is it unethical not to protect these groups; it makes no sense from a health perspective. It hurts all of us (United Nations General Assembly 2009).

Mr. Ban's argument suggests that the protection of the human rights of these vulnerable groups ensures their health from threats of AIDS and lowers the prevalence of the disease. The globalist approach pays attention to the fundamental or structural aspects of the epidemic. HIV/AIDS and other infectious diseases have been spread throughout the world, but disproportionately so; HIV/AIDS is concentrated in the most underdeveloped regions, such as Africa, and among the most disadvantaged groups such as sex workers, drug users, and men who have sex with men. Poverty is a social cause of HIV infection. Furthermore, HIV/AIDS worsens poverty (Bancroft 2001; Parker 2002). The globalist approach pays close attention to the fundamental causes of health threats, such as poverty, illiteracy, and class inequality (Nakajima 1997). It stresses that the fundamental solution for the health crisis is dependent on the upgrading of the quality of life of the disadvantaged or socially isolated people. Empowerment of vulnerable people or advocacy for their health could be managed well by local NGOs and their international networks. Thus, they are regarded as major actors in the governance structure of global health.

In this paper, I will compare three country case studies. First, I will review the case of the Chinese government's failure to conceal the outbreak of SARS. The world-wide monitoring system on infectious disease makes the Chinese government's effort to conceal useless, meaning that the nation state is no longer the sole agent of public health—it is necessary to establish cooperation with transnational organisations.

Second, I will discuss the case of the Australian government's successful control of the HIV outbreak. Instead of implementing statist policies such as tracking down the infected people and making testing mandatory, the Australian government emphasised community involvement and advocacy for voluntary testing and condom use, and the formation of partnerships between the government and gay and sex worker groups. As a result, the HIV prevalence rate has been kept at a very low level. Also, the infected people are not socially isolated because of the efforts of managing AIDS stigma successfully.

Third is the case of the AIDS policy in Korea. The country is a good example the merits and demerits of the statist approach to health issues. On the one hand, it succeeded in keeping the prevalence of HIV to less than 0.1 per cent. On the other hand, it failed to successfully reintegrate the victims of HIV into society; severe stigma has been produced as a by-product of the policy emphasising the tight control of HIV virus. Those infected with HIV may have survived medically, but most have become figuratively "almost dead" socially. The limitations of the Korean AIDS policy will be discussed and compared with other countries such as Australia and Taiwan.

2. SARS and the Statist Approach by the Chinese Government

The SARS outbreak occurred from November 2002 to August 2003 in 32 countries worldwide; 8,422 people were infected and about 10 per cent of them were killed (World Health Organization 2003). Most patients were found in the East Asian countries of China, Hong Kong, Taiwan, and Singapore. Most other countries had an occurrence of fewer than 10 patients, except in Canada with 251 patients. SARS was a typical infectious disease that threatened the Asian region.

The SARS crisis led the way for a world-class quarantine system to be established. Under the situation of frequent exchanges of commodities and persons between countries and the weakened sense of borders, the outbreak of the epidemic in a country is no longer a domestic affair, but a transnational issue. In response, the World Health Organization (WHO) has established the worldwide disease surveillance system created in 1997, called the Global Outbreak Alert and Response Network (GOARN). The system collects new information and rumours from multiple sources of information channels for infectious diseases, and conducts systematic analysis of this information. Based on this, the WHO arrives at a decision and takes necessary measures to prevent the spread of the epidemic (Grein 2000). Despite these surveillance systems, however, SARS spread from China to countries overseas. WHO and the Canadian Broadcasting Company tracked down the occurrence of the SARS epidemic and provided a timeline that summarised the following story of SARS:[3]

> In the fall of 2002 in Guangdong, occurrences of a new type of pneumonia patients were reported at least in seven places on its own. In November of the same year, in the provincial capital of Guangzhou, city of Guangdong, people flocked to the hospital with pneumonia; doctors were infected. The illness spread to other regions of China. By December, these instances were

[3] Summarised from the Canadian Broadcasting Corporation SARS timeline. 15 December 2003. Accessed on 21 August 2012 from http://www.cbc.ca/news/background/sars/timeline.html.

> reported to the Chinese government. In early 2003, the Chinese government dispatched a professional team for a field survey, and a red alert soon followed among the hospitals in the region. WHO's GOARN found out about the SARS outbreak and the shutdown of hospitals on 10 February. The next day, the Chinese government reported to WHO of the occurrence of a new type of respiratory disease in Guangdong since November 2002; by then, 300 people were infected and five had already died.

On 21 February, one physician who had treated SARS patients at a hospital in Guangdong, and who was eventually infected with SARS, visited Hong Kong to attend a relative's wedding. He stayed overnight at the Metropole Hotel. The next day, his symptoms worsened; he was hospitalised and died. The 12 guests on the same floor of the hotel, unaware that they had been infected, departed for Singapore, Hanoi, Toronto and elsewhere. This was the point where SARS was spreading in the world. After obtaining more evidence, WHO issued a SARS alert on 12 March and international travel regulations on 15 March.

In this case, the Chinese government tried to control the information about SARS. From the fall of 2002 to February 2003, the government denied the incidence of the respiratory disease itself. From February to mid-April 2003, the Chinese government recognised the occurrence of SARS, but argued that it was successfully treated and had not dispersed to other areas. It was only after 17 April, when a decision taken by the Communist Party of China, that all information related to SARS was open to the public (Fiedler 2004).

The failure to disclose the SARS information by the Chinese government was due to the effects of international and internal information networks. Ahead of the disclosure of information, WHO requested that the Chinese government identify the occurrence of SARS on the basis of evidence obtained through its own information system. SARS was not included in the disease list that each country has the duty to report the outbreak of diseases to WHO. Thus, the Chinese government was able to legitimately decline the request. Without the Chinese government's support, WHO was not able to inspect local hospitals to identify the outbreak of SARS. However, once SARS spread internationally and it became evident that China was the epicentre of SARS, the Chinese government no longer had control over information on SARS.

In everyday life, it is important to block the spread of fatal infectious disease such as SARS. It was found that traditional public health methods such as case detection, isolation, and tracking contacts, worked well (Smith 2006). Since SARS occurred in the West and Asia, with advanced public health systems, it was combatted successfully. What is more important is the fact that epidemic prevention is not entirely dependent on national institutions. Propagation of the epidemic can be monitored through global information systems and the occurrence of an epidemic can be reported to the world by the people who witnessed it through Internet bulletin boards, Facebook or Twitter in real time. Since the government does not regulate these private sector activities, the former had to formulate partnerships with private agents.

However, as shown in the case of SARS-related information control, the Chinese government overemphasised national security. Since national security is thought to be its own unique work, the government is reluctant to cooperate with the private sector and international organisations. In fighting the common enemy, the people have to trust and support the government's public health policy unilaterally. Nowadays though, more people prioritise personal health and safety and, having been dissatisfied with the government's policy, they try to get help from the outside by informing the external world of the realities and the possible health risks. Thus, the government's aim to control information is unsuccessful.

3. AIDS and the Community Approach in Australia

Unlike other infectious diseases, HIV/AIDS has provoked social debates as to which methods of prevention are the most effective from the beginning of the outbreak. Facing the HIV crisis, American gays developed the solution of "safer sex" to prevent AIDS infections, and to protect their sexual freedom (Escoffier 1999). However, the American government was reluctant to fully adopt these "safer sex" methods, since safer sex implies the maintenance of multiple sexual partners by wearing condoms to ensure sexual safety. Rather, the American government adopted a strategy emphasising monogamy and abstinence. The Australian government selected a different method of AIDS prevention from that in America. Looking back on the American chaos of homophobia and the uncontrollable spread of AIDS, the Australian government took a community-based approach emphasising the active role of homosexuals in developing health education materials and peer education and in practising safer sex, which successfully lowered HIV infections over the short-term (Senziuk 2003). Sexual identity as a social discourse was fully developed, and homosexuals were well-organised in both America and Australia. However, the political climate of two countries was quite different. The American government was headed by conservative forces who viewed homosexual behavior with suspicion; conversely, the Australian government was governed by progressives, who took a relatively generous attitude toward homosexuality. As Epstein (1996) argued, the critical factor in choosing an AIDS prevention strategy is to define the fundamental cause of the AIDS crisis either as a lifestyle, or as a virus. The statist approach regards the HIV virus as the cause of the AIDS crisis and attempts to control it. The community approach focuses on the lifestyles of vulnerable people and attempts to improve them through empowerment and advocacy, as well as networking and partnership.

The Australian strategy has diffused to some other Asian countries. The notion of the "Seven Sisters" is a good example (Seven Sisters 2008). It refers to the coalition of seven broad-based alliances of networks in Asia Pacific on HIV/AIDS, working with vulnerable groups such as sex workers, gay men, transgender individuals, drug users, women, youth, indigenous people, and migrant workers or transients. Each group formulates its own network, such as APN+ for the HIV positive and APNSW for sex workers. Furthermore, these groups are regular members of the AIDS Society of Asia and the Pacific, an international NGO representing Asia and the Pacific in AIDS-related affairs. These organisations are committed to encouraging, promoting, and sustaining coalition building, partnerships, and alliances with regional intergovernmental and non-governmental bodies, and are involved in HIV and AIDS policy development, and actively engaged in fostering public and private partnerships, advocacy, and communication management efforts with regard to major issues related to HIV and AIDS (Sarkar 2010). Additionally, it is worth noting that the partnership between the government and gays or other vulnerable groups has become a trend in AIDS prevention in Asian countries (APCOM 2010) and other regions such as Latin America (Barnes 2008; 2010).

4. AIDS and the Korean Government

Unlike Australia, Korea has taken the statist approach to HIV prevention. To the Korean government, AIDS is simply a new lethal disease threatening the nation's health and national security. Thus, while the government has faithfully carried out the tasks of detecting and monitoring virus infection, and providing free medical treatment, it has to some degree neglected the protection of the rights and welfare of the infected. The community approach, or the role of NGOs in this situation, was not taken into significant consideration. The current prevalence rate of HIV infection in Korea is less than 0.1 per cent among adults,[4] one of the lowest in the world. The Korean government has hailed such a low prevalence of HIV as result of a successful prevention policy.

Korea experienced the successful control of tuberculosis and other infectious diseases in the 1960s and 1970s. Major infectious diseases, including sexually transmitted infections (STIs), were designated by law and strictly monitored by the government. Sex workers were required to have STI testing at government health centres once a month. When the first HIV infection reported in 1985 occurred among US soldiers stationed in Korea, the government quickly tracked down the homosexuals and sex workers who had had contact with those soldiers, and tested them to ascertain whether they were infected with HIV (Lee 1994). People who were found to be HIV-positive were placed under special governmental monitoring (Cho 2008).

The detection and monitoring of risk groups is a basic public health measure necessary for the prevention of infectious disease in most countries. The Korean HIV policy is unique in terms of its unusually strict and harsh implementation. In order to exercise exceptionally strong public health measures, the government enacted the AIDS Prevention Act in 1987. The enactment of a special law for the purpose of AIDS prevention was, at that time, fairly unique in the world. This law gave the government extra power to coercively inspect and test those suspected of infection, particularly the family members of the infected. The law also imposed upon the infected the responsibility to report monthly to government health centres regarding their health status and their observance of safe sex

[4] Central Intelligence Agency. "The World Fact Book: HIV/AIDS Adult Prevalence Rate." Accessed on 21 August 2012 from www.cia.gov/library/publications/the-world-factbook/rankorder/2155rank.html.

rules, that is, they are required by law to wear a condom for sexual intercourse. They were prohibited to work at bars and restaurants where they would serve clients, even though they do not have any sexual relationships with them. They were also prohibited from donating blood. The law even specified that these individuals could not refuse medical treatment. If these regulations were violated, the individuals were to be punished as criminals, and could be imprisoned for up to three years. In cases in which infected individuals lost their jobs and had no means of livelihood, they were entitled to state subsidies. Thus, the infected were treated almost as criminals or enemies. Infected people bemoaned that they could not tolerate the government's surveillance more than the fact that they were infected. Human rights issues were almost neglected (Lee 2005). Some gays and HIV positive people spoke of their experiences, and made a caricature of Korean society as an acquired human-rights deficient society alluding to HIV, a human-acquired immunodeficiency virus (Jee 2011).

5. Limitations of the Statist Approach

There were several limitations of the Korean government's HIV policy. First, mandatory testing was found to be not very efficient in detecting the HIV virus. The government inexorably expanded the number of people obligated to take an HIV test in order to completely stop the spread of the virus among the people. As the government began to see the threat as a national security concern, the target for monitoring inevitably expanded. The first target risk group was the full-time sex workers. However, the risk group soon expanded to include "part-time" sex workers and even to ordinary service workers in coffee shops, restaurants, hotels, and baths. The target population enlarged yearly, consequently vitiating the efficacy of the testing policy. In 1996, the government conducted 1.9 million tests, but detected only 33 infected people. This meant that one infection was detected per 58,000 compulsory tests. The government allocated more than 60 per cent of its AIDS budget to this testing. It was estimated that voluntary tests at hospitals and anonymous tests at health centres would be a more cost-effective measure, roughly ten times more so than compulsory tests in terms of finding one infected case (Yang 1997). Voluntary and anonymous testing was conducted to a minimum extent, since the government did not believe in the authenticity of voluntary testing, as it simply relied on compulsory testing. This attitude might be interpreted as a result of the long history of military dictatorship or authoritarian leadership in the country.[5]

The second limitation was that it intensified AIDS-phobia and furthered social discrimination against HIV-positive people. As the government strengthened viral detection and behavioral monitoring of infected people, people became overcautious, with some who even attempted to break off relationships with those who are infected, in an effort to protect themselves against infection. Thus, the HIV-positive people hid or moved to another place without notifying the government to avoid discrimination from their neighbors, and to seek new means of living.[6] The government openly searched for them like criminal suspects, and the newspapers reported about this widely.[7] When they were traced down, the entire community was seized with horror. This invisible, anonymous, and hidden characteristic of HIV escalated the people's fear of the disease.

The most extreme form of AIDS-phobia occurred in the form of rejection of infected family members. A 2005 survey demonstrated that only 49.9 per cent of Korean respondents were willing to care for an infected family member in their home (Cho & Sohn 2005). This is in sharp contrast with attitudes in other countries; for example, more than 90 per cent of Vietnamese and Thailand migrant workers residing in Korea were willing to do the same for their families (Cho 2006). In Korea, HIV-positive individuals had trouble with their own families, to the point of breaking off contact with their family members (Lee 2003). Infected people were not generally able to obtain social support from family, friends, colleagues, and even churches. Thus, they experienced severe depression and emotional disturbances. Lee et al. (2005) estimated from evidence that infected people had a suicide rate 10 times higher than that of the general public.

---

[5] The authoritarian AIDS policy could be also found in Thailand, one of the highest prevalent area of AIDS in the 1990s. The military government after the coup in 1991 enforced to implement the strongly effective AIDS policies such as "100 per cent Condom Campaign" for sex workers. The government unilaterally pushed the policy instead of reaching social consensus (Porapakkham, et al. 1995).

[6] Chosunilbo (1994). "A sex worker infected with AIDS flitted from one pub to another for eight years" (in Korean). 24 July.

[7] Kyunghyang Daily News (1991). "29 HIV positive people in hiding; government requested health authorities to report their presence" (in Korean). 9 December.

The third limitation was that the statist approach did not affect behavioral change, though it was fairly effective for viral detection. Early HIV infections were transmitted primarily through sexual contact with infected foreigners and sex workers. As sex workers have been closely monitored and have begun to use condoms, their infection rate has declined. However, infections among homosexuals increased in the 1990s. Since they were unorganised and hidden from society, the government had insufficient information to contact and persuade them to take HIV tests. Given this changing epidemiological trend, the government had to loosen its compulsory testing protocols to introduce anonymous testing (Lee 1995).

Korea's AIDS policy has changed gradually since the late 1990s. First of all, the government abolished mandatory testing and adopted the principle of voluntary counseling and testing (VCT) in 1999. That same year, service workers began to be exempted of their HIV testing obligations. The government initiated such a change partially in order to observe global human rights standards. However, the more important reason for the change in testing policy was the fact that most new infections can be detected through hospital testing, usually during the ordinary treatment of illness; thus, mandatory testing was no longer considered as an effective measure in detecting the virus. The government also established anonymous testing centres in 2003: two for homosexuals, three for heterosexuals, and one for foreign migrant workers. The new testing centres were designed to guarantee privacy in terms of location, access, and the internal process of testing. They also provided quick test results (within a half hour) and subsequent counseling services. The centres, in addition, allowed gay clients to use their facilities, including seminar rooms and computers. The centres became a gathering post among the gay community. These centres were staffed by volunteer gays. They ran the testing procedures and provided counseling services. Gay personnel also carried out peer education programmes and designed education materials and moving pictures for advertisement. Since they were skillful in managing sexual materials and familiar with gay lifestyle, these personnel could produce appropriate educational materials that are tailored to gays.

However, the government continues to maintain its distance from LGBT (lesbian, gay, bisexuals and transgender) groups and HIV-positive people. The testing centres and other caring activities are implemented by "civil organisations" which are supported by the government. Gay groups are not permitted to run these facilities on their own, since the gay community is considered not to have sufficient human capital and organisational capacity to run such types of sexual health programmes. The real issue appears to be that the government is reluctant in sharing the management function of HIV and AIDS issues with these types of organisations.

Two situational factors contributed to the stubborn attitude of the government concerning AIDS policy. As an economically developed country the Korean government has the capability to procure all of the necessary resources for HIV prevention and treatment. In developing countries, global funding agencies provide local NGOs with considerable amounts of money. Thus, local NGOs or gay health organisations are able to run HIV prevention programmes even without support from their respective governments. Unlike them, Korean gay groups and other NGOs have no resource providers aside from the government.

The other factor was that the Korean government faithfully followed the medical model of public health (Cho 2008). In the early stage of the HIV epidemic, the Korean government had focused on the detection and monitoring of the HIV virus. In the late 1990s, the government shifted its focus to medical treatment of those infected. Unlike the governments of other developing countries which cannot guarantee regular and sufficient access to medical care, the Korean government can ensure medical treatment for all HIV-positive and AIDS patients. This reliance on the government's medical measures, in turn, lowered the necessity of enhancing an NGO's active role or empowering HIV-positive people. The Korean government makes available relevant HIV statistics and other HIV information to the public, and provides free medical care to the infected. Thus, transnational organisations such as WHO, UNAIDS or Seven Sisters have no opportunity to make recommendations for the government to enhance its AIDS policy.

6. CBOs and NGOs within the Transnational Context

The active role of community-based organisations (CBOs) and NGOs in AIDS prevention began with the relative indifference of governments to the AIDS issues in many developing countries (Rau 2006), due to the lack of resources, effective drugs and therapies, as well as due to the lack of concern on health problems experienced by social minority groups. Thus, the CBOs and NGOs fill the gap between governmental indifference and these people. Community organisations not only provide care for AIDS victims, they also mobilise the people in the community, including risk groups, to advocate for change in their behavior towards safe sex. Thus, those in danger of catching AIDS have changed their role, from being members of the risk group, to being agents of prevention in this community-based approach (Kammerer et al. 2001). Their sexual identity was respected and socially included (Caceres 2008). In this context, community approach represents the attributes of the globalist approach such as concern on human security or welfare, empowerment of local people, and emphasising human rights values. CBOs and NGOs in developing countries procured most of their resources from international funding agencies. The newly developed theory and methods for prevention, and the values of human rights as a new guiding principle for AIDS prevention, have been diffused and practised through the network of recipient and donor organisations. Their strategies conformed to global standards, which are usually requested by the funding agencies.

Unfortunately, Korean gays have had no opportunity to mobilise a "gay health movement," primarily due to the lack of resources, both domestic and international. Korean gays have had only about one decade of history as a social group. The first coming-out of gays in Korea took place in 1994. Some gay groups were organised on campuses in the 1990s. Currently, it is not difficult to find gay bars in large cities. The gay community in Korea is largely congregated in ghetto-like areas. The majority of gays in the country still hide their identity from the heterosexuals.[8] AIDS has made them even more reluctant to reveal their identities and furthermore they are exposed to the double discrimination associated with both AIDS and homosexuals. Nevertheless, the government was not, until recently, concerned with this issue.

To tackle this problem, gay groups began to be active in calling for the protection of human rights to secure their privacy and eliminate social discrimination. Groups of gay activists requested that the government change its

---

[8] The mature gay identity influenced significantly the formation of the gay health movement. Sawazaki (1997) described the Japanese gays' efforts of organising for gay health. But Korean gays have had a relatively shorter history of identity formation.

AIDS policies to promote the human rights of infected people (Nanuri Alliance for Promoting Human Rights of People with HIV/AIDS 2006). They organised conferences and street campaigns, and formulated political alliances among gay activists, the progressive party, and concerned scholars. This alliance pushed the government to abolish the AIDS Prevention Act, which was emblematic of the statist approach. The National Human Rights Commission, in support of the group and its advocacy, provided funding in a form of a research grant for the first systematic survey of human rights for the HIV-infected in 2005. The report submitted to the Human Rights Commission uncovered a great deal of discrimination cases experienced at various places such as firms, hospitals, and health centres (Lee 2005). The gay alliance did not succeed in abolishing the AIDS Prevention Act, but the government is now under pressure to abide by the human rights standards for the HIV-infected. Currently, the government no longer monitors the behavior of those infected, and has become careful not to leak the identities of the infected to the public or violate their privacy. However, it might be too early to expect that partnerships will form between the government and gays or infected groups.

This situation is compared with the case of Taiwan. Due to Taiwan's diplomatic isolation within the transnational community since its exclusion from the UN, the role of Taiwanese NGOs was limited. However, in terms of AIDS prevention, Taiwanese NGOs actively participated in regional organisations such as APN+ (Asia Pacific Network of People Living with HIV/AIDS), TREAT ASIA (Therapeutic Research, Education, AIDS Training in ASIA), SEA-AIDS Forum, and PWHA-NET. New ideas, research trends, successful policies, and discussions on human right issues were adopted through these transnational networks, which strongly influenced the formation of the Taiwanese AIDS policy (Rollet 2005). Taiwanese AIDS-related NGOs were invited to collaborate with the government, and also had sufficient autonomy.

Korean AIDS NGOs are less engaged with the government; they also do not actively participate in transnational networks. The primary reason is their weak capacity for resource mobilization. CBOs and NGOs are usually small in size and are not well prepared with administrative skills and bureaucratic rules. Thus, the government tends to be reluctant to grant much credibility to community groups. It was very difficult for Korean AIDS NGOs to gain the legal status of a corporate body, which is necessary to obtain government support. But the CBOs and NGOs are too small to meet the conditions in forming a corporate body. Without the government's support, those groups have to be self-sufficient with small amounts of personal donations (International Planned Parenthood Federation 2011). An international cooperative network can be made possible by participating in international workshops, or by inviting international professionals to visit Korea, and organising short-term seminars. The financial condition and language barrier of Korean AIDS groups have made them less active in transnational networks. Some members have participated in transnational meetings and conferences on AIDS, but usually have had no chance of reporting the results to the government, since there is no relationship between the government and these groups.

7. Conclusion

The globalisation of the AIDS epidemic teaches us lessons about both transnational outbreaks of infectious disease and the transnational partnerships that can be formed to cope with such epidemics. The Korean government is currently attempting to conform to transnational standards and regulations. For instance, it has accepted the new HIV testing standard, called VCT, the elements of which are in accordance with human rights. However, the Korean government is still not particularly aware of the role of NGOs in HIV prevention, and it maintains an immigration ban for migrant workers with HIV, which the United Nations and other transnational organisations attempted to lift.[9] It appears evident that the Korean government basically adheres to a statist approach. The government regards HIV/AIDS as a domestic health issue where it plays a sole role by using medical methods. It tends not to pay an attention to other possibilities such as transnational governance, partnership formation with domestic and global NGOs, and empowerment and advocacy for gays and HIV-positive individuals.

While the government has given up harsh measures for containing HIV and HIV-positive individuals, it continues to maintain a government-based

[9] As of 22 July 2012, the Republic of Korea has lifted these HIV-specific travel restrictions, joining 10 other countries who have lifted their restrictions since 2010. There are, however, 45 other countries, territories and areas still employing certain types of restrictions (Joint United Nations Programme on AIDS/HIV 2012).

HIV policy. The element of national security that used to dictate the policies concerning HIV and AIDS has been dropped. However, AIDS is still regarded as a disease, rather than a lifestyle or a sexual identity issue. Insofar as the government keeps this stance toward AIDS, it will continue to allocate the majority of its resources to medical treatment. In contrast, the role of gays and other community groups will continue to be neglected or undervalued. In a word, the Korean government adheres to a medical discourse in regard to the HIV epidemic, but is indifferent to the socioeconomic context of being HIV-positive. It is tragic that the emphasis on HIV detection and medical treatment has resulted in social discrimination for the HIV-positive, which is the fundamental flaw of the statist approach to HIV/AIDS.

In East and Southeast Asia, transnational networks of HIV-related community groups are well organised. If the solid connection or alliance between Korean community groups and these regional networks is to be built in the near future, the issue of Korea's isolation from the global trend of partnerships that respond to AIDS could be resolved.

References

Aaltola, M. (1999). "International Relations and Epidemics: A Short Expedition to Places Inhabited by States and Mad Cows." *Medicine, Conflict and Survival*, 15, 235-254.

Bancroft, A. (2001). "Globalization and HIV/AIDS: Inequality and the Boundaries of a Symbolic Epidemic." *Health, Risk & Society*, 3, 1, 89-98.

Barnes, N. (2010). "Social Network Analysis in Transnational Settings: The Case of Mexico City's AIDS CBOs." *Social Medicine*, 5, 1, 6-14.

________ (2008). "Paradoxes and Asymmetries of Transnational Networks: A Comparative Case Study of Mexico's Community-based AIDS Organizations." *Social Science & Medicine*, 66, 4, 933-944.

Caceres, C., Aggleton, P. and Galea, J. T. (2008). "Sexual Diversity, Social Inclusion, and HIV/AIDS." *AIDS*, 22, Suppl. 2, S45-S55.

Canadian Broadcasting Corporation. SARS timeline. 15 December 2003. Accessed on 21 August 2012 from http://www.cbc.ca/news/background/sars/timeline.html.

Central Intelligence Agency. "The World Fact Book: HIV/AIDS Adult Prevalence Rate." Accessed on 21 August 2012 from www.cia.gov/library/publications/the-world-factbook/rankorder/2155rank.html.

Cho, B. H. (2008). *Sexuality, Risk & HIV/AIDS*. Seoul: Nanam.

_________ (2006). *Report on the Migrant Workers' Understanding of AIDS, Sexual Risk Behaviors and the Utilization of Prevention Services*. Seoul: Korea Federation of HIV/AIDS Prevention.

Cho, B. H. and Sohn, A. (2005). *Report of the 2005 National Survey on Knowledge, Attitude, and Behavior Related to HIV/AIDS*. [in Korean] Seoul: The Korea Center for Disease Control and Prevention.

Davies, S. E. (2010). *Global Politics of Health*. Malden, MA. Polity.

d'Evie, F. (2003). "SARS and the High Moral Ground." Peace and Conflict Monitor, The University of Peace. Accessed on 23 August 2012 from http://www.monitor.upeace.org/archive.cfm?id_article=59.

Epstein, S. (1996). *Impure Science: AIDS, Activism, and the Politics of Knowledge*. Berkeley: University of California Press.

Escoffier, J. (1999). "The Invention of Safer Sex: Vernacular Knowledge, Gay Politics and HIV Prevention." *Berkeley Journal of Sociology*, 43, 1-30.

Fiedler, D. P. (2004). *SARS, Governance and the Globalization of Disease*. New York: Palgrave, Macmillan.

Grein, T. W., Kamara, K. B., Rodier, G., Plant, A. J., Bovier, P., Ryan, M. J., Ohyama, T. and Heymann, D. L. (2000). "Rumor of Disease in the Global Village: Outbreak Verification." *Emerging Infectious Disease*, 6, 2, 97-102.

International Planned Parenthood Federation (IPPF) (2011). "Sex between Men in Your City." Accessed on 21 August 2012 from http://ippf.org/resources/publications/sex-between-men-your-city.

Jee, S. H. (2011). *Outing the Acquired Human-Right Deficient Society*. Seoul: Sidaebooks.

Joint United Nations Program on AIDS/HIV (UNAIDS) (2012). "HIV Travel Restrictions: Latest Developments." 22 July. Accessed on 23 August 2012 from http://www.unaids.org/en/resources/presscentre/featurestories/2012/july/20120722travelrestrictions.

Kammerer, N., Mason, T., Connors, M. and Durkee, R. (2001). "Transgenders, HIV/AIDS, and Substance Abuse: From Risk Group to Group Prevention." In W. Bockting & S. Kirk (eds.), *Transgender and HIV: Risks, Prevention, and Care*. Binghamton: The Haworth Press. pp. 13-38.

Lee, D. H. (1994). *The Korean Government's AIDS Policy*. [in Korean] In Ministry of Health and Social Affairs, Health Professionals and AIDS. pp. 89-105.

Lee, H. J. Han, C. Y., Jeong, H. M., Kim, H. K., Kim, H. S., Kim, Y. M., Lee, H. S., Lee, M. Y.

and Park, K. S. (2005). *Report of Human Rights Realities of the People with HIV/AIDS.* [in Korean] Seoul. National Human Rights Commission of the Republic of Korea. Accessed 21 August 2012 from http://www.humanrights.go.kr/03_sub/body02_4.jsp?m_link_url=03_sub/body02_4.jsp&m_id1=27&m_id2=378&m_id3=392&m_id4=410?NT_ID=17&flag=VIEW&SEQ_ID=483241.

Lee, J. Y. (2003). *Report on Sexual Behaviors and AIDS Perception of Homosexuals and People with HIV/AIDS.* [in Korean] Seoul. Korea Federation of HIV/AIDS Prevention.

Lee, S. Y. (1995). *Efficient Management of Korean AIDS Programs and Surveillance System.* [in Korean] Seoul. Korea Institute for Health and Social Affairs.

Nakajima, H. (1997). "Global Disease Threats and Foreign Policy." *The Brown Journal of World Affairs*, 4, 1, 319-332.

Nanuri Alliance for Promoting Human Rights of People with HIV/AIDS (2006). "Our Opinion for the Amendment Bill of the AIDS Prevention Act." [in Korean] 20 April.

Parker, R. (2002). "The Global HIV/AIDS Pandemic, Structural Inequalities and the Politics of International Health." *American Journal of Public Health*, 92, 3, 343-347.

Porapakkham, Y., Pramarnpol, S., Athibhoddhi, S. and Bernhard, R. (1995). The Evolution of HIV/AIDS Policy in Thailand: 1984-1994. Accessed on 21 August 2011 from http://pdf.usaid.gov/pdf_docs/PNACG546.pdf.

Rau, B. (2006). "The Politics of Civil Society in Confronting HIV/AIDS." *International Affairs*, 82, 2, 285-295.

Rider, D. (2003). "Fear of virus fuels racism." Canwest News Service. 4 April. Accessed on 23 August 2012 from http://www.buzzardpress.com/acla/sars/virus_racism.html .

Rollet, V. (2005). "Taiwanese NGOs and HIV/AIDS: From the National to the Transnational." *China Perspective*, 60. pp. 1-17. Downloaded from http://chinaperspectives.revues.org/498.

Sarkar, S. (2010). "Community Engagement in HIV Prevention in Asia: Going from 'for the Community' to 'by the Community'—Must We Wait for More Evidence?" *Sex Transm Infect*, 86, i2-i3.

Sawazaki, Y. (1997). "Gay Men and HIV in Japan." *Journal of Acquired Immune Deficiency Syndromes and Human Retrovirology*, 14, Suppl. 2, S47-S50.

Senziuk, P. (2003). *Learning to Trust: Australian Responses to AIDS.* Sydney: University of New South Wales Press.

Seven Sisters (2008). *Minimum Standards for Civil Society Participation in the Universal Access Initiative. The Coalition of Asia-Pacific Regional Networks on HIV/AIDS.* Bangkok: Asia Pacific Network of People Living with AIDS (APN+).

Smith, R. D. (2006). "Responding to Global Infectious Disease Outbreaks: Lessons from SARS on the Role of Risk Perception, Communication and Management." Social Science & Medicine, 63, 3113-3123.

The Economist (2003). "Epidemics and Economics." 11 April. Accessed on 23 August 2012 from http://www.economist.com/node/1698814.

United Nations General Assembly (2009). "Progress Made in the Implementation of the Declaration of Commitment on HIV/AIDS and the Political Declaration on HIV/AIDS." Report of the Secretary-General. 63rd Session Agenda Item 41.

Yang, B. M. (1997). "Economic Cost-effectiveness of AIDS Testing in Korea." Paper presented at the 10th Anniversary of the World AIDS Day of Korea. 1 December. Seoul: Korea.

World Health Organization (WHO) (2003). Summary Tables of SARS Cases by Country, 1 November 2002 - 7 August 2003. Accessed on 21 August 2011 from http://www.who.int/csr/sars/country/2003_08_15/en/index.html.

State Centrism and East Asian Regional Cooperation: The Case of Cooperation on Natural Disasters and Environmental Issues[1]

Jaehyon Lee

1. Introduction

East Asia has been plagued by many transnational natural disasters and environmental catastrophes over the last decade. Only recently however, did it earn newly-acquired publicity, largely due to two new developments. First, the level of awareness of the people and societies in the region of such problems has grown substantially in the past few years. This is mainly because of more frequent media coverage of the cases, and of economic affluence. Endeavouring to achieve economic growth and affluence, countries in the region overcame, to a certain degree, immediate challenges posed to the people in the region—such as severe starvation and social unrest, including war and conflict. This economic development provided people with an opportunity to look beyond the immediate threats of daily life; at the same time, it turned the focus of public concern to human security and non-traditional security issues including natural and environmental disasters.

Second, regional cooperation in East Asia has brought about a new perspective to people in the region. Traditionally, the prevention of and response to disaster was considered a national duty. Although a country could expect help from

[1] This chapter is a revised and developed version of the author's article published in IFANS Review in 2011. See Lee (2011).

neighbours or international organisations in the case of severe damage from disasters, it was fundamental to the national agenda to protect citizens from natural disasters. It must be highlighted though, that regional cooperation has driven people and individual countries in East Asia to search for a regional solution to those issues since many of these disasters take place on a transnational scale.

The disasters addressed in this paper are "transnational" in nature because their origins and impacts are not confined to a single country. Quite often, natural and environmental disasters originate from multiple sources. Once disasters happen, they can easily cross geographical borders from the country of the origin to affect the lives of people in neighbouring countries. Since disasters have a transnational character, preventive actions should also be transnational. Problems resulting from such phenomena are expected to be resolved not by the efforts of a single country, but by neighbouring countries and regional countries in a collaborative effort.

Academic concern over transnational cooperation for environmental and natural disasters has increased as interest in general human security and non-traditional security issues have grown in East Asia. This has led to substantial research results on environmental cooperation among the Association of Southeast Asian Nations (ASEAN) countries (Badenoch 2002; Elliott 2004; Koh & Robinson 2002; Nishikawa 2009; Tacconi & Grafton 2008; Tay 2002a; 2008). In Northeast Asia, there has also been increased research interest on environmental cooperation (Lee 2001; Kim 2007; Schreurs 1998; Shim 2000; Yoon 2003). However, it is uncommon for a researcher to look into Southeast Asia and Northeast Asia in a single study. A survey of existing research would indicate that the close relationship between Southeast Asia and Northeast Asia tends to be overlooked, although the former and the latter have been increasingly identified as constituting one integrated region, which is East Asia. This tendency is particularly problematic, given that various East Asian regional cooperation frameworks, notably ASEAN+3 and the East Asia Summit (EAS), deal with transnational environmental issues as a major aspect of the agenda. In addition, there is limited existing research (regardless of its regional focus) concerned with natural disaster issues, coupled with the dearth of regional disaster initiatives, particularly in Northeast Asia. Thus, this paper intends to fill the void in areas of existing research on regional cooperation for transnational natural disasters and environmental issues in East Asia.

This paper examines two sets of issues. The first focuses on transnational natural disasters and environmental issues. Details of such environmental issues include the haze caused by the Indonesian wildfires in Southeast Asia, and the yellow sand (*huangsa*)[2] phenomenon in Northeast Asia. These two issues have the widest coverage in terms of their impact and are well known cases in each region. There are of course many types of natural disasters both at the regional scale such as drought and floods and at the national, including tsunamis, typhoons, earthquakes and volcanic eruptions. This paper deals with the latter.

The second set of issues concerns regional governance and cooperation. The natural and environmental issues addressed in this paper have a transnational nature that requires regional cooperation to solve the problems. East Asian regional cooperation schemes such as ASEAN+3 and EAS, and ASEAN have created various mechanisms and dialogues to find a regional solution to the issues. Regional governance includes basic rules and customs that govern regional cooperation required to solve collective issues.

This paper will evaluate regional governance and cooperation in the fields of regional environmental and natural disasters. First, an analytical framework—state centrism—will be introduced, with the aim of finding specific answers to questions raised throughout the paper. Following this, the article will survey the status of transnational environmental and natural disasters in the region. It then goes on to analyse how regional cooperative institutions and inter-governmental institutions are dealing with the transnational issues discussed in this paper, together with an assessment of the effectiveness of those institutions in coping with regional transnational issues. The following section is dedicated to answer why the institutions in the region are not efficient enough in dealing with these transnational issues, further discussing symptoms of state centrism in East Asia.

2. State Centrism in East Asia

In this section, a framework to understand East Asian regional responses to natural disasters and environmental issues will be explained. As is the case in

---

[2] Other names include Asian dust, yellow dust, yellow wind and Chinese dust storm. It is originally derived from the Chinese characters 黃砂 or 黃沙.

other countries and regions in the world, the East Asian regional response to these transnational problems should be analysed at two different levels—the individual country level and international relations level. Obviously, the initial responses are taken at the national level first. Therefore, regional responses to transnational issues should be discussed within the context of the nature of individual countries. The next stage of analysis should be done through a transnational framework. In other words, the origin and spread of such problems, together with the appropriate response is a concern not just of individual countries, but also of all the countries in the region that are affected by these transnational problems. In this sense, the dynamics among regional countries and the characteristics of a region as a whole, matter in the analysis of transnational issues.

The most important concept in understanding state and regional responses to transitional issues in East Asia is state centrism. State centrism denotes a tendency that prioritises the state over other values and institutions in the society, wherein other important values and goals are sacrificed in its name. It is particularly strong in security discourse, where referent objectives have been expanded since the end of the Cold War. In contrast, the core of security discourse is still national security, and the expansion of these objectives has not taken place under state-centrism (Acharya 2001a & 2006; Haacke 2003).

While security discourse goes beyond the simple concept of national security—which means a military threat to a state—the idea of state-centrism is to prioritise development and economic growth that is required for national security survival, over other objectives and security goals. Such unbalanced emphasis on the state brings about some undesirable consequences, such as the disregard and exclusion of social movements that constitute an important part of society.

State centrism in the region stems from the distinctive nationalism of East Asia formed during the course of decolonisation. Nationalism that flourished in the countries that achieved independence after World War II has distinctive characteristics. Theories of nationalism indicate that a nationalist movement that emerges later than others often becomes very hierarchical—being organised from the top by nationalist elites. Nationalism and nationalist movements in Asia developed during the colonial times when these countries' colonial masters had already well-established nation-states, with their own brand of nationalism. The nationalist elites in these Asian countries were in a hurry to form their own nation-states and "develop" nationalism in their own countries. Thus it can be deduced that the nationalist movement and nationalism in these countries were organised from the top, towards efficiently building nation-states. With this process, states led by nationalist elites often become very powerful proponents of nationalism and the nation-state (Berger 2004, pp. 30-31). In this way, states become the embodiment of nationalism, enforcing the nationalist way of thinking to people in the region. Since then, the state, in its vision of nation-building after independence, has received too much emphasis as an embodiment of nationalism. It must be emphasised that the state is not just a simple tool for the realisation of the nationalist sprit and nation-state building, but more of a goal that nationalism and the nation-state has to achieve. The state, not nationalism, is sacrosanct in East Asia.

The states in East Asia that have become strong and revered in the course of achieving independence became even stronger in the process of nation-state building after independence. In many cases, newly independent countries after World War II experienced economic difficulties, the malfunctioning of a democratic political system, and the presence of an international environment that constrained the autonomy of newly born countries. In Southeast Asia particularly, newly born countries have been plagued by intra-regional conflicts and disputes, and difficulties towards national integration—a consequence of arbitrary national boundary drawing by the colonial forces. All these symptoms were great challenges to the survival of these states. They thus have reproduced discourses that justify and protect themselves, in overcoming challenges and safeguarding the political power of nationalist elites running them. These developments have strengthened state-centrism even further, with the state becoming something that has to be preserved at all cost.

In practice, state centrism takes various forms and has a diverse impact on the many aspects of national, regional and international governance. Later in this paper, it will be argued that state centrism in East Asia, as far as transnational environmental issues and natural disaster management issues are concerned, has three distinctive symptoms: (1) mutual suspicion and the issue of relative gain among regional countries which are required to cooperate among themselves; (2) regional cooperation prompted by developmentalism, led by individual states rather than a collective, for regional common good; and (3) exclusion of civil society from the realm of governance of transnational issues, which is a definitive management weakness of the state.

3. Situation of Issues and Regional Cooperation

3.1 Natural disasters in East Asia

The most well known case of a transnational natural disaster in East Asia is the 2004 Indian Ocean earthquake and tsunami. On 26 December 2004, a massive earthquake (originating from an epicentre near Sumatra) shook the Indian Ocean. The shockwaves from the earthquake devastated coasts in Southeast and Southern Asia, and even reached the East coast of Africa, particularly Kenya, Somalia and Tanzania. According to the comprehensive assessment of the phenomena published by Risk Management Solutions (2006, p. 6), the total number of casualties resulting from the tsunami was 174,500; Indonesia recorded the highest number of casualties—126,900. In addition, about 500,000 people in Indonesia and about 70,000 people in Thailand were indirectly affected (British Broadcasting Corporation 2005).

The tsunami also created huge economic expenses for both the individuals and countries affected. Indonesia tops the list of tsunami-led economic losses at USD4.5 billion. The Maldives recorded a USD500 million economic loss (almost half of its national GDP) (Risk Management Solutions 2006, p. 10). However,

Table 1 Tsunami Casualties in 2004 (per country)

Country	Number of Casualties
Indonesia	126,900
Sri Lanka	31,000
India	10,700
Thailand*	5,400
Somalia	300
Maldives	80
Malaysia	70
Myanmar	60
Tanzania	10
Others**	9

* Including tourists.
** Seychelles, Bangladesh, South Africa, Yemen, Kenya
Source: Risk Management Solutions (2006, p. 10).

Table 2 Economic Losses Countries Incurred during the 2004 Tsunami

Country	Amount Lost (US$ Million)
Indonesia	4,500
Thailand	1,000
Sri Lanka	1,000
India	1,000
Maldives	500
Others	2,000
Total	10,000

Source: Risk Management Solutions (2006, p. 10).

Table 3 Major Earthquakes in Indonesia since 2006

Date		Region	Magnitude (Richter Scale)	Casualties
2006	26 May	Java	6.3	5,749
	17 July	South of Java	7.7	730
2007	21 January	Molucca Sea	7.5	4
	06 March	Southern Sumatra	6.4	67
	08 August	Java	7.5	-
	12 September	Southern Sumatra	8.5	25
	12 September	Kepulauan Mentawai	7.9	-
2009	03 January	North Coast of Papua	7.7	5
	02 September	Java	7.0	81
	30 September	Southern Sumatra	7.5	1,117

Source: United States Geological Survey Website. Accessed on 14 January 2011 from http://earthquake.usgs.gov/earthquakes/world.

individuals (especially the poor) were most affected economically. According to an Asian Development Bank (ADB) report (2005), the GDP loss in many affected countries were marginal, i.e. less than 0.5 per cent; however, the most significantly affected were the areas of agriculture and fisheries that sustain a large portion of the poor people in these distressed countries. The economic impact of the tsunami was substantial in terms of the effort towards poverty eradication.

Another major natural disaster in East Asia (especially in Southeast Asia) is the prevalence of earthquakes and volcanic eruptions. Indonesia has been particularly vulnerable to both. A United States Geological Survey shows that since 2006, there have been 28 earthquakes of more than 6.0 on the Richter scale that killed 7,796 people in Indonesia. Table 3 shows the major earthquakes (significant casualties or greater than 7.5 on the Richter scale) in Indonesia since 2006. Northeast Asia (notably China) is not earthquake-free as well. There were 36 reported earthquakes of a magnitude greater than 4.0 in China since 2000, and a third of these earthquakes were in Yunnan Province.

Typhoons and cyclones are another major natural disaster in East Asia that causes considerable socio-economic losses. While the Philippines has experienced quite a number of typhoons, the most deadly was the tropical cyclone Nargis that devastated Myanmar in May 2008, where it hit Ayewarwady and the Yangon Divisions of the country. Over 140,000 people were killed or remain missing, and more than 2.4 million were affected (Association of South East Asian Nations 2009). The cyclone's after-effects were a significant problem in addition to the wind that created more problems for the people of Myanmar. The people in the affected areas were exposed to unsafe environments due to the lack of shelter, unsafe water, poor sanitation and crowded living conditions in the shelters. These conditions led to the proliferation of communicable diseases such as malaria and dengue fever (World Health Organization 2008, pp. 5-6). In addition to the physical effects, the affected people were plagued by psychological trauma as well.

3.2 Environmental issues in East Asia

The haze is one of the most notable environmental challenges in the Southeast Asian region and falls into the parameters that define a natural disaster. Its occurrence in Southeast Asia attracted the attention of the international media in 1997-1998 when extraordinarily severe haze occurred in the region. Originating in Indonesia, there remains a debate however, over the cause of the haze or the wildfire that caused it. Some argue that it is caused by slash-and-burn type agriculture practised in some areas of Indonesia (King & Wilder 2003), while others blame the commercial greed of plantation owners (Jempa 1995). Others attribute the cause to meteorological factors such as El Niño and drought conditions (Nicholls 1993). Peat land is widespread in Southeast Asia (60 per cent of tropical peat land is found in Southeast Asia) and becomes a significant fire hazard when drained.

While the ASEAN region accounts for just 3 per cent of the world's land area, about 40 per cent of all animal and plant species on earth can be found in Southeast Asia. Mountains cover 45 per cent of the ASEAN region while the global average is just 30 per cent. The region has more than 1,000 natural parks (600,000 km^2 or 13 per cent of the total land area of Southeast Asia) reserved for biodiversity protection. The haze caused by the fire threatens the environment and biodiversity as well as causes damage to both health and society. This phenomenon takes place almost annually; however, the most serious one was in

Table 4 Economic Losses from the 1997 Haze Occurrence

Sector	Estimated Economic Losses (in US$ Million)	
	Minimum	Maximum
Agriculture		
Farm	2,431	2,431
Plantations	319	319
Forestry		
Timber from natural forest	1,461	2,165
Lost growth in natural forest	256	377
Timber from plantation	94	94
Non-timber forest products	586	586
Flood protection	404	404
Erosion and siltation	1,586	1,586
Carbon sink	1,446	1,446
Health	145	154
Transmigration /buildings/ property	1	1
Transportation	18	49
Tourism	111	111
Fire-fighting	12	11
Total	8,870	9,725

Source: Asian Development Bank (1999).

1997. The 1997 haze was not limited to Indonesia but also affected Singapore, Malaysia, Brunei and even Thailand. Schools, airports, and private businesses had to shut down and public transportation operations were affected as well. Overall, the 1997 haze resulted in USD9.3 billion of economic losses in terms of agricultural production, destruction of forests, health, transportation, and tourism in the Southeast Asian region (Kamal 2001, p. 11). Table 4 shows the ADB's estimate of the economic losses caused by 1997 haze in Indonesia.

Yellow Sand originates from the Taklamakan Desert and the Gobi Desert in China. The average annual rainfall in these areas is less than 400 mm. The main cause of the Yellow Sand problem is the desertification of Mongolia and some parts of China. The sand from these dry areas is sucked up by the wind, crossing mainland China into the Korean Peninsula and Japan, which sometimes can be observed in the U.S. and Southern Canada. About 30 per cent of the sand particles fall in the areas of origin; however, 20 per cent of them are carried to neighbouring areas. The remaining 50 per cent is carried deep into the Korean Peninsula, Japan, and Pacific Ocean. In Japan, the sand particles are observed 300 days a year. According to the observation, the amount of deposition is about 15 tons/km^2 a month in Beijing, China and about 1 to 5 tons/km^2 in Japan in a year.[3] Severe Yellow Sand is observed a few times a year on the Korean Peninsula, with the number of days of Yellow Sand warnings issued by the Korea Meteorological Administration increasing every year. The Yellow Sand used to be a phenomenon that takes place during spring in the country; however, it is now observed in winter as well, since the phenomenon has become more frequent.

On the Korean Peninsula, it is not even a new phenomenon. According to historical records, Yellow Sand—at that time called Woo-To (雨土 or "rain of soil")—was observed as early as the second century on the Korean Peninsula (Chun et al. 2008). Yellow Sand was not known to be harmful in the past; however, it has become a serious environmental, economic and health problem in recent years. It is known to cause soil acidification that damages the agricultural industry in affected countries. It also causes health hazards since it contains significant chemical particles such as lead and cadmium. Since the sand particles

---

[3] Asia Pacific Economic Cooperation (APEC) Virtual Center for Environmental Technology Exchange (website). "Yellow Sand or dust and sandstorm." Accessed on 20 January 2011 from www.apec-vc.or.jp/e/modules/tinyd01/index.php?id=23.

and the chemical elements contained in Yellow Sand are harmful and toxic, schools and nurseries in Korea (especially those along the western coast) had to shut down for a few days in 2008 when severe Yellow Sand weather anomalies occurred. Over the years, the socio-economic damage to Korea caused by Yellow Sand is estimated to range from USD3.9 billion to a maximum of USD7.3 billion in 2002, with the average of USD5.6 billion (0.8 per cent of GDP) or USD117.00 per South Korean inhabitant (Jeong 2008). The problem of Yellow Sand is an environmental issue due to the toxic chemicals found in the substance, mainly caused by the rapid industrialisation of China and the uncontrolled emissions of chemicals into the air which has damaged agriculture, the environment, health and economy.

3.3 Regional cooperation schemes

The level of cooperation by ASEAN on these transnational issues reflects international and collaborative developments in the late 1990s and early 2000s, i.e., the 1997 Economic Crisis, the severe haze in 1997-1998, and the tsunami that hit Southeast Asia in 2004. Natural disasters have always occurred in Southeast Asian countries, and cooperation over natural disaster is one of the oldest agenda items for these countries. In 1976, ASEAN announced the ASEAN Declaration on Mutual Assistance on Natural Disaster that recommended the voluntary assistance of ASEAN member countries to another member country affected by a natural disaster (Association of South East Asian Nations 1976). Long after the declaration, ASEAN convened the ASEAN Expert Group on Disaster Management, which in 2003, was transformed into the more permanent ASEAN Committee on Disaster Management (ACDM). The ACDM was tasked to (1) establish an ASEAN Action Plan for natural disasters; (2) develop a programme for capacity building; (3) form a communication network to share information on natural disasters; (4) strengthen partnerships with NGOs; and (5) increase public awareness by ASEAN members on natural disasters. In addition, the ASEAN Regional Forum (ARF), led by the association, has dealt with disaster relief issues and participated in various symposiums and inter-session meetings since 1997.

The 2004 Indian Ocean earthquake and tsunami became a turning point for ASEAN to increase efforts to prevent and respond to natural disasters. Members reached an accord on the ASEAN Agreement on Disaster Management and Emergency Response (AADMER) after the tsunami. It was announced in 2005 and all countries endorsed it by the end of 2009. The agreement has three main arms: the ASEAN Coordinating Centre for Humanitarian Assistance on Disaster Management (AHA Centre) in Jakarta, the ASEAN Disaster Management and Emergency Relief Fund, and the ASEAN Standby Arrangements for Disaster Relief and Emergency Response (ASADRER). The AHA Centre coordinates national focal points and acts as a first responder for disasters. ASADRER provides information on reserved material for disaster management in individual countries. It is also used as a disaster information centre. In addition to these, the ASEAN countries conduct exercises for disaster response and search-and-rescue operations on rotational basis.

The level of institutionalisation of ASEAN cooperation on environmental issues is higher than those in other fields, as demonstrated by two binding agreements: the "ASEAN Agreement on the Establishment of ASEAN Centre for Biodiversity 2005" and the ASEAN Agreement on Transboundary Haze Pollution 2002. ASEAN's response to these transnational environmental issues consists of two strategies. One is on general environmental issues and the other is specifically on the haze problem (since it is recognised as a serious regional issue). For general environmental issues, the highest-level meeting among

Table 5 Natural Disaster-Related Cooperation Mechanisms in ASEAN

Organisation	• ASEAN Committee on Disaster Management, ACDM (2003)
Agreements and Declarations	• ASEAN Declaration on Mutual Assistance on Natural Disaster (1976) • ASEAN Regional Programme on Disaster Management (2004) • ASEAN Agreement on Disaster Management and Emergency Response, AADMER (2004) • ASEAN Coordinating Centre for Humanitarian Assistance on Disaster Management, AHA Centre (2011) • ASEAN Disaster Management and Emergency Relief Fund (2005) • ASEAN Standby Arrangements for Disaster Relief and Emergency Response, ASADRER (2005)

Source: Compiled by author.

ASEAN countries is the ASEAN Ministerial Meeting on Environment (AMME), comprising a senior officers' meeting (ASEAN Senior Officers Meeting on Environment (ASOEN)) and six working groups.[4] Based on the Agreement on the Establishment of the ASEAN Centre for Biodiversity (2005), ASEAN (supported by the European Union) has set up the ASEAN Centre for Biodiversity. Other major initiatives in this field include the ASEAN Environmental Education Inventory database that promotes environmental education and builds an environment-related database, and the ASEAN Wildlife Enforcement Network (ASEAN-WEN) that monitors poaching activities in ASEAN member countries.

Since the 1980s, ASEAN countries have dealt with transnational air pollution, such as the haze issue, with various schemes that were strengthened after the 1997 haze outbreak. Concrete action was taken even before the 1997 haze. In 1995, ASEAN set up the Haze Technical Task Force (HTTF) through AMME. Alarmed by the 1997 haze, ASEAN announced the Regional Haze Action Plan (RHAP).[5] It stipulated the following member country duties: (1) prevention of wildfire through a national level policy and heightened monitoring; (2) establishment of national action mechanism to monitor wildfires; and (3) strengthened cooperation to prevent wildfires. In 2002, the ASEAN countries

Table 6 ASEAN Cooperation on Related Environmental Issues

Meetings	• ASEAN Ministers Meeting on Environment (AMME) • ASEAN Senior Officers Meeting on Environment (ASOEN) • 6 Working Groups
Organizations	• ASEAN Centre for biodiversity • ASEAN Environmental Education Inventory Database • ASEAN Wildlife Enforcement Network, ASEAN-WEN
Agreements / Declarations	• ASEAN Agreement on the Establishment of the ASEAN Centre for Biodiversity (2005)

Source: Compiled by Author.

[4] The following working groups deal with the following issues and causes: (1) multilateral environmental cooperation; (2) ocean-coastal environment; (3) preservation of nature and biodiversity; (4) water-resource management; (5) eco-friendly and sustainable cities; and (6) environmental education.

[5] Association of Southeast Asian Nations (ASEAN) Website. "Regional Haze Action Plan." Accessed on 23 August 2012 from http://www.aseansec.org/9059.htm.

Table 7 Tsunami-Related Cooperation Strategies in ASEAN

Mechanism	• Regional Haze Action Plan, RHAP • Haze Online
Agreements and Declarations	• ASEAN Agreement on Transboundary Haze Pollution (2002) • Conference of the Parties to the ASEAN Agreement on Transboundary Haze Pollution, COP to AATHP

Source: Compiled by Author.

formed a consensus on the ASEAN Agreement on Transboundary Haze Pollution (AATHP), immediately sent to individual countries for ratification. The agreement has two main tools to respond to the issue. The first one is the Conference of the Parties (COP) to the agreement wherein the countries convenean annual ministerial level conference on haze to coordinate their actions against the regional haze problem. Another major attempt to coordinate solutions is Haze Online (http://haze.asean.org), a website created in 1999 by RHAP, providing haze-related information to the public, and acting as a depository of related information and documents produced by the government meetings of the association.

The main carrier of regional cooperation is ASEAN+3 in East Asia. While EAS is a larger framework for regional cooperation, it has not developed solid cooperation mechanisms yet. At the ASEAN+3 level, environmental cooperation developed relatively well compared to other areas. The ASEAN+3 Environmental Ministers' Meeting was set up in 2002, and a senior officers' meeting has been annually held since 2004. Natural disaster cooperation at the level of East Asia did not develop much, and so far it only had a senior officers' meeting that was first convened in 2006. Cooperation in East Asia is not just taking shape through multilateral platforms such as ASEAN, ASEAN+3 and EAS. It is also important to note what kind of cooperation takes place at the ASEAN+1 level. Each of the so-called +3 countries (i.e. Korea, Japan and China) has its own cooperation schemes with ASEAN in the field of transnational crime and regional pandemic diseases. However, each country's bilateral cooperation with ASEAN in the field of environment and natural disaster is much weaker. Only Japan has a senior officers' meeting with ASEAN in the field of environmental issues. There are other smaller ad hoc bilateral cooperation initiatives between +3 countries and

ASEAN; however, institutionalised cooperation on a permanent basis remains unseen.

Regional cooperation that can address the Yellow Sand issue is beyond the purview of an East Asian regional cooperation mechanism. An East Asian regional cooperation mainly deals with issues covering the entire East Asian region, and Yellow Sand (mainly an issue of Northeast Asia) is beyond the coverage of the said initiative, although there are bilateral and multilateral efforts by concerned parties in Northeast Asia. For example, Korea and China setup a Yellow Sand joint surveillance network in 2003 with USD3 million invested by the two countries in the establishment of ten observatories in China. Two stages of the joint effort have been completed and the third stage will start soon with the creation of 5 additional observatories. At the multilateral level, the ministries of the environment from the three concerned countries, i.e. China, Japan and Korea, convened a Yellow Sand joint research team in 2007. It formed two working level research groups, with an annual meeting to exchange information, technology and progress reports. In a recent meeting, the working groups decided to extend the exchange of information (which has been confined to just Korea and China) to Japan and Mongolia (Korea Meteorological Administration 2010). Prior to this, some countries and concerned international organisations have established a fund (although very small) to tackle the Yellow Sand problem in 2002. Under this initiative, Korea, Japan, China, Mongolia, UNEP, GEF and ADB participated. In addition, some private sector efforts are progressing (such as greening works) to prevent the further desertification of Mongolia and China.

The list of regional mechanisms to cope with transnational natural disaster and environmental problems looks impressive, especially in the case of ASEAN. There are many cooperation mechanisms for various issues including binding agreements among member countries; however, it is unknown if they are effective at preventing and responding to the various transnational issues in the region.

Regional cooperation on transnational issues in East Asia is comparatively new and underdeveloped compared to the experience of the Southeast Asian region and ASEAN. Thus the evaluation of regional cooperation on transnational natural disasters and environment issues in this paper has focused on the experience of ASEAN. Existing evaluations on the organisations recognise that the ASEAN countries have done much to develop regional cooperation; however, they simultaneously and clearly point out the negative side of cooperation. Some existing studies argue that they are mostly ineffective despite the impressive set of ASEAN cooperative mechanisms (Nishikawa 2009, pp. 226-229).

It must be noted, however, that existing evaluations are not specifically for transnational natural disasters and environmental issues, but deal with the issues in the context of human security and non-traditional security issues in which natural disasters and environmental issues are included. Ralf Emmers (2002) argues that the association's responses to human security issues have "primarily consisted of a rhetorical device" (p. 16). Emmers adds that these various cooperative mechanisms of ASEAN are nothing but expressions of good intentions. He points out that the ASEAN mechanism comprises "non-binding and unspecific measures, without addressing the question of funding, setting target dates and establishing monitoring mechanisms to assess progress." Simon Tay (2002a) is more specific on the problems of ASEAN. He argues that the organisation could build a cooperative mechanism that has gravitas because of the "ASEAN Way"; however, the ASEAN Way itself is simultaneously a problem that prevents ASEAN from developing human security and non-traditional security cooperation further (pp. 162-176).

4. State Centrism and Its Symptoms in East Asian Regional Cooperation

The breadth and the depth of transnational environmental and natural disasters in East Asian region are important to take note of, in understanding its institutional dynamics. Reflecting on this significance, there are a number of regional cooperation mechanisms at the level of ASEAN, ASEAN+3 and EAS; however, the overall evaluation on the cooperation mechanism is not so positive. This raises the question, "What went wrong in East Asia, and what prevents such regional associations from cooperating to solve the problems effectively?" For ASEAN, the immediate answer points to the ASEAN Way (Acharya 2001a; Bellamy 2004; Haacke 2003). However, blaming the ASEAN Way does not reveal more historically deep-root causes of regional cooperation in this part of the world.

There might be a few different paths to approach the problem; however, this paper intends to emphasise on the issue of states in East Asia. It can be said that the traditional security discourse has been monopolised by states in the region; in addition, security in East Asia has been a state-centric discourse. State-centrism in East Asia (as widely argued) has its roots in colonial rule and in the process of independence. The state-centric approach to security (including human security and non-traditional security) results in limited consequences that render regional cooperation on human security and non-traditional security ineffective in East Asia such as mutual suspicion and the issue of relative gain, regional cooperation prompted by developmentalism, and exclusion of civil society from the realm of human and non-traditional security issues.

This state-centric characteristic of these East Asian countries has a few implications for regional cooperation. First, the East Asian region is characterised as a region of mutual suspicion despite currently ongoing regional cooperation schemes such as ASEAN, ASEAN+3 and EAS. Among the nation-states that have mutual suspicion, the inter-state relationship is dominated by the discourse of national interests and relative gain. ASEAN, formed in 1967, has a longer experience of regional cooperation than ASEAN+3 which began in 1997. Since ASEAN is still the core of ASEAN+3, it is difficult to expect the ASEAN+3 regional cooperation platform to perform better than ASEAN, an organisation that has longer institutional experience. It is widely recognised that despite its 40 years or more experience, the ASEAN region is also characterised by mutual suspicion among member countries. For example, the current ASEAN secretary-general and former Thai foreign minister, Surin Pitsuwan argues that "If there is any region that is suspicious of external involvement and jealous of the concept of sovereignty, it is Southeast Asia. The concept of sovereignty is still very sacred here" (cited in Acharya 2001b, p. 21). Surin Pitsuwan's observation was made at a very abstract level, citing concepts such as the state and sovereignty; however, Emmers' (2002) argument is more concrete and pinpoints what causes the persistent mutual suspicion in the region: "Bilateral relations [in the region] have continued to be troubled by minor matters that can lead to larger diplomatic incidents" (p. 17). Indeed there have been, and still are, plenty of small cases of past intramural disputes within the boundary of ASEAN (Weatherbee 2005, pp. 120-151).

Mutual suspicion among ASEAN countries (despite a good and cordial relationship on the surface) and the state-centric worldview of Southeast

Asian countries that brought about a thick panoply of nationalism, have made the political elites and the domestic audiences of each individual Southeast Asian countries sensitive to "relative gain" (Baldwin 1993). Even if regional cooperation could bring gains for all member countries, individual countries would not be satisfied with regional cooperation if the "absolute gain" of one or more of the other is larger than theirs. Although cooperation actually benefits participants in absolute terms, national elites and a domestic audience that are suspicious of their neighbours cannot accept such advantage over their own. Sovereignty, in pushing for a successful regional cooperation, is rarely achieved and results in a very weak regional cooperation.

Regional cooperation might have the potential to make state-centric individual countries cooperate to resolve transnational environmental issues and natural disaster issues in the region. In reality, however, regional cooperation in East Asia has been ineffective in changing the behavior of individual countries. Regional cooperation in East Asia is mainly prompted by the developmentalism of individual countries, not by the pursuit of a common good in the region. In East Asia, individual countries in regional cooperation schemes pursue the maximisation of national interest rather than the regional common good. This again is related to the issue of relative gain. One of the notable cases is the formation of ASEAN+3. It was before the onset of the 1997 Asian Economic Crisis that ASEAN countries invited +3 countries to the ASEAN Summit. However, it was definitely the 1997 Asian Economic Crisis that strengthened the ASEAN+3 scheme and provided crucial momentum (Bowels 2002; Higgott 1998; Tay 2002b). In the early ASEAN+3, each individual country's motive to join the regional cooperation body was to overcome the 1997 Asian Economic Crisis as early as they could. However, soon after the countries got out of the crisis, the momentum for regional cooperation became significantly weaker and exposed differences in opinions toward the direction of regional cooperation.

Other problems embedded in East Asian regional cooperation have contributed to ineffective regional cooperation. For example, East Asian regional cooperation is often characterised by soft regionalism (Katzenstein 1997). Weak institutions and rules for such types of regional cooperations do not motivate individual states to put aside narrow national interests. The region (which is often described with mutual suspicion) does not have a credible and effective mediating state to lead the regional cooperation. Unlike the European Union, in which regional powers like France and Germany acted as providers of common good assurance, East Asian regional powers (notably China) have not provided such a common good until recently. All these factors have contributed to the less than satisfactory regional cooperation in East Asia.

A country resorting to concessions for the bigger benefit of a whole region is hardly normal. Although they work together for regional cooperation, a concession (thus a short-term loss) is accepted as a defeat in the race for national interests and is not acceptable to national elites. Furthermore, the domestic audience does not accept such concession for a bigger benefit in the long term either. In this extreme situation, regional cooperation among these countries is an arena of a beggar-thy-neighbor strategy, rather than a mechanism for common and shared prosperity and progress. This does not mean that East Asian countries are such extreme countries—some countries are more sensitive to national interests and sovereignty than the common good, so it is not easy to reach a consensus on how to cope with transnational issues. Furthermore, a bidding norm and regulation for regional cooperation (which necessarily limits the full exercise of national sovereignty) is very hard to emerge.

The state-centric nature of East Asia has another negative implication for regional cooperation on transnational issues. It has effectively prevented NGOs and civil societies in the region from speaking out on the issues. In many East Asian countries, the management of non-traditional and human security issue is still monopolised by the state. Amitav Acharya (2006) observes:

> The state is the critical actor in any securitisation process. Securitisation in Asia is fundamentally a state-centric project, meaning that the state plays the instrumental role in deciding which issues are to be securitised, when are they to be securitised, and what would be the method of securitisation, that is, whether it will be principally a rhetorical speech act, or carried out through concrete policy and institutional adjustments (p. 247).

This state-centric nature of the security issue in East Asia has two implications. First, when it comes to transnational issues under scrutiny (human security or non-traditional security issues) the public or ordinary citizens are excluded from the discussion of human security, when it is these very individuals that are be protected or to be secured against transnational threats and danger. As such the cooperation and cooperation mechanisms for transnational issues in East Asia do not correctly reflect the needs and voice of the protected because they exclude NGOs and civil societies from the process. Therefore it proves more questionable if the cooperation cannot protect these individuals who are supposed to be protected in a proper and effective manner.

The state-centric approach to human security and non-traditional security in East Asia has failed to utilise the expertise of NGOs and civil society on the issues involved. Mely Caballero-Anthony (2004) argues that traditionally, security has been the domain of the state, excluding civil society. This tradition (despite the big gap in the natures of traditional security and human/non-traditional security) still applies to human and non-traditional security in East Asia. She further notes that "whatever attempts were made to challenge the dominant security discourse and offer alternative perspectives were not found in the track-one or track-two circle" (pp. 164-165). This state-centric approach to human and non-traditional security is a great loss for regional cooperation in effectively dealing with transnational issues, and the not so simple exclusion of a part of society. Caballero-Anthony adds that "the domain of state authority had contracted and its capacity to handle an increasing number of security threats was already being stretched to the limit" (p. 176). Civil society and the NGOs in the region have a lot to contribute to regional cooperation on those issues in such circumstance. These organisations have accumulated grass-roots expertise, knowledge and wisdom on what the problems are, how to handle those issues, and what people want. These are actually what states in regional cooperations lack. In addition, NGOs and civil society organisations have built their own transboundary networks as well. Thus, regional NGOs and civil society organisations have much to offer to the states' efforts towards human security and non-traditional security cooperation. Regional cooperation on human and non-traditional security becomes ineffective and irrelevant when it lacks such valuable contributions that could be brought in by the involvement and input of civil society and NGOs.

5. Conclusion

This paper has discussed the issue of transnational natural disasters and environmental problems in East Asia from the perspective of regional cooperation. The topics dealt with in this paper include environmental issues in the region—natural disasters such as earthquakes, tsunamis, and cyclone-typhoons, also the Yellow Sand and haze phenomena. These are transnational issues, having originated and experienced from a single country, but dispersed regionally. The impact of such disasters is not confined within the boundaries of a single country and the transnational nature of the problem requires effective regional cooperation to prevent such disasters from happening again, to protect people and be able to respond to such circumstances more effectively. This paper has also evaluated the cooperative measures in place in East Asia and analysed the weakness of the various provisions, after surveying the status of regional cooperative mechanisms in the region.

The paper has argued that the state-centric tradition of East Asian countries has made regional cooperation ineffective with regards to human security and non-traditional security issues that include transnational natural disasters and environmental problems. The impact of colonial rule, the state-led independence process and historical experiences ingrained state-centric tradition into these East Asian countries. It has been shown that the state-centric tradition has created three legacies with implications for East Asian regional cooperation. These are (1) mutual suspicion and the issue of relative gains among member countries; (2) regional cooperation prompted by developmentalism; and (3) the exclusion of civil society from the realm of human and non-traditional security issues. These factors negatively affect the development of regional cooperation in East Asia.

It is difficult for countries in the region to give up state-centrism voluntarily, and find a quick way to fix it. East Asian states are bound by their respective historical legacies as baggage. However, it should be added that the states in the region are moving in the direction of more effective regional cooperation, although very slowly. Some propose external input, arguing that it is not easy for member countries to fix the problem and that the inclusion of external countries in the regional cooperation is needed to stimulate progress. However, external countries would not have a great stake and interest in the issue of human security and non-traditional security since such issues do not directly influence their interests except in a limited number of areas, making it more difficult to find a quick solution in the region. The states in the region should be under continued pressure to shed state-centrism and make their first move towards regional cooperation with additional pressure from regional civil societies, NGOs and intellectuals.

References

Acharya, A. (2006). "Securitization in Asia: Functional and Normative Implications." In M. Caballero-Anthony, R. Emmers and A. Acharya, eds. *Non-Traditional Security in Asia: Dilemmas in Securitization*. pp. 247-250. Aldershot: Ashgate.

_________ (2001a). "Human Security: East Versus West?" *Working Paper*, No. 17. Singapore: Institute of Defence and Strategic Studies.

_________ (2001b). *Constructing a Security Community in Southeast Asia: ASEAN and the Problem of Regional Order*. London: Routledge.

Asian Development Bank (ADB) (2005). "An Initial Assessment of the Impact of the Earthquake and Tsunami of December 26, 2004 on South and Southeast Asia." Accessed on 23 August 2012 from http://www.adb.org/Documents/Others/Tsunami/impact-earthquake-tsunami.pdf.

_________ (1999). Final Report on Planning for Fire Prevention and Drought Management Project, TA 2999-INO. Jakarta: Asian Development Bank.

Asia Pacific Economic Cooperation (APEC) Virtual Center for Environmental Technology Exchange (website). "Yellow Sand or Dust and sandstorm." Accessed on 20 January 2011 from www.apec-vc.or.jp/e/modules/tinyd01/index.php?id=23.

Association of South East Asian Nations (ASEAN) (2009). "ASEAN's Post-Nargis Humanitarian Assistance-Fact Sheet." Accessed on 23 December 2010 from http://www.aseansec.org/CN-FactSheet-1.pdf.

_________ (1976). "ASEAN Declaration on Mutual Assistance on Natural Disaster." 26 June. Accessed on 17 January 2010 from http://www.aseansec.org/1431.htm.

Badenoch, N. (2002). *Transnational Environmental Governance: Principles and Practices in Mainland Southeast Asia*. Washington: World Resources Institute.

Baldwin, D. ed. (1993). *Neo-realism and Neo-liberalism: The Contemporary Debate*. New York: Columbia University Press.

Bellamy, A. J. (2004). "The Pursuit of Security in Southeast Asia: Beyond Realism." In M. Beeson, ed. *Contemporary Southeast Asia: Regional dynamics, National Differences*. pp. 156-177. Houndsmill: Palgrave.

Berger, M. T. (2004). "Decolonizing Southeast Asia: Nationalism, Revolution and the Cold

War." In M. Beeson, ed. *Contemporary Southeast Asia: Regional dynamics, National Differences*. pp. 30-49. Houndsmill: Palgrave.

British Broadcasting Corporation (2005). "At-a-glance: Tsunami Economic Impact." 22 March. Accessed on 15 January 2011 from http://news.bbc.co.uk/go/pr/fr/-/2/hi/business/4154277.stm.

Caballero-Anthony, M. (2004). "Revisioning Human Security in Southeast Asia." *Asian Perspective*, 28, 3, 155-189.

Chun, Y., Cho, H., Chung H., and Lee, M. (2008). "Historical Records of Asian Dust Events (Hwangsa) in Korea." *Bulletin of American Meteorological Society*, 89, 823-827.

Elliott, L. (2004). "Environmental Challenges, Policy Failure and Regional Dynamics in Southeast Asia." In M. Beeson, ed. *Contemporary Southeast Asia: Regional dynamics, National Differences*. pp. 178-197. Houndsmill: Palgrave.

Emmers, R. (2002). "The Securitization of Transnational Crime in ASEAN." Working Paper No. 39. Singapore: Institute of Defence and Strategic Studies.

Haacke, J. (2003). *ASEAN's Diplomatic and Security Culture: Origins, Development and Prospects*. London. Routledge.

Higgott, R. (1998). "The Asian Economic Crisis: A Study in the Politics of Resentment." *New Political Economy*, 3, 3, 333-356.

Jempa, C. J. (1995). *Tropical Deforestation: A Socio-economic Approach*. London: Earthscan.

Jeong, D. (2008). "Socio-Economic Costs from Yellow Dust Damages in South Korea." *Korean Social Science Journal*, 35, 2, 1-29.

Kamal, A. (2001). "ASEAN's Response Strategy in Addressing Transboundary Haze Pollution." *ASEAN Biodiversity*, July-September, 11-14.

Katzenstein, P. (1997). "Introduction: Asian Regionalism in Comparative Perspective." In P. Katzenstein & T. Shiraishi, eds. *Network Power: Japan and Asia*. pp. 1-44. Ithaca: Cornell University Press.

Kim, I. (2007). "Environmental cooperation of Northeast Asia: transboundary air pollution." *International Relations of the Asia-Pacific*, 7, 3, 439-462.

King, V. T. and Wilder, D. (2003). "Ecology and Environmental Change." *The Modern Anthropology of South-East Asia*. pp. 231-261. London: Routledge.

Koh, K. L. and Robinson, N. A. (2002). "Regional Environment Governance: Examining the Association of Southeast Asian Nations (ASEAN) Model." In C. Daniel and M. H. Ivanova, eds. *Global Environmental Governance*. pp. 101-121. New Haven: Yale School of Forestry and Environmental Studies.

Korea Meteorological Administration (2010). "Korea Meteorological Administration Press release" (in Korean). 5 November. Accessed om 23 August 2012 from http://web.kma.go.kr/notify/press/kma_list.jsp?bid=press&mode=view&num=1191641&page=4&field=&text=.

Lee, J. (2011). "Transnational Natural Disasters and Environmental Issues in East Asia: Current Situation and the Way Forward from the Perspective of Regional Cooperation." *IFANS Review*, 19, 1, 25-52.

Lee, S. (2001). "Environmental Regime-building in Northeast Asia: A Catalyst for Sustainable Regional Cooperation." *Journal of East Asian Studies*, 1, 2, 31-61.

Nicholls, N. (1993). "ENSO, Drought and Flooding Rain in South-East Asia." In H. Brookfield & Y. Byron, eds. *South-East Asia's Environmental Future: the Search for Sustainability* (pp. 154-175). Japan: United Nations University Press.

Nishikawa, Y. (2009). "Human Security in Southeast Asia: Viable Solution or Empty Slogan?" *Security Dialogue*, 40, 2, 213-236.

Risk Management Solutions (2006). *Managing Tsunami Risk in the Aftermath of the 2004 Indian Ocean Earthquake & Tsunami*. Newark: Risk Management Solutions. Accessed on 23 August 2012 from http://www.rms.com/publications/indianoceantsunamireport.pdf.

Schreurs, M. A. (1998). "Environmental cooperation in Northeast Asia." *Global Economic Review*, 27, 1, 88-101.

Shim, S. (2000). "Transboundary Air Pollution in the Northeastern Asian Region." Paper presented at the International Workshop on Environmental Peace in East Asia. 5-6 July. Seoul and Wonju Korea.

Tacconi, L, F. J. and Grafton, R. Q. (2008). "Local Causes, Regional Cooperation and Global Financing for Environmental Problems: The Case of Southeast Asian Haze Pollution." *International Environmental Agreements*, 8, 1, 1-16.

Tay, S. S. C. (2008). "Blowing Smoke: Regional Cooperation, Indonesian Democracy, and the Haze" in D. K. Emmerson, ed. *Hard Choices: Security, Democracy and Regionalism in Southeast Asia*. pp. 219-240. Stanford: The Walter H. Shorenstein Asia-Pacific Research Center.

_________ (2002a). "Fire and Haze in Southeast Asia," In P. J. Noda (ed.). *Cross-Sectoral Partnership in Enhancing Human Security*. Tokyo: Japan Center for International Exchange.

_________ (2002b). "ASEAN Plus 3: Challenges and Cautions about a New Regionalism." In M. J. Hassan, S. Leong & V. Lim, eds. *Asia Pacific Security: Challenges and Opportunities in the Twenty-first Century*. pp. 99-117. Kuala Lumpur: ISIS Malaysia.

United States Geological Survey Website. *World Earthquake Information*. Accessed on 14

January 2011 from http://earthquake.usgs.gov/earthquakes/world.

Weatherbee, D. E. (2005). *International Relations in Southeast Asia: The Struggle for Autonomy*. Lanham: Rowan & Littlefield.

World Health Organization (WHO) (2008). *Communicable Disease Risk Assessment and Interventions: Cyclone Nargis-Myanmar*. Accessed on 23 August 2012 from http://www.who.int/diseasecontrol_emergencies/MyanmarCycloneNargis090508.pdf.

Yoon, E. (2003). "The Growth of Environmental Cooperation in Northeast Asia: The Potential Roles of Civil Society." *The Good Society*, 12, 1, 46-51.

Transnationalism and Crime:
Victims, Perpetrators and the Law

Mike Hayes

1. Introduction

The association between transnationals and crime is at times contradictory, sensationalist, under researched, and racist. Various media stories and political groups have attempted to link the increase in immigration with rising crime rates. The reasons, while overlapping and confusing, are clear: a mixture of discrimination, lack of opportunities, and selective information on immigration gives an impression to people that immigration leads to crime waves. The facts are still debatable in some areas, but the overall picture suggests, quite strongly according to some, that there is a weak or non-existent association between migration and crime rates. A study of the related literature for the past century on immigration and crime in the United States concludes that "immigrants are generally less involved in crime than similarly situated groups, despite the wealth of prominent criminological theories that provide good reasons why this should not be the case" (Martínez & Lee 2000, p. 501). Yet regardless of the evidence of at most a weak connection, the link between transnationalism and crime persists.

This paper has two objectives: first, to detail the multiple ways in which the transnational is legally, politically and culturally related to crime; second, the paper examines how this myth of immigrant and crime is constructed, particularly in South East Asia, and the consequences of these perceptions of the "criminal migrant." It is important also to critically engage with ideas of "international crime," a term which is much favoured in the popular media, in order to understand how the threat of international crime should be understood, and the impact this has on the rights of the non-citizen. The paper has two sections. The first section covers the responses of the state to international crime, covering the political and legal contexts. The next section addresses the view from the transnational, in particular connections between migration and crime, and migration networks.

2. The "Image" of the Transnational Criminal

The image of the transnational criminal, and the idea of an international organised criminal network has become a common and recurring feature in the global media. Providing a quick list of what is considered to be the growing threat of international crime is simple. In late 2010 these were some of the many stories making headlines, in this case mainly in Thailand: the Russian Mafia is gaining influence in Thailand, and throughout Asia, Japanese Yakuza members are on the run in South East Asia. The suspected arms dealer Victor Bout was extradited to the United States, causing tensions in Thailand's relationship with Russia who also wanted Bout to be extradited to face charges in Russia. The Thai media has also focused on the arrest of British paedophile Charles Taylor, who was on the run for twelve years and arrested in late December (BBC 2010). Transnational crime also has its victims, from tragedies such as the people-smuggling boat carrying around 90 asylum seekers, which ran aground and capsized on Christmas Island killing about 45 people, including children. These recent events highlighted are predominantly that of the media's representation of crime: migrants are frequently represented as either the criminals or the victims; either way they are a burden that demands arresting or assistance. It is incorrect to consider these merely as media stories, as this perception of international crime resonates throughout politics, policy and society. Asian states emphatically declare they are involved in an incessant battle against organised crime which impacts the lives of its innocent civilians. The international legal framework criminalising activities across borders have been significantly increased in breadth and strength in the last decades. However, has this change in the response climate been of benefit to everyone? One would consider that citizens feel safer, and that crime is on the decline. But the picture is more complex than this.

As a counter example, in Chiang Mai, a city in Northern Thailand, a young female student was tragically raped and murdered in her dormitory. The suspects, two ethnic Shan construction workers, were arrested. After the arrest, students started to rally and, supported by the police, asked for the expulsion of all migrant construction workers in Chiang Mai. A number of raids and forced expulsions occurred over the following days, with estimates of hundreds of people expelled to Burma. The expulsions were illegal, and in some cases several Thai citizens were caught up in the raids and were also expelled (Weng 2009; Fah 2009; Fry 2009). Mass expulsions are a rare yet dangerous violation of human rights, and an action clearly in contravention of a number of human rights and national laws. Yet people's fears of the non-citizen criminal and the state's acquiescence let this occur. Often it is stated that transnational crime such as piracy, forgery, or smuggling is victimless. The recent groundbreaking United Nations Office for Drugs and Crime (UNODC) report on Transnational Organized Crime (TOC) states as much in its opening chapter (United Nations Office on Drugs and Crime 2010a). But as the case in Chiang Mai shows, the transnational can be more prone to responses to this type of crime because public sentiments lead to their discrimination and sometimes expulsion. As this paper develops further, the non-citizen is often the victim of transnational crime itself, as the trafficked person or the exploited worker. These examples show the developing complexity of international crime and security in a transnational world. We have a greater media concentration on the image of the international criminal—whether as a paedophile or gang member—and a growing complexity of the legal framework, which is often mired in political and diplomatic issues. Often overlooked in this context is the tragedy that can accompany the rise of transnational crime: we do hear of cases of those losing their lives during illegal transit to countries through human smuggling, yet we do not hear of the discrimination facing innocent people, mostly non-citizens, who are like "collateral damage" in the increasing securitisation states make in dealing with crime.[1] These people are branded as criminals merely because of their non-citizen status.

[1] The term "collateral damage" was also used in a 2007 GAATW report on exactly this same issue: that of traffickisssng victims who also became victims of the trafficking laws themselves (Global Alliance Against Traffic in Women 2007).

3. Transnationalism and Transnational Crime

It has been widely accepted that we are in an era of transformed criminal activity. As has been well documented by Manuel Castells (1998), the rise of globalisation has also seen the transformation of the nature of international crime. This expansion is neatly summed up by the blogger Kathleen Millar (2010), who in discussing the UNODC's *The Globalization of Crime* report, stated:

> In our "open economy," in cyberspace, in a marketplace where licit and illicit trade are densely integrated and impervious to the border-bound efforts of national law enforcement agencies, criminals are not only able to conduct their "business" openly and with impunity, but to use market penetration to dig into the fabric of legitimate society, to use criminal revenues to buy political power, and to set themselves up as viable alternatives—as providers of social welfare and security—to civil institutions unable to compete in terms of budgets and revenue.

Some crucial points are underscored here: crime today is a new phenomenon made possible by technological and social transformations; that illegal trade commonly works alongside the legal; that law has been limited by the territoriality of the country, and that criminal networks compete with transnational social networks.

These factors which have led to the expansion of crime in Asia are almost identical to the reasons for increased transnationalism. First, the increased movement of people across borders with the concomitant porosity of the borders has also opened opportunities for crime to flourish in these areas. Where people regularly and illegally cross borders (and examples of these borders in Asia are between Thailand and Burma, Vietnam and China, Indonesia and Malaysia) are also areas where there is a significant amount of smuggled goods and people. It is clear that migration patterns are also shadowed by patterns of criminal behaviour. As Susan Kneebone notes in terms of trafficking, "The patterns of trafficking vary between countries, but generally they follow established migration and trading patterns" (2010, p. 148).

Second, the globalisation of the economy has in a number of ways created more transnational communities of labourers, and also made remittances an important part of national economies. The flow of money has also made crime easier, with money laundering and repatriating profits easier with the use of electronic banking. Similarly, increased capacity in communications has made it easier for transnational cultures to flourish, and also to organise and coordinate criminal activities. The network structure of society nowadays, perhaps best exemplified by the ubiquitous Facebook, is also a feature of transnational communities. The positive aspects of a network structure are also an advantage to criminal organisations: they can isolate and dislocate the people committing the crimes from the leaders of the organisation; they can divide the criminal task into disparate unconnected cells, minimising risk to the organisation; they can also separate the person giving the commands from the legal jurisdiction of the crime, in a sense making the commander inviolable to the law.

What can be clearly inferred from this brief description is an inter-relationship between transnational movements and international criminal activities. This does not imply that transnationals are more involved in crime, but perhaps it could be assumed that the kind of crime that occurs in their community tends to be internationalised, and this is greatly stigmatised by the media and state authorities. Further, as the UNODC report states, crime mostly occurs in populations of young, poor, urban and foreign males. In addition, as a UNODC report notices, most irregular migrants need or must resort to the assistance of profit-seeking smugglers (2010b, p. 2). While the range of internationalised crime is great, this paper seeks to describe crime by focusing on those associated with migration. However, in order to more fully flesh out this relationship between transnational communities and crime, an understanding of how networked societies operate to increase financial incentives will also be discussed.

4. The State and Security

This changing environment of international crime, as recent phenomena, has most commonly been responded to by states through the lens of security. This is not, unfortunately, referring to the security of the person, but rather a traditional view of security in which the state and the law are the subjects of protection. States tend to focus on models of state or national security that are more concerned about protecting the values, economy, and governance of a state.

The consequences of these responses to international crime is thus a double-edged sword; the increased power given to states to boost their ability to secure themselves from crime can have the negative result of making transnationals more vulnerable to the power of this law. Indeed when we ask whose security is being protected in the movements against organised crime, it appears that the state protects itself while often leaving the transnational vulnerable to both the state's security forces and vulnerable to the exploitation through international crime itself.

An alternative approach is the human security response, which highlights how traditional security responses to crime are frequently not about protecting human life, but rather have been used to discriminate, penalise and ostracise transnational communities. The 'value added' of this type of response is the argument that the subject of security—that is what is being protected logically and efficiently should be the human. While human security is one policy improvement that can be implemented to ensure that government activities have few victims, there is a constellation of forces working against this idea: the power of the media promoting a representation of an ever growing menace of the international criminal gang that is ruthlessly evil; the historical and cultural discourses of discrimination in many countries in the region which means citizens often have little sympathy (and more likely have open hostility) to non-citizens in their country; and the standard operating procedures of states which take the simple path of increasing traditional security forces and laws rather than addressing the more complex but sustainable solutions available through human security planning, such as regularising undocumented workers, treating drug problems as also a public health concern, and educating citizens on non-discrimination.

The relationship between the transnational and crime cannot be reduced to a simple set of relationships; the fluid nature of transnationalism means people are differentially subject to (though in clearly definable ways) the changing nature of international crime and, to further add complexity, this occurs as both subjects of crime and criminals themselves. The task of this paper is not to map out the variety of relationships, but rather provide the context of the law and the transnational, and show where the transnationals are vulnerable to crime, or not receiving the protection which they should be getting. When the laws of states in the region tend to penalise non-citizens, most transnationals find themselves labeled as criminals for doing nothing more than existing in the country, even if they were born there. Transnationals may participate by buying smuggled products, which could be anything from drugs to pirated DVDs. Further, because migration in many areas has been criminalised, the participation in recruitment or organising travel or labour may label these people as smugglers or traffickers. This is not to say that all smugglers or traffickers are innocent, but rather that the law is a blunt instrument that can easily target people who were only trying to help a family member get a better job by crossing a border. Indeed it is because of their transnational identity that international crime takes an increased importance in their lives, and one that cannot be simplified as either being a criminal, benefiting from the criminal activities, or being victims. The transnational criminal is an ubiquitous figure not because non-citizens are prone to crime, but rather because criminal laws seek non-citizens out as easy targets.

Another exaggeration commonly used is the idea of non-citizens being involved in international crimes, normally to imply that the crimes themselves are crossing borders and becoming more prevalent countries. A simple confusion here is between international crimes and crimes of an international nature. International crimes are legally defined and occur within different laws and understanding, or legal jurisdiction; crimes of an international nature—or crimes that cross borders—are not defined legally, and are often subject to national jurisdictions. A strict legal definition of an international crime would categorise those international crimes as ones whose severity demands that states produce specific mechanisms to sanction those who commit them (such as universal jurisdiction), or establish mechanisms whose task is to put on trial people accused of these crimes (such as the International Criminal Court). Generally, according to Antonio Cassese, international crimes are considered to be violations of international customary law or treaty law of a general nature, and not crimes specific to international organisations or states only (2005, p. 436). There is often little connecting these transnationals to international crimes, and this mistake may come about through the mis-association of any crime of an international nature to non-citizens, as if transnational criminal networks are only populated by cosmopolitan criminals. Rather, as this paper details further, the technologies of globalisation make the criminals often much more local.

It is useful to outline the increasing interest given to transnational crime for this often results in increased perceptions of threat to a state. The change in level of interest does have ramifications in the broadening scope of the power of international criminal law and potential for it being misapplied. The cases of people being accused of terrorism, subject to internal security acts, or branded as traffickers, are more commonly associated with transnationals: foreigners are associated with "foreign" crime. Though in order to more clearly detail this misapplication it is necessary to understand how "crimes of an international nature" are defined. The UNODC report gives the following definition: "'transnational organized crime' encompasses virtually all profit-motivated criminal activities with international implications" (2010a, p. 3). Such an extremely broad definition is necessary because the nature of crime is forever changing, and in order to be flexible enough to continually include new forms of crime (for example, cyber crime or the smuggling of environmental goods). There have been attempts to define the number and scope of the crimes, from Gerhard Mueller's (2001) list of 18 crimes given in the 1990s,[2] to the most recent UNODC (2010a) report which examines eight areas (though these eight crimes are considered the most severe, and not an exhaustive list).[3] However, crimes such as trafficking and people smuggling, drug and weapons smuggling, piracy, money laundering, and counterfeiting regularly appear in these lists.

While international crimes and crimes of an international nature may be distinct, there are areas of overlap. The tool of universal jurisdiction is used in both categories. Since World War Two the international community has witnessed an increasing number of crimes which states apply universal jurisdiction to. Genocide was one of the first, along with Crimes Against Humanity, war crimes (or Grave Breeches of the Geneva Convention), and torture—all of which are considered international crimes. Added to this list are hijacking planes, terrorism, drug trafficking, human trafficking, and enforced disappearances. Some states use universal jurisdiction for the crimes of corruption and paedophilia.[4] Apart from universal jurisdiction, the two areas of international crime relate when regimes which commit international crimes often

---

[2] Mueller gives 18 categories for TOC, which even 10 years later, is showing its age and missing some important new crimes.

[3] Among the eighteen crimes are: money laundering, drug trafficking, a range of corruption like crimes, computer crimes, intellectual property theft, arms trafficking, terrorism, hijacking on land air and sea, trafficking and body part trading, art theft, and environmental crime.

[4] For instance these crimes both have universal jurisdiction in USA and EU.

include crimes of an international nature as well, such as firearms smuggling, or drug exporting.

An interesting point of relationship, but one that cannot be developed much here, is the support and advocacy for international crimes by transnational communities because it is one method to weaken displaced undemocratic regimes in their home country. Many people in Southeast and East Asia are outside of their country because the government has ineffectively managed the country, and corruption and insecurity means people have to search elsewhere for their economic security. In a sense their transnationalism is a result of corrupt regimes, which engage or condone transnational crime. For these transnational communities—exiled Burmese, Indonesian, or North Korean communities[5]—pressure on their government's corruption can be given legitimacy when classified in terms of international crime. The results are numerous. It means that state officials are more reluctant to travel for fear of arrest under universal restriction. It means that the advocacy of transnational groups is taken more seriously when they couch their grievances in terms of non-law abiding states, rather than as differing political opinions. It also means that states are far more cautious about openly condoning illegal activities for fear that some time in the future, the law will catch up with them. It also demonstrates that the relationship between transnationals and crime is not merely that of the former being victim, but also in some cases the laws are strategically used for specific political purposes.

5. The State and the Law

The changes in criminal activities do imply a transformed position of the nation state. The concept of the nation is a privileged form of identification in transnational theory, and the most commonly used identification. Contesting nationalism is safe and a too easily taken path in terms of analysing the advent of globalisation. It is too easy to talk of the weakened state or the end of the

[5] For example, see the *License to Rape* report, which structures the rape of ethnic Shan women as a crime against humanity, and therefore punishable through international criminal law (Shan Women's Action Network 2002). Similarly, civil society groups in Australia have attempted to arrest Indonesian generals for war crimes. In a different sense, many senior North Korean military and their families are restricted from traveling to USA and EU countries.

nation state (in Kenichi Ohmae's (1996) famous claim), when in some areas—such as security and crime, we see a great reach for power by the nation state. In studies of international crime the position of the state can be invigorated through its increased powers to police crime, and to strengthen policies on security. But it is often these strengthening powers that are used to consolidate a monolithic state identity in contrast to a reality of transnationalism. The powers relegated to police crime enable stronger monitoring of the borders and surveillance of non-citizen communities. The emergence of transnational organised crime has seen two distinct responses. On one side is the development of international laws. On the other side is the failure of states to see the multi-dimensional threat of crime to a range of people.

A recent example of the strengthening of the state is the ratification of the United Nations Convention against Transnational Organized Crime. The law itself emerged out of a state need to address its significant weakness in addressing the new global forms of crime, and ensure that transnational crime would not fall between the cracks in the law. States first started to address this with the work towards the International Criminal Court, an on-again off-again project for the international community since the Nuremburg trials in Post World War Two Europe. The debate was invigorated in the early 1990s when Trinidad and Tobago asked for some kind of criminal court to address transnational organised crime, particularly the drug gangs which operated through the Caribbean smuggling cocaine into the USA. As it turned out, the attempts to include organised crime and terrorism into International Criminal Court jurisdiction were quickly dropped. The issue did not disappear but rather manifested as a treaty administered by the UN's Office for Drugs and Crime (which was previously known as the Drug Control Program). The treaty, and its three protocols (on trafficking, smuggling in humans, and smuggling firearms), is perhaps a limited gesture to address problems of international crime, but it has enabled the state to play a much stronger role. Simply stated, the TOC ensures that international crime is a crime that a state can prosecute. As the UNODC summarises,

> States that ratify this instrument [the Convention on Transnational Organized Crime] commit themselves to taking a series of measures against transnational organized crime, including the creation of domestic criminal offences (participation in an organized criminal group, money laundering,

> corruption and obstruction of justice); the adoption of new and sweeping frameworks for extradition, mutual legal assistance and law enforcement cooperation; and the promotion of training and technical assistance for building or upgrading the necessary capacity of national authorities.[6]

While gestures towards stopping international crime are very worthy, little has been done to address either the victims of crime (though there are some rights mentioned in the TOC treaty), or states (or other organisations) that misuse their power in combating transnational crime. From the very beginning—with the formulation of the optional protocols on smuggling and trafficking; "these negotiations had never really been about human rights" (Gallagher 2009, p. 791).

So far the paper has detailed the legal and political context to transnationalism and crime. The paper will now turn to provide the context of migration to crime.

6. Migration

It is common knowledge that wherever there are large flows of people across borders, there is also a flow of undocumented people who are frequently engaged in or subject to criminal activities. As an example, the UNODC Report states, "the world's biggest trading partners are also the world's biggest markets for illicit goods and services" (2010a, p. 1). Determining the flows and numbers of migrants in the South East and East Asian regions is an extremely complex undertaking, and there is some speculation involved. However, as highlighted in recent reports, some of the fundamental principles are that documented and undocumented migrant workers tend to migrate to bordering countries. There are significant flows of people from the Philippines, Indonesia, Vietnam and Burma to Singapore, Thailand and Malaysia. There are also smaller, but still significant flows of people from Laos, Cambodia and Bangladesh into the three more developed countries. In terms of size, the International Organization for Migration (IOM) has given a figure for the region of South East Asia at an estimated 5.6 million in 2005 (Sciortino & Punpuing 2009, p. 139). However, given that some

[6] See UNODC's homepage for the treaty: http://www.unodc.org/unodc/en/treaties/CTOC.

consider that Thailand and Malaysia alone have about 6 million migrant workers between them, this could be a conservative figure. It is necessary to highlight that just because a person enters a country without the proper documentation, which some may call illegal, it may not be appropriate to call these people criminals. Current UN and other International Organizational practice is to consider these people undocumented; to call people in a country without a visa illegal is to label them as the criminal when they may be merely seeking asylum from conflict, searching for work to sustain their family, or attempting to find the basic needs for their livelihood and development.[7]

Two forms of criminal activity are associated with these flows of people across borders. First, the act of smuggling, which is assisting people to illegally cross borders into another country, is widespread among many borders in Asia. People smuggling has been an international security issue since the 1970s when Europe was seeing an increase in people entering the continent undocumented, to undertake work in the expanding industrial economies of Germany, France and England (Cholewinski 1997). The issue was highlighted through cases where smuggled people were sometimes trapped and killed in shipping containers or overcrowded boats, tragic events that are still occurring today. Smuggling has become a dominant crime in Asia because of the proximity of poor countries to developed or developing ones. This juxtaposition is greater in Asia than in the other continents, and thus smuggling in the region is widespread and substantial. With an estimated 3 million undocumented workers in Thailand and five million in Malaysia (International Federation for Human Rights 2008), even if only a small proportion of these were smuggled it does give an idea how large this industry is, region wide. Also, it does imply that there is a close relationship between transnational communities and smuggling networks, to ensure people can travel to and from their country of work. The state response has unfortunately been to increase criminalisation in this area.

A more distressing crime is that of people trafficking, which is the transporting of people through coercion or deception into situations where the person finds themselves in slave-like conditions—whether for unpaid labour,

[7] This position is clearly detailed in the International Convention on the Protection of Migrant Workers and Members of their Families. While it does give the documented more rights, the undocumented status does not seriously impede any fundamental rights of migrant workers.

sexual services, or being trapped on a fishing boat. Trafficking estimates vary greatly because of the clandestine nature of the crime, and also the regional variations of the definition (for instance some countries like Vietnam still do not recognise trafficked males, whereas Thailand and Cambodia consider that anyone regardless of gender can be trafficked). Even determining why people are trafficked in the region is unclear. Reports tend to show that trafficking for sexual slavery is the dominant (with some reports placing the number at between 60-80 per cent of all trafficked victims) (Kneebone 2010, p. 143), yet the majority of anti-trafficking organisations only collect data on sex trafficking, leaving trafficking for labour reliant mainly on guesswork. Where there have been attempts to detail numbers of labour trafficking, it seems that this is a huge industry. For example, in a recent preliminary survey of repatriated Cambodians from Thailand, it was found that perhaps up to 24,000 Cambodians a year were victims of trafficking, nearly all of which were trafficked for labour, a number which dwarfs the number of sex trafficking victims which is somewhere in the low thousands (Olivie 2008). Trafficking for sex work in the region starts from sending countries like Burma, Vietnam, the Philippines and Indonesia, to destination countries in the region such as Japan, Thailand and Malaysia. Hopefully the trafficking sector realises that sex trafficking is only a small portion of the trafficking industry, and that work on labour trafficking will receive some of the research it deserves. Examples of labour trafficking scenarios are factories where people are locked inside and cannot leave, the fishing industry where people are trapped on boats at sea, and in the agriculture and domestic labour sectors.

As already mentioned, transnational communities play a double-edged role in these crimes. While there is an incentive to end these practices and support the security systems to eliminate these crimes, the transnational communities themselves create pull factors which increase a person's willingness to risk being smuggled: they may act as a kind of faulty insurance, or the fact of a community's existence may encourage others to risk migration. Furthermore, in many cases of trafficking for labour, the middlemen or labour recruiters are commonly from the transnational communities. Obviously, transnationalism does not imply innocence, though the overwhelming number of victims is from the transnational communities.

7. Migration and Networks

Manuel Castells' influential work, *The Rise of Network Society* (1996) provides perhaps the strongest and most expansive description of the evolving and unique features of globalisation in contemporary transnational society, through his broad analysis of the rise of the network structure. The network structure itself must be seen as a neutral structure. However, it can be put to multiple uses. The features of the network's social structure itself are partially the reason for the rise in transnational crime. Such features include the lack of a central organising unit, with no disciplinary centre to order the structure. This allows simultaneously for anarchy and participation. Transnational criminal organisations thrive in a network structure because it is much easier to embed and hide an organisational centre in this model—one of the greatest difficulties in policing international crime is finding a central criminal to sanction.

An example of this is the tragic case of the 54 Burmese migrant workers who suffocated as they were smuggled into Thailand in 2008 (Agence France-Press 2008). Even though there were 54 people who were killed, there were no serious prosecutions for this case, showing that either the police could not locate a hidden central organising person, or that there was no central person responsible for this crime, going against the commonly perceived image of a single responsible criminal put forward in media discussions of cases like this. The smugglers, based in Burma, escaped any scrutiny because they were on the other side of the national border, outside the jurisdiction of the crime. Those who got the people onto the truck only received light sentences for the crime of harbouring. The truck owner claimed he did not know the crime was happening, and there are no reports of what happened to the truck owner. Perhaps the severest punishment was given to the 66 survivors. Some of the women were classified as trafficking victims and repatriated. The males were arrested as illegal immigrants, detained and ultimately deported. As this paper has argued, this case shows that it is generally the transnationals who suffer the impact of the crime and the law—they were either arrested or killed. Partially this is the result of a changing nature in society towards network structures that enable criminal organisations to escape punishment. Unfortunately, the response is in some cases, may mean more punishment for the victims.

A second feature of the network structure found in migration is the ability for connections to move from the local to the global. Information travels further and faster, for example—information about work, smuggling routes, or life outside of the village. While these connections are multiple and weak, a range of things are connected now as they never were before, whether in products, ideas, media, values, or technology. This is mostly through what Malcolm Gladwell calls "weak ties"; for example, as he points out "you can have a thousand 'friends' on Facebook, as you could never have in real life" (2010). The phenomena of weak ties means the communities built though migration networks are often fragile and ever changing. The reality of their multiplicity can be seen in the transnational's trans-cultural life, as cultural products, whether through media, food, objects, communication, and easier trans-border travel. Creating a sense of home in foreign countries is far easier, yet this does not necessarily mean a protected and respected community. For example, with the transnational cultures comes transnational crime. Much transnational crime relies on a network of disparate groups, the transporters, harbourers, recruiters and so on, who often do not know each other. They are weakly brought together in these syndicates to undertake criminal enterprises. Improvements in communication have made it easier to organise exercises like this. More disturbing examples have been the spread of honour killing from places like Pakistan and Iraq to Western Europe and North America. Other results have been the increasing prevalence of the commercial sex industry in places where there are large numbers of migrant workers. So, for example, much of the Burmese sex trafficking into Thailand is mainly to cater for the Burmese migrant workers. Further, within the transnational community are organised crimes around loan sharking, gambling, or protection rackets. Where many transnationals are in vulnerable positions as undocumented migrants, they are most prone to exploitation. This may be by the police, for example the harrowing report "Above the Law," which documents police abuses of Burmese migrant workers in Mae Sot (Human Rights Documentation Unit 2002), and of the US Committee's report on the Malaysian immigration police's exploitation and trafficking of Burmese nationals in Malaysia (Committee on Foreign Relations 2009). These people may also be exploited by their own community members—loan sharks, even people who work for local employees or the police, informing on them.

Though the connections are weak, networks are persistent structures that can withstand significant damage. With no central core, any part of the network destroyed can be easily replaced. And this is seen in international crime as well, where the arrest of one part of the network has negligible impacts on the other parts. So for instance, the continuous arrest of people carrying drugs through airports has little impact on the amount of drugs transported because these people who act as couriers can always be replaced. On a more damaging level was the "War on Drugs" in 2003 in Thailand in which the arrest of around 2,600 minor and middle level drug dealers did result in a hiatus to the amount of drugs circulated in Thailand, albeit only momentarily, as drugs have quickly become available again. Hence responding to this crime through policing and arrests only will have little impact. Rather, the response needs to be much more multi-dimensional. The source of the problem needs to be addressed (for example the ability of countries like Burma to produce enormous amounts of methamphetamines). Further, the market for the problem needs to be reduced, whether this is reducing drug use through public health or regularising migrant labour through formalised registration.

8. Conclusion: Transnational Victims

International crime is an emerging threat to transnational communities, both as victims of crime and subject to the power of criminal law. Transnational crimes shadow the routes, needs, and economies of migrants. As a response states are increasing their power to combat this problem, but such power is not necessarily to protect the rights of the transnational. Instead states have the ability to sanction anyone who may be associated with these crimes with the media, prompting popular responses that tend to attack the foreigner. The strengths of the networks remind us that transnationalism is going to be a permanent feature of today's society, and that attempts by groups to expel non-citizens, whether by expelling Burmese migrants from Chaing Mai, displacing Christians in Indonesia, or Vietnamese communities in Cambodia, are reactions against an inevitable fact towards heterogeneous societies. In face of the almost indestructible nature of international criminal networks are the transnationals who can become the targets of society's blame. Hence we see in a recent drug raid in Bangkok a situation where, according to the reporter Maximilian Wechsler, "While questioning one African, a policeman repeatedly told him in a gentle voice 'why don't you go back to your homeland?'" (2011, p. 8). Here, in this unequal relationship between the state and the transnational under the securitisation of international crime, a belief stands that crime comes with the foreigner.

With criminal networks becoming harder and harder to dissolve, and states grasping (often legitimately) for more power to control this problem, the brunt of state power is directed at the nearest foreign substitute—the non-citizen. Yet what is the aim? It is an attempt to dissolve the crime by expelling the foreign person from the country. The direct costs are apparent and dangerous. Not only is the violation of rights a degrading precedent that should be avoided, but the only effect is to further enflame discrimination and mistrust. Transnational networks cannot be destroyed through expelling the transnational migrant, as they perhaps were in pre network society countries such as Burma (which expelled Indians). Networks just do not disappear. People who are expelled frequently return because they are needed for jobs. The resolution is for a more holistic and cross sectoral response, working with both source and destinations of crime, attacking the money (as profit is the main reason for crime) and addressing inequality which leads to risky migration. When a policeman whispers into a non-citizen's ear, "Why don't you go home?," it voices the state's attempt to eradicate crime by sanctioning the only person available to blame, as if the mere expulsion of the non-citizen will end the reason for crime. In another example, we see Thai University students responding to the rape and murder of a fellow student—though undoubtedly sincere in their convictions and outraged at the violation—by calling for a vigilante style mass eviction of construction workers. For the students this is perhaps their only means to respond to the crime—again through expulsion. For in the rise of transnational crime and its elicited response, the double-edged victims are the transnationals themselves who, by being outside their state protection (or being citizens of states who never offered protection in the first place) are made to be the vulnerable scapegoats of these feared transnational crimes, and whose images are regularly featured in our media today.

References

Agence France-Press (2008). "54 Myanmar migrants die in seafood container: Thai police." 9 April. Accessed on 12 August 2012 from http://afp.google.com/article/ALeqM5is334VG__3Wkx5Ztz9SnouZvEg5A.

BBC News Asia Pacific (2010). "British paedophile suspect arrested in Thailand." 23 December. Accessed on 27 August 2012 from http://www.bbc.co.uk/news/world-asia-pacific-12065348.

Cassese, A. (2005). *International Law*. Oxford: Oxford University Publisher.

Castells, M. (1998). *End of Millennium, Volume 3: The Information Age: Economy, Society and Culture*. London: Blackwell.

_________ (1996). *The Rise of the Network Society, Volume 1: The Information Age: Economy, Society and Culture*. Cambridge, MA; Oxford, UK: Blackwell.

Cholewinski, R. (1997). *Migrant Workers in International Human Rights Law: Their Protection in Countries of Employment*. Oxford: Clarendon.

Committee on Foreign Relations (2009). "Trafficking and Extortion of Burmese Migrants in Malaysia and Southern Thailand: A Report to the Committee on Foreign Relations." United States Senate. 3 April.

Fah, H. K. (2009). "Crackdown Continues in Chiangmai." *Shan Herald Agency*. 17 February.

Fry, E. (2009). "Vigilantes Take to the Streets of Chiang Mai." *The Bangkok Post*. 22 February.

Gallagher, A. (2009). "Human Rights and Human Trafficking: Quagmire or Firm Ground? A Response to James Hathaway." *Virginia Journal Of International Law* 49, 4, 789-848.

Gladwell, M. (2010). "Small Change: Why the Revolution will not be Tweeted." *New Yorker*. 4 October.

Global Alliance Against Traffic in Women (GATTW) (2007). *Collateral Damage: The Impact of Anti-Trafficking Measures on Human Rights Around the World*. Bangkok: GAATW.

Human Rights Documentation Unit, NCGUB (2002). "Above the Law: Systemic Human Rights Violations by Thai Authorities Against Burmese Migrant Workers in Mae Sot, Thailand." Bangkok. N.P.

International Federation for Human Rights (FIDH) (2008). *Undocumented migrants and refugees in Malaysia: Raids, Detention and Discrimination*. March 2008 - N°489/2

Kneebone, S. (2010). "The Refugee-Trafficking Nexus: Making Good (The) Connections." *Refugee Survey* 29, 1, 137-160.

Martínez, R. Jr. and Lee, M. T. (2000). "On Immigration and Crime." *Criminal Justice 2000: The Nature of Crime, Vol. 1*. Washington, DC: U.S. Department of Justice, Office of

Justice Programs. July. 485-524.

Millar, K. (2010). "Global Organized Crime: A World Affairs Blog." 15 July. Accessed on 12 August 2012 from http://globalorganizedcrime.foreignpolicyblogs.com/tag/millar.

Mueller, G. (2001). "Transnational Crime: Definitions and Concepts." in D. Vlassis and P. Williams, eds. *Combating Transnational Crime Concepts, Activities and Responses*. London: Routledge.

Ohmae, K. (1996). *End of the Nation State: The Rise of Regional Economies*. New York: Simon and Schuster.

Olivie, A. (2008). *Identifying Cambodian Victims of Human Trafficking Among Deportees from Thailand*. December, Bangkok: UNIAP.

Sciortino, R. and Punpuing, S. (2009). *International Migration in Thailand*. Bangkok: International Organization for Migration.

Shan Women's Action Network (SWAN) (2002). *License to Rape*. Chiang Mai: SWAN.

United Nations Office on Drugs and Crime (UNODC) (2010a). *The Globalization of Crime: A Transnational Organized Crime Threat Assessment*. Vienna: UNODC.

_________ (2010b). "Issue Paper: Short Introduction to the Migrant Smuggling." Vienna: UNODC.

Wechsler, M. (2010). "Busted or Bullied?" *Bangkok Post, Spectrum*. 9 January. pp. 8-10.

Weng, L. (2009). "Student's Murder Leads to Migrant Roundup." *The Irrawaddy*. 12 February.

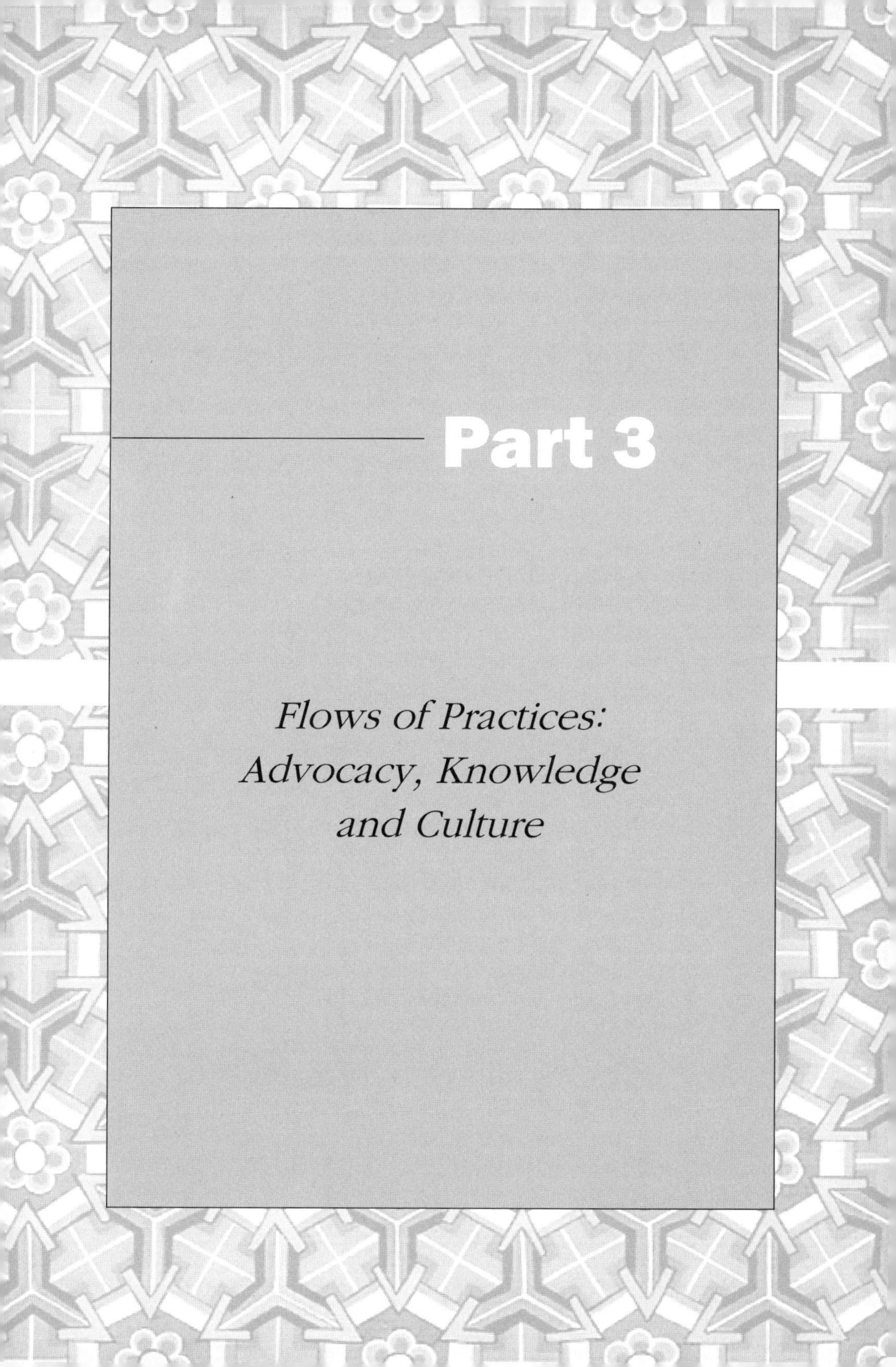

Part 3

Flows of Practices: Advocacy, Knowledge and Culture

Transcending Traditional Security in Southeast Asia:
The Relevance of Peoples' Agendas

Chantana Banpasirichote

1. Introduction

The rising awareness in transnational security issues implies that national borders, which for a long time were regulated under the state security command, are being significantly transcended by a range of ideas, people, products and activities (Mittleman 2011). The Association of South East Asian Nations (ASEAN) has recognised these emerging transnational issues in official meetings as: the environment, transboundary haze, transnational crime, drugs and narcotics, immigration and legal matters (ASEAN Secretariat 1999). Based on the assumption that the predominant national security thinking plays an influential role in the present state of transnationalism, particularly in Southeast Asia, this paper deals with transnationalism from the security issue angle. It argues that Southeast Asia can be better off by shifting out of a traditional security framework and governance structure, and preparing for a broader coverage of people's security concerns. Using the reflections from civil society organisation networks, this paper contends that the concept of people's security lays an important foundation for regional security and stability in the long run. It is observed that several ad hoc and horizontal networks of multi-stakeholders have been active outside the official processes and challenge the prominent state-centric security. The policy implications of transforming from traditional security responses to more human security will eventually lead to a basic redefinition of common threats and interests, and in the long run provide a regional public space for greater regional democratic governance.

2. Perceptions of Security Threats and Transnational Implications

The dominant transnational security agenda after 9/11 has undoubtedly been anti-terrorism. However, as much as it has been internationally propagated, the anti-terrorism agenda has not been internalised equally in the region (National Defense University 2002). Countries within the ASEAN have not perceived terrorism to the same degree; Indochina in particular does not seem to be much influenced by the impact of terrorism (Gerstl 2010). As time passes, it appears that terrorist acts are nurtured more by homegrown problems. What seem equally important but often forgotten are other aspects of transnational crimes such as drugs, smuggling, small arms transfer and money laundering. Ironically, security laws in the region are known to be more targeted at government opposition activities than what may be classified as terrorism.

Recent literature on security in the region often ignores the business of open wars, acknowledging that violence is no longer driven by battle deaths. One major analysis of the situation through the Regional Security Outlook 2009-2010 made the Council for Security Cooperation in the Asia Pacific (CSCAP) features major security problems such as nuclear disarmament, internal conflicts, and maritime security; it nevertheless recognises issues on refugee and internally displaced people, and captures new emerging security concerns such as natural disasters and human trafficking. While the perception of security as transnational and multi-dimensional has been more pronounced, the move toward policy options or a new mode of regional governance is still lagging. CSCAP's security outlook is concerned with the fact that the increasing knowledge on emerging new security issues has not sufficiently influenced states' security policy. CSCAP impact on regional policy, argues Hassan & Cossa (2009), is limited:

> [CSCAP] has also influenced policy formulation in areas such as preventive diplomacy. However, CSCAP has yet to succeed in making itself more centrally relevant to the work of ARF in particular. Proposals contained in several of its memoranda have not been reflected in ARF policy or strategy (pp. 44-45).

It is also surprising to find reports from the Asian Regional Forum (ARF) which should represent official security thinking, also covering issues other than state security such as natural disasters, small arms trade, and narcotics. In their discussion on anti-terrorism, the ARF regional mechanism in their security policy referred to non-military approaches to security such as interfaith dialogues or civilisation dialogues among religious groups, which in a way acknowledges the complexity of responses to terrorism.

While it is assuring also to learn that the Asia Pacific was assessed by some scholars as an area of "relative peace" from the end of 1970s (Kivimäki 2010), this only indicates a decline of violence from war, crimes and armed violence. There are reasons to believe that the region has not achieved positive peace when structural violence—that is violence that arises from poverty, discrimination, and other structures in society, which impact people's security—is still widely prevalent. Structural violence comes out of political structures; as Kivimäki (p. 524) asserts that the region might be vulnerable to authoritarian regimes. In addition, there are also blind spots in the region such as the situation in Myanmar and the Philippines (and maybe the Korean Peninsula and southern Thailand) where state repression and battles with insurgents have not been overcome. The terms "comprehensive," "non-traditional," "extended," "peoples" and "human security" have been used with increasing frequency in security studies of the region. Scholars see the coming trend of security transformation as inevitable and thus responses within a realist paradigm need a rethinking (Dupont 2001, p. 7). Needless to say the new threats to the people in the region go beyond borders and seem to surpass the capability of traditional security actors like the military. The crises of financial collapse, climate changes, tsunami, pandemic diseases, influx of immigrant workers, as well as environmental risks are self-evident of the extent and ramification of emerging new threats. This broad spectrum of threats, from economic to health to environmental, are resulting from untamed globalisation, such as rapid population increase, migration, urbanisation, resource competition and so on; in sum, it is simply the consequence of the nature of our modern development.

While the increasing transnational elements of security threats should be appreciated by the regional community, the responses so far have not been addressed at the regional level, as one might expect. There are certain challenges. First, certain norms—for instance, the respect for human rights—has become increasingly universal but is yet to take on a regional role. It can be reiterated here that regional initiatives to cope with transnational human rights issues constantly face a non-interference principle particularly when the state under question does not respect human rights. Further, even though ASEAN will become unified under a treaty by 2015, concrete mechanisms (such as the human rights commission) have not been given full power to exercise human rights protection. Second, East Asia has a long tradition of state-centric regimes, democratic and non-democratic alike. The security actors have always been primarily the state and political elites and public participation is accommodated only to a minimal extent. Third, in ASEAN in particular, different country priorities can still be a limiting factor for common regional responses. There are discrepancies for instance in the respect for human rights, environmental standards, or social security for migrant workers (Gerstl 2010). This is mostly due to the lack of a real concern for security of the people by the states. These self-contradictions in the course toward new transnational security norms and mechanisms reflect the lag between regional norms and domestic politics. The regional norms and standards, which are supposed to guide national practices in responding to new securities, unfortunately have limited themselves by respecting the non-interference tradition (in the case of ASEAN); additionally, national polity in most member countries has little awareness of transnational norms. The political developments in Myanmar indicate that constructive engagement works to some extent, with Myanmar preparing for ASEAN Chair, though the relationship between the military government and the opposition is equally a determinant factor.

Regional cooperation does have some success and positive momentum. The anti-human trafficking measures, for instance in mainland Southeast Asia, cannot be overlooked. The Memorandum of Understanding (MoU) among countries in the Mekong Sub-region, including Thailand, Myanmar, Lao PDR and Cambodia to handle trafficking cases exclusively has been established in order to protect the rights and security of children and women. Regional coordination on the prevention of avian flu epidemic, despite stumbles in information sharing at the beginning, has eventually contributed to the control of the incident. The most notable has been the regional cooperation over the mitigation of the impact of the 2004 Tsunami. Threats from natural disasters bring out the spirit of humanity of the region. The new norms work well for these soft issues.

3. Transnational Advocacy: The Role of Civil Society Networks

An important ingredient in regional cooperation on transnational social issues is the role of civil society organisations as advocates in transnational social networking. A study of the ASEAN norm of socialisation, for example, identifies the role of non-governmental organisations as instrumental in changing security norms (Cheeppensook 2012, p. 185). This part of the paper will therefore examine civil society organisations working on human security related issues to show how a platform for an alternative security agenda is opening up within civil society. Due to the fact that traditional security actors are confined within the state and political elites, Civil Society Organisations (CSO) working directly on hard security issues like anti-terrorism, provide a useful counter narrative in the security discourse. Most security studies and policy recommendations are carried out by track two (academic) institutions such as the ASEAN Institute of Strategic and International Studies (ASEAN ISIS) and CSCAP. Interestingly enough, the connection between track one (official) and track two does not guarantee policy influence and change. The relationship between the two tracks is more of a complementary relationship than a critical or analytical assessment of security policy. The shift of security policy towards protecting people, and being more "human oriented," has led to a higher number of regional CSOs working on issues such as migration, migrant workers, human trafficking, climate change, human rights protection, global justice, human development, non-violence, and post-conflict peace building. Most of them are policy advocacy and development practice groups. This makes track three (people and civil society organisations) more vibrant, grounded, and provocative than track two in their agenda setting (Chavez 2006, p. 17; Cheeppensook 2012, p. 192). This does not indicate that track two is now defunct but, rather that tract three and the trend of multi-track governance is where the innovation is originating.

Local and national civil society organisations in the past did not usually pay sufficient attention to the regional movements. It is only in the past two decades that regional, national and local NGOs and CSOs have formed alliances across a variety of issue-based sectors. The phenomenon of people's organisations around the world gathering initially in the anti-globalisation movement then more recently in the World Social Forum event in 2001 in Brazil, with the slogan

"Another World is Possible," has changed the strategy and the mentality of many people's movements worldwide. In the age of globalisation, it is almost imperative for CSOs to link with international networks because transnational actors like multinational corporations or threats from international trade regimes, demand transnational responses. Transnational activism has become an instrument for solidarity, empowerment, policy framing and changes within the civil society sector.

There are a number of regional and international NGOs working on transnational issues, including human security, at the ASEAN level; their collective voices are represented by network organisations, among others, the Solidarity of Asian People Advocacy (SAPA),[1] ASEAN's Civil Society Conference (ACSC)[2] and the ASEAN Peoples' Forum (APF).[3] These networks link with a larger international circle organised through the website People's Agenda for Alternative Regionalisms (www.alternative-regionalisms.org). The reality is that the people around the world are seeking to shape regional integration that affects their lives. These networks have become vocal and their statements, to a large extent, are the only alternative sources apart from official and track two analyses. Indeed, within the region, people have been working cross-nationally and cross-culturally for the past two decades.

The connection among the people in the region is mobilised from the regional level down to the national and the grassroots. It is almost imperative that the work of the national level reflects the realities of the people (Chavez 2006, p. 17). Transnational networks of civil society organisations work to make

---

1 SAPA is a consultation forum aiming to seek cooperation between various people's organisations in the ASEAN region, which play an important role in conducting direct negotiations with the government of ASEAN member countries. Members of SAPA mostly consist of working groups on democracy, human rights and human security, sustainable development and the environment, trade and finance in the globalisation era, and labour (ASEAN Peoples' Forum 2009, p. 6).

2 The ASEAN Civil Society Conference (ACSC) is an alternative conference instigated by the Malaysian government and was held for the first time in 2005 in parallel with the ASEAN Summit. It involves groups such as FTA Watch, Thai Labour Solidarity Committee, Farmer's Federation Association for Development Thailand, and the People's Empowerment Foundation.

3 The ASEAN Peoples' Forum is an alternative people's forum instigated by the Malaysian government and was held for the first time in 2005 in parallel with the ASEAN Summit. It is collaboration between the national and regional civil society sector and NGOs. The forum is meant for people to share their thoughts and analyse the situation faced by the people themselves, and collectively seek solutions at the regional level (*ASEAN Peoples' Forum 2009*, pp. 6-7).

people visible in the regional area. People's visibility might not immediately lead to policy change, but it empowers those who are usually excluded, which is particularly important for disadvantaged and ethnic minorities groups (such as women or indigenous peoples). Because peoples' empowerment eventually crosses into the policy agenda, the peoples' agendas should play a role in socialising new norms. The effort of CSO alliances and networks, however, is not without problems. Civil society organisations experience a different level of social activism in their joint actions. In some new democratic countries, such as in those new emerging democracies in the Mekong sub-region, civil society organisations are still controlled by the state. Furthermore, the sustainability of regional organisations is still precarious due to institutional dilemmas such as too much dependence on external funding and too little support from within the region.

4. Peoples' Security Agendas

The effort of the peoples' networks in responding to regional security policy deserves a consideration. The most notable collective action of CSOs responding to the debate on people's meaningful participation in the regional mechanism is the ASEAN Peoples' Forum (APF). The APF launched two reports titled *Advancing a Peoples' ASEAN* (2009) and the *Position of Solidarity of Asian People Advocacy (SAPA) on the ASEAN Charter* (2008), both of which were responses to the ASEAN NGO Summit (2009) which took place in Thailand after the ratification of the ASEAN Charter. Other organisations following regional issues have also produced statements from meetings and seminars such as Focus on the Global South (Bangkok),[4] Initiatives for International Dialogue

[4] Focus on the Global South is a non-governmental organisation with twenty staffs working in Thailand, the Philippines and India. It was established in Bangkok in 1995, and their works combine policy research, advocacy, activism and grassroots capacity building in order to generate critical analysis and encourage debates on national and international policies related to corporate-led globalisation, neo-liberalism and militarisation (Accessed on 7 September 2012 from http://www.focusweb.org/content/who-we-are).

(IID) (Davao City),[5] and Forum-Asia (Bangkok).[6] The concerns reflected in reports from these organisations are twofold: seeking a critical view of security framework, and providing input to the policy agenda.

The statements of civil society organisations in the parallel meeting of the 15th ASEAN Summit in 2009 directly addressed the group as a regional organisation.[7] The advocacy emerging from the ASEAN's People Forum shows that ASEAN has become a subject of concern for civil society. Pressing local issues is in fact common across the region. It is interesting that those progressive citizens who once advocated for less-government in the democratic polity are now calling on member states' governments to unite their act against the impact of the global market, and to follow a universal standard regarding the protection of the people. Based on the content of civil society deliberation, two important points will be discussed: security and policy agendas.

4.1 Security

The ASEAN's People Forum statement is quite comprehensive since it covers the concerns of all four pillars of the ASEAN community, *viz* economic, socio-cultural, political-security, and environment. To focus on their discussion particularly on security, members of civil society networks pay attention to the ASEAN Political and Security Community (APSC) by stressing that:

> APSC needs to further elaborate on its support of a comprehensive approach to security, especially concerning gender mainstreaming—encouraging women's participation on all levels, especially as agents and decision makers in conflict resolution, and protecting women's security in their homes,

---

[5] Initiatives for International Dialogue is an advocacy and solidarity organization promoting south-south solidarity and people-to-people internationalism. Thematic priorities are conflict prevention and peacebuilding, democratisation and right to self-determination. Focus areas include Mindanao, Burma, Timor-Leste, South Thailand, Aceh and West Papua (Chandra 2009).

[6] Forum-Asia is a membership-based regional human rights organisation committed to the promotion and protection of all human rights including the right to development. It was founded in 1991 in Manila and its regional Secretariat has been located in Bangkok since 1994. At present, it has 46 member organisations across Asia (Asian Forum for Human Rights and Development 2010).

[7] Statements since 2009 can be found on the ASEAN Civil Society Conference website at: http://www.aseancivilsociety.net (accessed 21 March 2012).

communities, nationally, and regionally (2009, p. 9).

The state's changing position on comprehensive security in the region is recognised in these statements. However, further analysis of security issues discussed in the people's sector can be interpreted as stemming from economic social and political vulnerabilities as well. A preliminary survey of the literature from CSOs, as well as the statements from the ASEAN People's Forum, provide some highlights to the general background of comprehensive security as shown in Table 1. Traditional issues are considered what affecting directly state authorities, while emerging issues are more recent phenomena. There are issues of human security crossing between the two such as drug trafficking. Emerging issues indicate some tension or disagreement between the state's and civil society's perceptions and priorities.

There is no doubt that most of traditional security issues have been and still are the primary concerns of the states in the region. Some of the emerging issues are further discussed here to highlight how they transcend state securitisation measures.

Table 1 Comprehensive Security Agendas from CSOs

Traditional security issues	Emerging security issues
• Nuclear arms threat • State securitization (on anti-terrorism) • Small arms proliferation • Intra-state, and Intra-region conflicts • Militarisation • International crime • Narcotic drugs Trafficking	• Economic risks and vulnerabilities from free trade • Environmental and Social risks from large scale development • Migration and migrant workers • Human trafficking • Climate change and natural disasters • Stateless people and citizenship • Refugee and internal displaced people • Natural resource and energy crisis • Food security • Essential drug accessibility • Citizen and activists disappearance in conflicts and state suppression • Narcotic drugs trafficking

Sources: ASEAN Peoples' Forum 2009; Nonviolence International Southeast Asia 2009; Bangkok Declaration 2009.

First, traditional security evolved around direct or physical violence against individuals. It is an irony that this is far more commonly fear from state repression rather than terrorism. The measures of state securitisation have led to violations of human rights, including the use of special laws such as state emergency decrees, martial law, or Internal Security Acts. CSOs have not paid as much attention to international crimes as they have done to small arms proliferation and incidence of disappearances under state securitisation. These problems are transnational as security issues around protracted internal conflicts in individual ASEAN member countries and have effects on the regional political stability.

Second, the emerging security issues are the consequence of economic uncertainty, most notably under the influence of free trade agreements. Security in this sense signifies vulnerability and risks to peoples' livelihood. The people have witnessed the impact of financial crisis, natural catastrophe, and even the impact of large-scale projects and fierce economic competition in the free market economy. Trade-offs and trade wars have resulted in widening social and economic gaps, as well as social dislocations. To a large extent, the vulnerability and risks of the majority are closely attached to the nature of social and economic development in the region.

Third, CSOs have paid special attention to specific vulnerable groups that are not usually visible and received attention from the state. They are minority groups, the stateless, refugees, indigenous people, and internally displace people who are victims of internal conflicts and discrimination. The wellbeing and security of marginalised people does tell a lot about the stability of the regional community. Somehow an achievement of human security is indicated by the respect of minorities.

In summary, the peoples' call shows that that transnational security is human related, while traditional security is confined by that of the state. Perhaps it is not so surprising that in this part of the world state security is seen by the people as in conflict with people's security. This is particularly the case for minority and stateless groups. Paradoxes are found in realisation that most human insecurity is development driven, meaning the people are vulnerable because of the free market economy; and also that violence is perceived to be driven by state securitisation policy for the sake of national security.

4.2 Policy agendas

The overarching policy agenda used as reference in the People's Forum and most of CSOs' documents is "human rights protection and regional solidarity for alternative regionalism." Human rights violations lead to violence, both physical and structural, and create conditions of insecurity. The establishment of a regional human rights mechanism is hopeful. ASEAN member states have expressed a commitment to the ASEAN Inter-government Commission on Human Rights (AICHR), and also to the independent body for ASEAN Commission of the Protection and Promotion of the Rights of Women and Children (ACWC). Human rights protection should be stressed particularly in internal conflict when state securitisation is increasing. Strengthening dispute mechanisms in the region is an imperative to maintain regional stability and to minimise the impacts of armed violence. In particular, intra-state conflicts causing influx of refugee and internal displaced people call for a regional norms and measures to protect these vulnerable groups.

Alternative regionalism is advocated in order to enhance mutual cooperation. The current regional integration has not provided confidence to the people so that they can cope with new emerging transnational threats. The region is still at risk of intra-regional conflict and tension from economic competition in the free market environment (Bamford 2010). Alternative regionalism implies regional solidarity of sharing and caring, bottom up integration, people's participation, cultural diversity, and driven by sustainable development (Chandra 2009).

5. Transcending Traditional Security: Making Sense of Civil Society's Agenda

It is undeniable now that transnational security is primarily human security related. The existing transnational and regional mechanisms, despite the increasing recognition of changing security trends, are still state-centric. Adhering to the tradition of non-interference and not responding effectively to transnational problems will lead to human insecurity. Knowledge building on new securities and policy agendas provided by track two, such as the think tanks of CSCAP and ISIS, are not making sufficient progress in the regional policy agendas.

Besides making the people visible, transnational advocacy mobilised by alliances of international and national CSOs, organised in parallel to track one and two endeavours, has called for greater regional responsibility of the expanding phenomenon of human insecurity in the region. Despite the bottleneck of state-centric practices in inter-government organisations, the CSOs find the mechanisms of regional integration are crucial for transnational human security. However, a different kind of regional integration is still sought for. At this point, a simple yet fundamental question should be raised as to what sort of conditions lead to a favorable environment for the realisation of human security in the region? I believe the very rich and comprehensive agenda setting by civil society networks inform the national and regional policy community to deal with in the new context of transnationalism.

5.1 Regional common interest: soft cooperation for regional social protection

While people are still skeptical about the role of new regional mechanisms such as AIHRC, many are committed to shaping the direction of regional security frameworks to be more people-oriented. In order to make a more favorable environment for the protection of human security, the region needs to transcend the dichotomy of state versus human security. Naturally, human security which concerns individual safety and human development can help to expand mutual and common interests of the region. The dynamics in the region lead to progress more on matters of soft cooperation found in social protection issues such as migrant workers, health, and natural disasters. The increasing space for soft cooperation on human security issues in the medium and long term might gradually reduce the dominance of traditional and state centric security. Recent experience finds that the synergy between non-state and state actors, for example on the protection of migrant workers, is possible and yields results. Issues of human security have made a possible platform for soft cooperation on issues such as tsunamis, human trafficking, and SARs. Above all, in the area of human security, non-state actors, from both the private sector and CSOs, are mostly relevant and have played a pivotal role in crisis management. Strategically, an expansion of soft cooperation should lead to more mutual confidence among nation states. Soft cooperation can be expanded toward the protection of rights to development and safe environment, such as common labour standards, compatible environmental safety and impact assessments and health protection. Those imperative issues help divert tension from economic competition and territory disputes among countries in the region. In summary, social protection can lead to genuine regional integration and prevention of transnational security threats.

The dichotomy of state versus people security can be closed by redefining new national interests according to common regional security concerns. Individual countries need to be exposed to real assessments of emerging threats so that they will realise the interconnection of security issues among individual countries. Awareness on new security concerns may have been created, but these issues are not sufficiently raised at the policy level.

5.2 The validity of peoples' networking for new alternatives

Alternative regionalism as propagated by peoples' networks cannot be achieved without a democratic space established in the region. In ASEAN, the state-to-state relationship among member countries is relatively equal. However, this democratic space does not necessarily extend to its people. One cannot imagine how a regional democratic space can be created without growing democratic spirit in individual countries. Democracy is therefore indispensable and integral to security, and the assumption that democratic activities causing political instability is a myth (Acharya 2010). Considering the importance of non-state actors in policy initiatives, their transnational advocacy is surpassing the state in forming alliances and developing clearer agendas for human security. In this regard, access to information on important decisions made in the region is a crucial stepping stone. CSO-engagement in the decision-making process at the regional level is a determining factor of meaningful political space for policy change.

Regardless of the seemingly promising new ASEAN Charter, multilateral cooperation might not be effectively exercised in track one diplomacy due to different perceptions of threats, lack of confidence on military matters, and internal competition over resources and economic opportunities (Jones & Smith 2007; Tepchatri 2009; Webber 2010). Likewise, the tradition of non-interference has proved that multilateralism, despite being inevitable, become only rhetorical.

On the contrary, people to people networks are promising even on hard issues like landmines, nuclear disarmament, and small arms proliferation. Alliances of CSOs function as connectors for local and regional agenda to flow. However, domestic politics does have an impact on the work of CSOs, especially with security laws (Muntabhorn, 2009; Southeast Asian Press Alliance (SEAPA) and Forum Asia 2011). The limit of peoples' networking is yet to be tested.

6. Conclusion

As ASEAN is approaching a single market economic community in 2015, a policy platform to increase the capacity of people to cope with the market forces and state securitisation is urgently needed. As far as security issues are concerned, civil society has discovered critical emerging issues that are not addressed by the old state security paradigm. CSOs' regional advocacy highlighting the idea of inclusive development in which marginalised people are respected in a just and sustainable development path, is fundamental to regional stability in the long run. The political space for the people in the region is being claimed by social activism. If the people are to march together with their fellow state authorities over the transnational hurdles to secure a reasonable decent life, a transnational democratic space in the region has to be mutually recognised and secured in the first place.

References

Acharya, A. (2010). "Democracy or Death? Will Democratisation bring greater regional instability to East Asia?" *The Pacific Review* 23(3), 335-358.

ASEAN Civil Society Conference (website). Accessed on 21 March 2012 from http://www.aseancivilsociety.net.

ASEAN Peoples' Forum (2009). "Advancing a Peoples' ASEAN." Proceedings of the ASEAN People's Forum–Fourth ASEAN Civil society Conference (ACSC). 20-22 February. Chulalongkorn University, Thailand. Bangkok: Working Group on ASEAN People's Forum.

_________ (2008). "Position of solidarity for Asian People's Advocacies (SAPA) working

Group on ASEAN and of the Philippines working Group on ASEAN." Hearing on the Ratification of the ASEAN Charter, Senate Committee on Foreign Relations. 28 August.

ASEAN Secretariat (1999). "Transnational Issues." Accessed on 18 August 2012 from http://www.aseansec.org/9930.htm.

Asian Forum for Human Rights and Development (2010). "SAPA Task Force on 3rd Regional Consultation Meeting on ASEAN and Human Rights." Press release: Asian Forum for Human Rights and Development. 20 September.

Bamford, C. C. (2010). "ASEAN in a changing world: The enemy is within." presentation at the 6th ASEAN People's Forum, Hanoi. Focus on the Global South - September 2010.

Bangkok Declaration (2009). "People's Call for Justice and Peace." ASEAN NGO SUMMIT. Islamic Center, Bangkok, Thailand. 16 October. Accessed on 7 September 2012 from http://www.thaingo.org/writer/view.php?id=1416.

Chandra, Alexander C. (2009). "Civil Society in Search of an Alternative Regionalism in ASEAN." International Institute of Sustainable Development. Accessed 20 on January 2011 from http://www.iisd.org/publications/pub.aspx?id=1136.

Chavez, J. J. (2006). "The Search for Alternative Regionalism in Southeast Asia." *Women in Action* 1, 7-18.

Cheeppensook, K. (2012). "Shaping Human Security in ASEAN: Transnational NGOs' Contributions." In C. Banpasirichote, P. Doneys, M. Hayes and C. Sengupta, eds. *Mainstreaming Human Security: Asian Perspectives*. pp. 185-201. Bangkok: Chula Global Network and International Development Studies Program, Chulalongkorn University.

Center for Non-Traditional Security Studies (2010). *Center for Non-Traditional Security Studies Year in Review 2010*. Singapore: S. Rajaratnam School of International Studies, Nanyang Technological University.

Focus on the Global South (website). Accessed on 18 August 2012 from www.focusweb.org.

Gerstl, A. (2010). "The Depoliticisation and 'ASEANisation' of Counter-Terrorism Policies in South-East Asia: A Weak Trigger for a fragmented Version of Human Security." *Austrian Journal of South-East Asian Studies*, 3(1): 48-75.

Hassan, Jawhar and Ralph Cossa (2009). "CSCAP and Track Two: How Relevant to Regional Security?" In B. Jobs, ed. *Regional Security Outlook 2009-2010: Security through Cooperation*. Council for Security Cooperation in the Asia Pacific (CSCAP).

Jones, D. M. and Smith, M. L. R. (2007). "Making process, not progress: ASEAN and the evolving East Asian Regional Order." *International Security*, 32, 1, 148-184.

Kivimäki, T. (2010). "East Asian Relative Peace-Does it Exist? What is it?" *The Pacific Review*, 23, 4, 503-526.

Mittelman, J. H. (2011). *Contesting Global Order: Development, Global Governance, and Globalization*. London and New York: Routledge.

Muntarbhorn, V. (2010). "National Security Laws: Key implications for Thailand." Bangkok Post Online. Accessed on 10 November 2010 from http://www.bangkokpost.com/opinion/opinion/202963/national-security-laws-key-implications-for-thailand.

National Defense University (2002). "Transnational security threats in the Asia-Pacific Region: 2002 Pacific Symposium Highlights." Accessed on 15 October 2010 from http://www.ndu.edu/inss/symposia/pacific2002/2002PACSUMMARY.html.

Non-violence International Southeast Asia. (2009). "Arming of Civilians and Firearms Proliferation Exacerbates Polarization in South Thailand." Accessed on 7 September 2012 from www.nonviolenceinternational.net/seasia.

People's Agenda for Alternative Regionalisms (website). Accessed on 7 September 2012 from http://www.alternative-regionalisms.org.

Solidarity for Asian Peoples' Advocacy (SAPA) Task Force on ASEAN and Human Rights (2010). "Hiding behind its limits." Performance report on the first year of the ASEAN intergovernmental Commission on Human Rights (AICHR). Bangkok: SAPA-TFAHR, Forum-Asia. Accessed on 12 January 2011 from http://forum-asia.org/2010/Report%20on%20AICHR's%20first%20year%20_for_dist.pdf.

Southeast Asian Press Alliance and Forum Asia (2011). "Joint statement by SEAPA and FORUM-ASIA on Proposed NGO Law in Cambodia." Accessed on 2 January 2011 from http://www.prachatai.com/english/node/2237.

Tepchatri, P. (2009). "จริงหรือฝัน สู่ 'ประชาคมอาเซียน' นกรัฐศาสตร์ ม.ธ. ชี้ต้องฝ่า ๙ อุปสรรค" (True or Not, toward 'ASEAN Community': A Thammasat Political Scientist Identifies 9 Obstacles). Accessed on 2 March 2009 from http://prachatai.com/journal/2009/19880.

Webber, D. C. (2010). "Regional integration that did not happen: Cooperation without integration in early twenty-first century East Asia." *The Pacific Review*, 23, 3, 313-334.

Decolonising the River: Transnationalism and the Flows of Knowledge on Mekong Ecology

Jakkrit Sangkhamanee

1. Introduction

One way of looking and understanding transnationalism is through a study of the flow of knowledge, and how this flow of knowledge instigates transnational flows of power. In the Mekong region, the production of knowledge related to the river has been an intriguing process in which different agencies employ different modes of production—folk and popular sciences—in order to claim for rights in resource access and the authority to manage it. In this chapter, I examine the transnational flows of two sets of knowledge on water management in the Mekong region, namely hydrological science and the local villagers' research. The first part investigates the transnational flows of "western" hydrological knowledge and technologies that came about to determine the development of the region from the late nineteenth century to the post World War II and until now. The latter part of the chapter examines the emergence and the transnationalisation of the villagers' research on cultural ecology of rivers produced region-wide, to counter-act the dominant approach in water management. By looking at the transnational feature of knowledge production and articulation, I argue that the Mekong current is now in a conjuncture where diverse trends in cultural ecology have spilled all over the region, thus creating a space of contestation over the issue of resource rights and control.

2. The Transnational Flow of Hydrological Science into the Mekong Region

The Mekong region prior to the second half of the nineteenth century was almost *terra incognita*, known mainly by "cartographic imagination" (Mayoury & Pheuiphanh 2002, p. 95). It was with the arrival of the French colonisers and their expedition team that the Mekong was seriously charted for commercial and political purposes. Besides the cartographic survey, explanation of the river exploration was tied to the then popular idea of the mission for civilisation through, and for, scientific knowledge. As mentioned in the book by Louise de Carné, a member of the survey team, "the mission of exploration was designed to serve at once the interest of science and colonial interests of the first importance" (de Carné 2000, p. xiv). This mission for "science and colonial interests" can be analysed against the criteria set for membership selection of the exploration team, which represented the demand of experts in the necessary fields of knowledge to serve the idea.

The mission, however, was not only about mapping the Mekong on a macro scale. Rather, as the team traversed its turbulent course, they were more interested

Source: A Pictorial Journey on the Old Mekong (Delaporte and Garnier 1998, p. 85).

Plate 1 A Drawing of Whirlpools in the Mekong by French Exploration Team

in studying and recording the hydrological features of the river from both local and regional perspectives. The detailed description and pictorial record of the geomorphology and hydrological features of the river was, however, not just a process whereby the information was amassed in the way that it was normatively and objectively described. As Pratt (1992) argued, within the procedures of colonial survey, the data collection was set in a way that the information would be delivered within familiar Western systems of natural classification to serve their scientific purposes and the advancement of colonial trade at that time.

The French exploration team's struggle through the mighty courses and enormous rapids of the river was not only focused on gathering knowledge about the river *per se*. Rather than imply knowledge, Osborne (2000) observed, they sought "souls, trade and power" derivable from a conquest of the river. The transnational attempt to map the river, for example, was primarily for the purpose of securing navigational trade with China as well as gaining control over "chaotic" riparian political entities (Gargan 2002; Keay 2005; Osborne 2000). In addition, such scientific knowledge can be considered as a means used by the colonialists to articulate their progressiveness and civility. The period of the survey was evidently an era of transboundary *mission civilisatrice*—the French concept of a civilising mission that they alone among the countries of Europe were capable of fulfilling (Osborne 1996). Through the production of knowledge of geographical features, the Mekong was turned into a strategic space for the colonialists to navigate and, later on, expand their political role in the riparian region administered under French Indochina (Nguyen 1999). The initial flow of western knowledge over the indigenous ways of practices in utilising the river, I argue, was part of this transnational river exploration. In other words, the political agenda of transnationalism was packaged, hidden and delivered under the discursive claims of the benevolence of civilisation and the neutrality of scientific knowledge.

3. The Optimism in Transnational Modernism

After the mission of "civilisation" by the French exploration team, came the mission of "modernisation," with a flood of international organisations led by the United States after the Second World War and the decolonisation of the region marked by the signing of the Geneva Accord in 1954. Cambodia, Vietnam and Laos, as a result of the accord, were granted independence from their former colonial master France. This created an opportunity for the lower Mekong Basin countries to engage in political collaboration and realise visions of economic development across the states. The already-working United Nations Economic Council for Asia and the Far East[1] saw an opportunity in the establishment of the first Mekong state-based cooperation. At that time, the Economic Council for Asia and the Far East was largely responsible for investigations toward possibilities and the promotion of regional trade cooperation. Other international development organisations such as the International Bank for Reconstruction and Development (IBRD), the International Development Association (IDA), and the United States Agency for International Development (USAID) were later established and became involved in the development of the Mekong River through the construction of dams and state-based economic cooperation.

"The Mekong Committee was born in an era of enormous optimism in science, technology and international development assistance," stated the Mekong River Commission (MRC) (2010) on its website regarding the development of its predecessor organisation, the Mekong Committee. The Committee for Coordination on the Lower Mekong Basin, popularly dubbed the "Mekong Committee," was established in 1957 by the initiation of the Economic Council for Asia and the Far East. The commencement of transnational cooperation among riparian states was then one of the most challenging steps as, prior to that, "no international river body had ever attempted to take on such encompassing responsibilities for financing, construction, management and maintenance of projects on an international river" (Mekong River Commission 2010). Eugene Black, then President and Chairman of the World Bank when the Mekong Committee was formed, described what he saw as a "gospel of multilateralism" in the Mekong region "designed to engage the energies of the leaders and the people of Southeast Asia in building things—durable things like hydroelectric dams, irrigation systems, new highways, and railroads" (Black 1969, p. 6; 1970, p. 11).

Many fields of technology and knowledge were employed to act upon the "untamed" river on behalf of transnational projects of modernisation. These

---

[1] A pre-cursor of the present-day Economic and Social Commission for Asia and the Pacific (ESCAP) located in Bangkok since 1947.

included geological surveys, aerial mapping, hydrological and soil studies, agricultural farm experiments, hydraulic and alluvial channel investigation, a study of fisheries as well as the introduction of mathematical modeling for river basin simulation. The United States offered to provide a hydrometric network, establish base levels for surveying, and undertake a hydrographic survey of the main channel, at an estimated cost of more than USD two million. Canada and Japan undertook aerial surveys and mapped the mainstream and major tributaries, while the Australian government was in charge of geologic mapping at major dam sites. France conducted soil and mineral surveys, and many more countries became involved with the production of technical knowledge in the region (Sewell 1968). The introduction of scientific methodology and technology into the Mekong basin, to a great extent, had created within the Mekong region an international atmosphere. As White (1963, p. 415) put it, it was a time when "a Japanese engineer team while working on Cambodian terrain may use Canadian maps, Australian geological studies, French soil maps and American hydrological observations."

Despite the assorted "modern" technical knowledge introduced into the region, it was a far cry from saying that the Mekong was a well scientifically-planned region. During its early decade from the mid-1950s to the mid-1960s, the data on the river were very much incomplete. Many writers have noted the paucity of hydrologic and climatic data as well as a serious shortage of local hydrological technicians to collect the exhaustive, precise information that was necessary to deliver sound riparian project planning and development (Ingersoll 1968; Jacobs 1995; White 1963). Despite the lack of information, however, the Committee had already carried out construction work on various tributary projects such as the Ubonrat Dam in the northeast of Thailand and Nam Ngum Dam in Laos (Jenkins 1968). Though the Committee enthusiastically praised the use of scientific studies and the arrival of modern technology into the region, ironically, the practice of scientific investigation seemed at times too slow to cope with the impatient, politically-driven minds of those steering the Mekong Committee. Once again, in this postwar era, the political feature of transnationalism was re-packaged under the discursive claim of regional modernity and technical advancement of development.

4. Knowledge as an Advocacy Tool

For the past several decades since 1950s, the production and the articulation of hydrological knowledge had become acute in Mekong Basin's post-war development. As we have seen from the subregional perspective, there have been attempts to stimulate a rapid move toward transnational river regulations led by development agencies. This transnational development had been planned and implemented, based mostly on the knowledge advancement in water engineering, hydrological science, as well as the improvement of irrigation technology. At the local level, however, there is an under-represented view on water-related knowledge practiced by villagers of northeastern Thailand at which this section will now turn to explore. This kind of "local knowledge" is rooted in everyday politics within the community as well as related to a wider context of bureaucracy at the national level and the process of modernisation in regional development.

The foundations and functions of knowledge are crucial factors underpinning development practices. In big river development, the use of sole scientific hydrological knowledge and the monopolisation/domination of one knowledge system over other kinds of knowledge to legitimise the development projects, it is argued, often came to the detriments of local ecological and social issues (McCully 2001). The issues of alternative knowledge in water management are now in a crucial position that calls for a paradigm shift and pragmatic alternative approaches in comprehending the issues beyond a single dominated set of epistemology. At this conjuncture, the knowledge of resource management especially in Thailand academic circles has widely turned into the interests of the hybridisation process of knowledge in shaping the individuals and communities' practices toward their community development (Anan 2000b; Kanokwan 2005; Krisada 2005). The question of how villagers conceptualise ecological knowledge has been taken into account as a critique of today's national, transnational, and modernised regime towards natural resource rights and control.

Under this advocacy for community rights in resource politics, social science academics have expanded, if not broadly turned, the attention in development and resource management into the alternative realm of acquaintance in so-called "local knowledge" (Agrawal 1999; Antweiler 1998; Yos 2003). Different modes of ecological knowledge and practices, it is claimed, can be manipulated and used for political purpose in accessing and controlling resources by changing power

Source: Living River Siam (website). Accessed on 6 September 2012 from www.livingriversiam.org .

Plate 2 Thai Baan Researches Derived from Different River Basins

relations among stakeholders (Agrawal 2005; Demaine 1990; Peluso 1995). In mainland Southeast Asia and especially in Thailand, the studies of "local knowledge" often pay attention to how such body of knowledge can be used as a way to criticise state control and monopolisation of science-based policy makings over the issues of community forest, river basin development, land uses, and coastal and marine environment. Particularly in debates within political ecology, "local knowledge" has often been deployed in redefining peoples' identity in accordance with alternative and sustainable development (Reynolds 2002; Yos 2003), the articulation of local resource rights and controls (Anan 2000a; Pinkaew 2002; 2005; Yos 2003; 2008) and the political tools utilised by new social movements in defining resource tenure (Missingham 2003).

Besides academic discussion, local ecological knowledge is also a crucial political apparatus of villagers and NGOs in determining the tendency of transnational politics of resource management. Formalised grassroots researches conducted by local riparian people being affected by development projects are examples of crucial, and obvious, bodies of knowledge being articulated under the debates of ecological knowledge in Thailand and the Mekong region. The key example is the Thai Baan Research of the Pak Mun riparian communities in northeastern Thailand which, after its success in policy negotiation, set a standard for local people in presenting their local knowledge in an accepted research format supported by local and international NGOs as well as academia (Southeast Asia Rivers Network et al. 2004); later on, this was used as a regional model to counter unjust policies on national water development and establish a regional trend in economic and technological-oriented use of water resources.

The first research of Thai Baan—which literally means "villagers"—emerged as a political response from grassroots environmental movement toward the dam construction on the Mun River, one of the Mekong tributaries. The research was aimed at first to counter-balance the hegemonic approach to the conventional form of knowledge production or, to be precise, scientific methodologies done by international water "experts." Later on, the model of Thai Baan research was applied to inspire conduct in other riparian areas in Southeast Asian countries where development projects were deemed to threaten local people's livelihoods (Centre for Children and Community Network & Southeast Asia Rivers Network 2005; Living River Siam et al. 2008; Southeast Asia Rivers Network 2006a; 2006b). It is, however, necessary to keep in mind that in locating this Thai Baan research in the debates of ecological knowledge, it is the politics of transnational river management and the resource conflicts that brought the research to its existence. Unlike Thai-style manual knowledge (Reynolds 2006) which is produced primarily for knowledge transfer, the research itself was produced to counter the dominant paradigm in water management and give villagers rights in claiming their own resources. In the preface of one Thai Baan research, it is stated that:

> "[t]his type of research is essentially meaningful for [villagers] because they can take control over the process of knowledge production and 'write' their own story on how they perceive and interact with their environment and how to coexist harmoniously with it. Thai Baan research presents a concrete example of how common villagers can do and use research to negotiate the unbalanced power relations existing in the process of knowledge production and development" (Southeast Asia Rivers Network et al. 2004, p. 4).

Realising the significance of knowledge in negotiating power relations, this research by the villagers is therefore intended to represent what they see as cultural aspects that had largely been neglected or ignored in river development discourse. By claiming that "without struggles of Pak Mun villagers, this research cannot be realised" (Southeast Asia Rivers Network et al. 2004), the Thai Baan knowledge production itself is politically driven and acts as a part of organised social movement in the politics of water resources.

While Thai Baan research has made a great contribution to the existing knowledge on water management and played a crucial role in the transnational politics of river development, it is however undeniable that there are some shortcomings that need to be scrutinised and taken into account when discussing hydro-related knowledge. When aiming to articulate local ecological knowledge as a tool in transnational political advocacy, there are some crucial aspects of knowledge that risk being left from the presented picture. I argue that contemporary and everyday pragmatic forms and roots of knowledge, viewed as less politically-driven, have often been excluded in the recent portrayal of "local knowledge," especially in Thai Baan research form. Aside from this kind of "knowledge" that is promoted and supported by transnational NGOs and local academics, it is undeniable that are also other roots and forms of existing water/river knowledge which emerged in the local context yet have remained outside the depiction of politically oriented "local knowledge" as they seem to be less political in nature. These subtle forms of knowledge are expressed through the local engagement with bureaucratic procedure, the adaptive social networks concerning water management and community development, and the transformation of religious rituals to fit the changing ways of life in the modernised communities.

It would be a mistake to assume that, by arguing for the collaborative nature of power and knowledge, I refuse to consider the series of confrontational events that emerged within the transnational scenes in river development. I admit that there have been serious malcontents in water management between villagers, state agencies, and transnational authorities especially in the case of dam projects in the region. This malcontent has caused widespread protests and confrontational actions by villagers through village-based organisation and networking with NGOs. Many of these have coalesced into nation-wide movement such as the Assembly of the Poor (Missingham 2003) and regional alliances of international

NGOs. While I argue that cooperation is part of the nature of knowledge production, I do not deny or downplay the significance of confrontational features of knowledge in resource conflicts. In other words, I do not want to present an overly benign view of power and knowledge and create an unjustifiable organic and functionalist model of state-village relations in modern water development. However, I feel that most of research on water development in Thailand during the past few decades has put too much emphasis on conflicting modes of knowledge and the contestation of powers between transnational, national and local levels. Such research may do well in opening space for community rights or showing the successes of the community in confronting and bringing the state and transnational authorities such as the MRC to negotiations. It is, however, the other side of the story—the everyday collaboration between villagers and government agencies—that is lacking and I argue that without an understanding of cooperative features of power and knowledge, the impasse in water management will not be overcome merely through the process of knowledge radicalisation and the transnationalisation of local knowledge.

5. Conclusion

As the chapter explores the process of transnationalism of knowledge on Mekong Basin development—starting from the era of colonisation to post-war modernisation and the post-modern critique of development by local activists and riparian villagers—it shows that power and knowledge are situated in development discourses and practices and can always be redefined for negotiation and empowerment. Transnationalism may entail a process in which dominant knowledge and power can be imposed on locality and enable the dominant authorities to manage and exploit resources to their own advantage. Transnationalism, however, can also provide a space for redefinition and negotiation for the subordinates to seek cooperation from a wider network to counter the hegemonic knowledge and practices that violate their rights and control over local resources. In that sense, transnationalism is an on-going, endless process that different stakeholders can manipulate in the politics of river basin development. It is in this process that, as I argue at the beginning of the chapter, the transnationalism in Mekong development is now in a conjuncture where diverse trends in cultural ecology have spilled all over the region and created a space of contestation over the issue of resource rights and control.

References

Agrawal, A. (2005). "Environmentality: Community, Intimate Government and Environmental Subjects in Kumaon, India." *Current Anthropology*, 46, 2, 161-190.

_________ (1999). "On Power and Indigenous Knowledge." In D. A. Posey, ed. *Cultural and Spiritual Values of Biodiversity: A Complementary Contribution to the Global Biodiversity Assessment*. London & Nairobi: Intermediate Technology Publications/ United Nations Environment Program.

Anan, G. (2000a). *Local Control of Land and Forest: Cultural Dimensions of Resource Management in Northern Thailand*. Chiang Mai: Regional Center for Social Science and Sustainable Development, Chiang Mai University.

_________ (ed.) (2000b). *Phonlawat Khong Chumchon Nai Kan Chatkan Sapphayakon: Krabuan That Lae Nayobai* (*Dynamics of Communities in Resource Management: Perspectives and Policies*). Bangkok: Thailand Research Fund.

Antweiler, C. (1998). "Local Knowledge and Local Knowing: An Anthropological Analysis of Contested 'Cultural Products' in the Context of Development." *Anthropos*, 93, 469-494.

Black, E. (1970). *The Mekong River: A Challenge in Peaceful Development for Southeast Asia*. New York: National Strategy Information Center, Inc.

_________ (1969). *Alternatives in Southeast Asia*. New York: Praeger.

Centre for Children and Community Network and Southeast Asia Rivers Network (2005). *Thai Baan Research in the Salween River: Villager's research by the Thai-Karen Communities*. Chiang Mai: Wanida Press.

de Carné, L. (2000). *Travels on the Mekong, Cambodia, Laos, and Yunnan: The Political and Trade Report of the Mekong Exploration Commission* (June 1866-June 1868). Bangkok: White Lotus Press.

Delaporte, L. and Francis G. (1998). *A Pictorial Journey on the Old Mekong: Cambodia, Laos and Yunnan: The Mekong Exploration Commission Report (1866-1868), Volume 3*. Translated by W. E. J. Tips. Bangkok: White Lotus Press.

Demaine, H. (1990). "Magic and Management: Methods of Ensuring Water Supplies for Agriculture in Southeast Asia." In P. Stott, ed. *Nature and Man in Southeast Asia*. London: School of Oriental and African Studies, University of London.

Gargan, E. (2002). *The River's Tale: A Year on the Mekong*. New York: Vintage.

Ingersoll, J. (1968). "Mekong River Basin Development: Anthropology in a New Setting." *Anthropological Quarterly, Dam Anthropology: River Basin Research* (*Special Issue*), 41, 3, 147-167.

Jacobs, J. (1995). "Mekong Committee History and Lessons for River Basin Development." *The Geographical Journal*, 161, 2, 135-148.

Jenkins, D. (1968). "The Lower Mekong Schemes." *Asian Survey*, 8, 6, 456-464.

Kanokwan, M. (2005). "Watthanatham Phuea Kan Phatthana Lae Fuenfu Setthakit Chumchon: Korani Sueksa Chumchon Lumnam Thi Dairap Phonkrathop Chak Kan Kosang Khuean Pak Mun" (Cultures for Community Economic Development and Recovery: A Case Study of Pak Mun dam Affected Riparian Communities). In *Khwamru Kap Kanmueang Rueang Sapphayakon* (Knowledge and Resource Politics), Proceedings from 3rd Sirindhorn Anthropological Center's Annual Conference. Bangkok: Sirindhorn Anthropological Center.

Keay, J. (2005). "The Mekong Exploration Commission, 1986-1988: Anglo-French Rivalry in South East Asia." *Asian Affairs*, 36, 3, 289-312.

Krisada B. (2005). "Krabuankan Torong Kap Kan Sang Khwamru Thongthin Nai Kan Chatkan Nam" (Negotiation Process and Local Knowledge Production in Water Management). In *Khwamru Kap Kanmueang Rueang Sapphayakon* (Knowledge and Resource Politics). Proceedings from the 3rd Sirindhorn Anthropological Center's Annual Conference. Bangkok: Sirindhorn Anthropological Center.

Living River Siam. Accessed on 6 September 2012 from www.livingriversiam.org.

Living River Siam, Towards Ecological Recovery and Regional Alliance, and Salween Post (2008). *Salween: the River of Three Lands*. Chiang Mai: Wanida Press.

Mayoury N. and Pheuiphanh N. (2002). "Early European Impressions of the Lao." In Mayoury N. and K. Breazeable, eds. *Breaking New Ground in Laos History: Essays on the Seventh to Twentieth Centuries*. Chiang Mai: Silkworm Books.

McCully, P. (2001). *Silenced Rivers: The Ecology and Politics of Large Dams*. London and New York: Zed Books.

Mekong River Commission (MRC) (2010). "MRC History." Accessed 31 January 2010 from http://www.mrcmekong.org/about_mrc.htm.

Missingham, B. (2003). *The Assembly of the Poor in Thailand: From Local Struggles to National Protest Movement*. Chiang Mai: Silkworm Books.

Nguyen, T. D. (1999). *The Mekong River and the Struggle for Indochina: Water, War and Peace*. Westport: Praeger Publishers.

Osborne, M. (2000). *The Mekong: Turbulent Past, Uncertain Future*. Singapore: Allen & Unwin.

_________ (1996). *River Road to China: The Search for the Source of the Mekong, 1866-73.* New York: Atlantic Monthly Press.

Peluso, N. (1995). "Whose Woods are these? Counter-mapping Forest Territories in Kalimantan, Indonesia." *Anthropode*, 27, 4, 383-406.

Pinkaew, L. (2005). "Khwamching, Watthanatham, Lae Khwamchuea: Kanmueang Lae Kan Phalit Khwamru Pa Mai Nai Thai" (Truth, Culture, and Myths: Politics and Production of Forestry Knowledge in Thailand). In *Khwamru Kap Kanmueang Rueang Sapphayakon* (Knowledge and Resource Politics), Proceedings from 3rd Sirindhorn Anthropological Center's Annual Conference. Bangkok: Sirindhorn Anthropological Center.

_________ (2002). *Redefining Nature: Karen Ecological Knowledge and the Challenge to the Modern Conservation Paradigm*. Chennai: Earthworm Books.

Pratt, M. (1992). *Imperial Eyes: Travel Writing and Transculturation*. London: Routledge.

Reynolds, C. (2006). "Thai Manual Knowledge: Theory and Practice." In *Seditious Histories: Contesting Thai and Southeast Asian Pasts*. Seattle and London: University of Washington Press.

_________ (2002). "Thai Identity in the Age of Globalization." In C. Reynolds, ed. *National Identity and its Defenders: Thailand Today*. Chiang Mai: Silkworm Books.

Sewell, W. (1968). "The Mekong Scheme: Guideline for a Solution to Strife in Southeast Asia." *Asian Survey*, 8, 6, 448-455.

Southeast Asia Rivers Network (SEARIN) (2006a). *Rasi Salai Thai Baan Research*. Chiang Mai: Wanida Press.

_________ (2006b). *Thai Baan Research in Keang Sue Ten*. Chiang Mai: Wanida Press.

Southeast Asia Rivers Network, Assembly of the Poor, and Pak Mun Dam Affected People (2004). *The Return of Fish, River Ecology, and Local Livelihoods of The Mun River: A Thai Baan (Villager's) Research*. Chiang Mai: Southeast Asia Rivers Network.

White, G. (1963). "Contributions of Geographical Analysis to River Basin Development." *The Geographical Journal*, 129, 4, 412-432.

Yos, S. (2008). *Flexible Peasants: Reconceptualizing the Third World's Rural Types*. Chiang Mai: Regional Center for Social Science and Sustainable Development, Chiang Mai University.

_________ (2003). *Biodiversity, Local knowledge, and Sustainable Development*. Chiang Mai: Regional Center for Social Science and Sustainable Development, Chiang Mai University.

YouTube and Girls' Generation Fandom[1]

Doobo Shim
Kwang Woo Noh

1. The New Shape of the Korean Wave

The Korean Wave, which refers to the phenomenon of Korean pop culture being all the rage abroad, has noticeably changed in recent years. In the early 2000s, it was characterised by scenes of middle-aged housewives from East Asian countries chasing after Korean actors whom they were enamoured of, from watching television and VCDs. Now, Korean pop (K-Pop) music has become the centerpiece of the Korean Wave, and it is largely enjoyed by teenagers around the world—not just in Asia. It is not uncommon for fans in Paris, New York, and Buenos Aires to perform "flash mobs" to demand K-Pop singers' concerts in their hometowns.

In this new stage of the Korean Wave, transnational diffusion of K-Pop is partly an outcome of socio-technological development. The rise of new technologies such as file-sharing and VOD (video on demand) have made compact disk-based media usage in the last decade outdated. The technology-savvy young generation plugs easily into fan networks in virtual space. Prosumers (producers and consumers of information) post, distribute and exchange video-recorded information on YouTube. With its slogan of Broadcast Yourself, YouTube, created in February 2005, was considered an embodiment of digital

---

[1] This chapter is a revision of an article of the same title in *Journal of Korea Contents Association* (2012) 12.1: 1-13.

empowerment of the individual. When the American newsmagazine *Time* lauded "You" for its annual "Person of the Year" issue at the end of 2006, it addressed YouTube as an exemplary element in the democratic digital revolution, emphasising its grassroots origin and participatory culture (Grossman 2006). Receiving hundreds of millions of views a day, YouTube is ranked as the third most visited website on the Internet, only behind Google and Facebook (Alexa 2012). As such, YouTube has become one of the most important sub-cultural centers of today's new media age.

YouTube has raised the issue of participatory culture and its conflict with mainstream media—such as the issue of copyright, that is, the control of distribution of mass produced cultural products in North America (Burgess & Green 2009). On the level of international communication, YouTube has brought out new issues: internet users' transnational reception of pop culture, such as the transnational fandom of Mexican female soap opera stars and the construction of international online fandom of K-Pop (Thornton 2010).

Since Google bought YouTube in November 2006, media corporations have become official YouTube users, being able to showcase their content directly to individual users through their YouTube channels. They have also made good use of YouTube's social networking services, engaging their channel subscribers to post messages and get alerts for new music videos (Brouwers 2008). YouTube's global reach and easy access also led major talent agencies/recording labels in Korea including SM Entertainment (SM) and YG Entertainment (YG), to launch their channels on YouTube to advertise their artists globally. This commercial infiltration is a strategic move for media corporations to incorporate the participatory practices of active fans. With their enthusiastic dedication, close textual readings, and growing numbers due to easier access to YouTube, active audiences are recognised as a significant part of the fan base. To this end, these active fans became "agents of consecration" (Bourdieu 1993, p. 77), who show loyalty to, and possess particular knowledge of the musicians they follow.

Since opening in August 2006, SM's official YouTube channel has recorded more than 502 million music video views and more than 14.8 million channel visits until 5 August 2011.[2] According to an executive of YG, "YouTube is important in disseminating K-Pop. In particular, YouTube has an advantage in

---

[2] See http://www.youtube.com/sment.

Table 1 Views of K-pop Music Videos on YouTube (by Continent) in 2010

Continent	Views	Continent	Views
Asia	566,273,899	Middle East	15,197,593
North America	123,475,976	Oceania	10,738,793
Europe	55,374,142	Africa	1,924,480
South America	20,589,095	South Pole	27

Source: Jeong 2011b.

Table 2 Views of K-pop Music Videos on YouTube (by Country) in 2010

Country	Views	Country	Views
Japan	113,543,684	Saudi Arabia	10,312,005
Thailand	99,514,297	France	9,707,334
USA	94,876,024	Australia	9,358,642
Taiwan	73,160,633	UK	8,278,441
Korea	57,281,182	Brazil	6,049,920
Vietnam	56,770,902	Germany	5,588,687
Philippines	38,833,639	Russia	1,287,345
Canada	20,859,251	Egypt	630,000

Source: Jeong 2011b.

providing real-time responses" (Ko 2010). Recently, international news media reports that the Internet and video-sharing websites such as YouTube have facilitated the global spread of K-Pop fandom (Jeong 2011a). Tables 1 and 2 above show the global composition of YouTube users who have viewed any of the 923 K-Pop music videos uploaded by the three major Korean talent agencies SM, JYP and YG in 2010.[3]

As shown in these tables compiled by the *Joong-Ang Daily* (Jeong 2011b), the total number of views of K-Pop videos by netizens from 229 countries total to around 793.5 million. As already noted, the reach of K-Pop fandom is not restricted to Asia. What is noteworthy is that non-Asian countries such as

[3] Registered users have to record their own personal information onto the YouTube database. There is, however, a possibility that some may fake their information.

USA, Canada, Saudi Arabia and France are ranked among the top ten countries the most K-Pop video views on YouTube. While we are not able to verify the authenticity of viewers' authentic citizenship and ethnicity, those figures at least suggest the globality of K-Pop fandom.

2. Girls' Generation on YouTube

Arguably the most globally famous K-Pop musicians, the nine-member girl band Girls' Generation (also known as 소녀시대, So Nyuh Shi Dae, SNSD, SoShi, and 少女時代) was formed by Korean music label giant SM Entertainment in 2007. The group's popularity in Asia was such that they attracted more than 24,000 attendees at their two-day concert in Taiwan in 2010. Girls' Generation's popularity is not limited to Asia—it is reported that their USA-based fan club "Soshified" boasts of 120,000 members (Jeong, 2011a). Soshified is a term coined by combining "SoShi" and "satisfied." As such, Girls' Generation has countless fan clubs scattered around the world, with an SM-sanctioned official fan club called S♡E (reads "So One"). S♡E symbolises fans' desire to be "so one" with SNSD, by changing "o o" in "so one" into "♡." "So one" is also an English literation of SNSD's Korean single 소원.

Among their releases, *Gee* in early 2009 is considered the most successful hit single in both home and abroad. It ranked at the number one spot for nine weeks in a row in the Korean Broadcasting System's Music Bank charts in Korea and for six weeks in the Thai charts (Hwang 2009; Kim 2009). Since spring 2009 when SM Entertainment uploaded the music video of *Gee* on its official YouTube channel, 76,649,207 page views have been recorded and 169,093 comments posted until 10 June 2012. *Gee*'s success is comparable to American pop sensation Lady Gaga's *Poker Face* (130,239,693 page views and 129,998 comments on its official YouTube channel as of 10 June 2012).

In addition to the *Gee* music video on SM's account, we can find more than fifty video clips of Girls Generation's various performances of *Gee* on television music shows, their domestic and international lives, and music award ceremonies on YouTube. We can also find many fan-made video clips of dance covers and music covers with their own musical instruments. Considering that some YouTube accounts were already suspended and their video clips erased due to the copyright infringement, it is almost impossible to count the exact number of *Gee* clips.

3. Research Methods and Questions

We used netnography as the main research method in this study. Netnography, which is also called digital ethnography or virtual ethnography, is an online practice of ethnography. According to the *Sage Dictionary of Social Research Methods*, it is "a qualitative, interpretive research methodology that adapts the traditional, in-person ethnographic research techniques of anthropology to the study of the online cultures and communities formed through computer-mediated communications" (Jupp 2006). A Canadian consumer researcher, Robert Kozinets is attributed to have started netnography as a research method. In 1995 when doing a field research of Star Trek fan convention, Kozinets discovered that some Star Trek fan clubs had established their own online communities based on the Internet bulletin board system.

An anthropologist by training, Kozinets adapted the traditional ethnographic research methods to understand online consumer cultures in a series of his research projects. For one, Kozinets appropriated netnography to examine the online fandom of *The X-Files*, a famous science fiction TV show (Kozinets 1997). Since then, many scholars have chipped in with their own research towards developing this online research method (Kozinets 1997; 2006). For example, Xun and Reynolds (2010) adopted netnography to understand the characteristics of electronic word-of-mouth which influenced significantly on the consumer's decision-making process. Jennifer Sandlin (2007) made use of netnography when she examined the consumers' learning process on informal consumer education sites.

In comparison with traditional ethnography, there are noted merits in netnography. First, it provides information that is unobtrusive and without needing the researcher's elicitation. Therefore, a netnographer is at a vantage point to understand "lived culture" that is naturally occurring in an online environment (Hogart 1992). In addition, it is relatively easy to download, summarise and analyse the data online. However, in order to avoid superficial and de-contextualised interpretation of the research object, a researcher must be adept in phenomenological *verstehen* (understanding). For this, he/she should be accepted as a member of the culture he/she studies, to obtain nuanced cultural understanding and interpretive subtlety.

At the same time, netnography poses its own ethical issues. While the anonymity in the fan site makes it possible for our informants to disclose their natural opinions, it also raises questions about their authenticity. Further, there were heated debates on whether online information should be considered private or public. For example, King (1996) argues that consent must be obtained from informants whenever the researcher uses the online information. On the other hand, Frankel and Siang (1999) argue that online information is one that is made public by the informant. From our communication with informants for this research, we concluded that many of the YouTube subscribers were aware that what they posted is publicly accessible. Above all else, the anonymity of informants poses an important question of how to handle the identity of the research subjects. Although we can find their age, sex, and nationality by clicking their IDs on YouTube, we have no reliable means to guarantee the veracity of this information.

Regardless of these concerns with and challenges of using netnography, however, we rely on this research method as it is the most suitable tool to understand the global K-Pop fan culture by examining various modes of fan interactions in the online environment. In order to protect their privacy, we renamed all the IDs of YouTube users whenever we cited their textual communication. We also endeavoured to retain the original texts to preserve the unobtrusive and naturalistic characteristics of the data gathered from netnography.

In this paper, we draw from recent theoretical discussions of online fandom and methodological discussions of netnography to explore global K-Pop fan culture on YouTube. In particular, we ask the following questions: "How do these fans experience a sense of community on YouTube?" and "How do fans articulate their fan identity in confrontation with challenges from non-fans?" For this, we analysed comment postings on the discussion threads attached to K-Pop girl group Girls' Generation's *Gee* music video within SM Entertainment's official YouTube channel.

Since it was difficult for us to examine all 169,093 comments on the *Gee* threads at SM Entertainment's YouTube account, we had to make a selection among such a vast amount of data. Therefore, we selected the first

2,000 comments posted, the second batch of comments posted in the period of December 2010 (approximately 2,000 posts) and a third batch of 2,000 comments posted in the period between June and July 2011—the period after SM held its Paris Tour, for our analysis.

4. Constructing a Transnational Imagined Fan Community

YouTube's primary function is the sharing of video files. Such transaction between uploaders and downloaders fosters the idea of "community." Giesler and Pohlman (2003) examined the music file sharing practice at Napster, in the frame of early anthropologist Marcel Mauss's concept of gift and Michel Serres's parasite (1980). Mauss (1924) considered gift giving as a behaviour which would lead to social network creation and individual integration. Gift giving in social networks does not necessarily involve the reciprocity between two individuals, but a different form of reciprocity among anonymous people within the network. Therefore, by accepting the "gift"—which are video files on YouTube—people feel the social obligation to "repay" his/her network. This transaction of gift giving and repaying is embedded on the whole in the YouTube community, leading to the sense of community.

Different from Napster (where the community is not based on textual communication), the concept of community on YouTube is based on textual communication among users as much as file sharing. What is important about the YouTube channel is not that it is a sum of videos, but that the videos attract users to post comments. In this process of textual communication, "popular cultural capital" (Fiske 1992) is transmitted as gift. Here, popular cultural capital refers to the fans' knowledge about their stars.

When the music video of *Gee* was initially uploaded on YouTube, many novices in K-Pop posted questions on the whole gamut of information about *Gee* and Girls' Generation. It did not take long time for the more knowledgeable users to respond to such posts. For example, when Xenga asked about each member's name of Girls' Generation, Athena answered it in 35 minutes:[4]

---

[4] All extracts are quoted ad verbatim.

> Can someone tell me there names? Cause they're hot xD
>
> 0:41 Seohyun, 0:52 Tiffany, 1:02 YoonA, 1:12 Jessica, 1:41 Sunny, 1:51 Sooyoung, 2:02 Hyoyeon, 2:11 Taeyeon, 2:40 (the one in the middle) Yuri.

Then, Koyashiki revealed his K-Pop knowledge as follows:

> the leader name is taeyeon.........she is wearing a scout cap and a purple jean....my fav is tiffany.....the one that said "listen boy, my first love story."....

A YouTube user MeRetarded responded to this posting:

> That's Tiffany? Shit... I thought she was the short-haired girl with big eyes.

Koyashiki corrected MeRetarded's mistaken recognition of each member's identity, and used this occasion as an opportunity to further disclose his knowledge of Girls' Generation.

> that is jessica......tiffany best pal.....both of them are good in english....
>
> taeyeon is the only one that have some kind a string on her jean.....thats how you can tell she is the leader....and also she always had a strong part at the end of their song coz she have a strong voice....

According to his profile on YouTube, Koyashiki, a 23-year old Malaysian man, subscribes to 179 YouTube channels as of 30 January 2011, most of which are K-Pop related ones. He even uploaded Tiffany's photo for his avatar, which is a small picture in his personal profile page on YouTube.

Novices also post questions about Korea and Korean culture in general, an interest which they derive from Girls' Generation. For example, on Gerald's question of each member's age, Charles18 replied to it briefly. Then, berman58 highlighted the Korean age reckoning practice:

> She's 22 in Korean age, and 21 is her international age. In korea you are one year old the day you are born. apparently Korean age is so complex there are

> considerations to be considered she might just be 20 not sure though^^.

Different from the international age system, newborns in Korea start at one year old, and each passing of a Lunar New Year adds one year to the person's age. As such, berman58 charmed novices by explaining the abstruse Korean practice of age reckoning. Some fans even posted their translation of Korean words and terms in relation to the lyrics of the Song. Sang, whose nationality is Singaporean, explicated Korean appellations in English for those who do not know Korean:

> Oppa is what girls say to boys who are similar in age or it also means older brothers.
> Unnie is the same only girls say it to girls.
> Hyung is the same as oppa but only boys say it to other boys. Noona is the same as unnie but only boys say it to girls.

In addition, when the average YouTube users asked the meaning of lyrics of the song *Gee*, fans who already knew the Korean language competitively (and, also virtuously) posted their answers. For example, Selah asked the meaning of 'bula bula bula' in the song:

> Oh, and another question...can someone tell me what "bula bula bula bula" means? And the point of rubbing fists together? (Selah)

Correcting Selah's 'bula' to 'molla', Mullens and Phantom posted their answers:

> Actually, Seohyun was saying molla molla molla, which translates to "I dont know, I dont know, I dont know" (in a cute, innocent way) in Korean;)) (Mullens)

> Bula means Don't know. Which part rubbing fist do you mean? (Phantom)

This altruistic behavior and expression of gratitude are what keeps online communities up and running. Fans enjoy not only gaining information about the TV show, but also sharing it with others (Baym 1998). Talk of distributing information helps the information-poor and novices to participate in the fan community as well as enjoy the content fully. Today, celebrity talk plays a huge role in social relations, "strengthening links and bonds between people ... and providing common ground for strangers to share" (Gray 2006; Shim 2007). It is suggested that such virtue of knowledge-sharing eventually leads to constructing and sustaining an imagined community of online K-Pop fans.

5. Defending Their Imagined Territory of a Fan Community

Since it is easy to join YouTube, and there are no restrictions on subscribing to a channel, channels and discussion threads are open to both fans and haters. Fans tend to regard themselves as protectors/defenders of Girls' Generation territory, against intruders who post negative and vulgar comments. In this vein, DorinaAmei56 posted what is called the S♡ne nationalist's Oath.

> S♡NE NATIONALIST's OATH
> As a Sone Nationalist, I shall uphold the pride of 9.
> I shall promote the girls to friends and non-worshippers and
> I shall detest all rumors against the girls.
> May our nation prosper for a thousand years!!!

The membership to a certain community is strengthened when its members actively promote the community's credos. Once formed, a fan club should make every effort to sustain itself, defeating outside challenges. Here is one example of fans showing their loyalty and devotion to Girls' Generation by vehemently responding to haters' negative comments or misconceptions:

> I wanna Slap their fuckin cute face! this group cant sing they just sell sex and surgery body ewh!actin cute and girly like chipmunk is so 2000 late hoek. (spikypushy)

> spikypushy shut up ! you dont wanna start a fight !
> these girls are much more than just cute, they are respectful, nice and just wonderful , they dont have surgery body ! If you would take care of your body and train and dance you could look like that !

> They are GIRLS and girls are girly and they can act cute thats totally fine
> These girls are just dancing and smiling like a girl can or should do
> they arent dancing like sluts and they dont look like sluts!
> We love SNSD <3 (mruntouchable22)

> This page is to listen to Girls' Generation's *Gee*.
> Theres no room for your hatred.
> So take your hatred and PISS off.
> Much Appreciated.
> From, the 31+ Million Viewers Who Watched '*Gee*' SujuuiiLoveYuu[sic] (helmetgirl24)

> If you hate SNSD so much, why are you even on this video? thats right. your just a little kid who has no friends and no like. you TROLL. (alaskaroyal91)

A Troll is an informal Internet term for a person who posts a message intended to provoke other posters or to disrupt the channel's intended purpose. In addition to such counters against trolls, some fans actively participate in quarrels out of rivalry with other girl groups. At some point of time in 2010, there broke out a bout of exchange of insults between S♡NE and Blackjacks, the 2NE1 fan club. K-Pop girl group 2NE1, a product of YG Entertainment, was then considered Girls' Generation's huge rivals, with the two groups releasing new songs almost at the same time. Sometimes rivalry among fan club members is reproduced and amplified through heated verbal exchanges on YouTube channels. When a fan of 2NE1 posted an abusive word on the *Gee* discussion threads, countless fans of Girls' Generation counterattacked with furious responses, eventually leading the 2NE1 fan to withdraw from the "battlefield of words":

> Sluuuuuuuuuuuuuuuuuuuuts. (2ne1forever3000)

> So you're trying to say SNSD's sluts and your id is like 2NE1 thing? Go away if you don't like SNSD's MVs or their looks .... (TheVenusVanitas)

> LOL. Who started this? go check 2ne1's vids and ull see that btch whos bashing 2ne1. And yeah for me theyre sluts got a problem?

> LOOOOOOOOOL (beazazama)
>
> shut up.. if you hate them so much, I don't see a need of you coming here to waste your time and post a comment to bash them. (Sujulove)
>
> ur just jealous of SNSD face the fact dun come here and bash on SNSD vids grow up u little kid ur srsly lifeless and u need to get alife soon xD. (SujuWife)

Some of the posts above were written by supposedly Super Junior fans, considering that their IDs such as "Sujulove," and "SujuWife" included "Suju," an abbreviation of Super Junior. Among fans, Super Junior is considered as Girls' Generation's "brothers," as they are also products of SM. In this vein, some Super Junior fans seemingly allied themselves with Girls' Generation fans, striking back the intruders. Different from Fiske's (1989) critical idea of an active audience, these participatory fans have been incorporated by the SM Entertainment's strategic move to expand and integrate different fan bases.

After going through this entire fracas, some fans made petitions to refrain from posting negative comments on rival idol groups' channels, and to behave and respect each other. Here is an example:

> HEY SONEs! if YOU call yourself a SONE. be a proper one, recently, i saw 'SONE' going around 2NE1's videos, bashing them. this ain't the right way to promote SNSD. you will only be flamed back and and the same time, staining the reputation of SNSD and SONEs. noe do you see where the anti's are coming from? no war doesn't mean you have to start one. respect other groups, just like SNSD does. if you see other 'SONE' doing so, please stop them. :) Jigeumeun So Nyuh Shi Dae! (Bezzie46)

A total of 125 YouTube users had clicked the "thumbs up" sign right after the post, as a gesture of agreement to the post as of 30 Dec. 2010.

These activities of defending community are not restricted to the rivalry among K-Pop groups and their fans but extended to the conflict among Asians and non-Asians. In May 2011, some newcomers, mostly from USA, confessed that Zach Porter, a lead singer of Allstar Weekend, brought them into this video. Allstar Weekend, composed of four male members, is a San Diego-based pop rock band, and Porter mentioned that he liked the *Gee* video on his Twitter feed. However, not all the US fans of Allstar Weekend seemed to like the music video. Some negative and apathetic responses written by Allstar Weekend fans provoked anger among the Girls' Generation fans and aroused furious controversy between both fan groups.

According to McMillan and Chavis (1986), community is "a feeling that members have of belonging, a feeling that members matter to one another and to the group, and a shared faith that members' needs will be met through their commitment to be together" (p. 4). In a sense, a community becomes a community through its members experiencing it. Through participation in warfare with its rivals, it is found that members' distinction from non-members is articulated, and shared emotional connection among members is strengthened. In the end, the sense of community among Girls' Generation fans is being reinforced.

6. Discussion and Conclusion

This paper suggests that YouTube plays an important role in setting the new stage of K-Pop fandom. As an Internet platform, it provides venues for fans to maintain emotional affinity, in which the sense of community is being formed. As noted by Hyun-ji Son (2010), emotion is still an important aspect in digital media performance. According to Anderson (1984), media is an important resource for constructing an imagined community. In a sense, the users of the same media will almost never meet or hear of their fellow users, but in the minds of each user lives an image of their communion. This is especially the case with YouTube where members from all over the world surpass physical boundaries to create a virtual network of fandom, taking advantage of the technological possibilities of the Internet. As such, the fans produce transnational dialogues, share cultural meaning, and form affective ties with each other.

Within this de-territorialised and virtual space, fans also help others to further indulge in K-Pop consumption, constantly educating each other using their popular cultural capital in K-Pop. Against outside attacks from trolls, Girls' Generation fans rally to defend and strengthen their online community.

It is known that these kind of online fights between different fan clubs are not

Table 3 Girls' Generation's Fandom

Imagined Community on YouTube	
Constructing Community	Defending the Community
Gift Change	Countering Negative Comments
Information Sharing	Making Distinction from Non-members
Showing Gratitude to Fellow Members	Alliance with Affiliated Fandom

Source: Compiled by the authors.

uncommon. There are, of course, other aspects of online fan community activities such as giving notice on new concerts, raising money for charitable causes, and so on. Our chapter, however, focused on the aspects of constructing and defending the community on account of space consideration.

According to Fiske (1989), fans today create their own popular culture by appropriating corporate media-produced mass culture. There exists a constant tension in the sites of cultural production, distribution and consumption. While media institutions control the flow and meaning of media products, media consumers try to distort the top-down processes (Barker 2004). Possibly because of the innate limitation of the research subject in this paper, however, the questions about a corporate media-organised community are left unexplored, except for a few comments that criticise SM's desire and intention to control the fandom. In fact, more and more corporate entertainment producers are trying to exploit these fan practices by engaging in YouTube to maximise their economic profits. In late 2010, when major Korean television station MBC (Munhwa Broadcasting Company) initiated a new talent search show, it made a strategic alliance with YouTube. With this, it seems that media corporations continue to hold a dominant position into the age of new media by having collaboration with active fans. A Foucauldian approach to power, however, suggests that we should look at diverse ways in which media institutions influence ordinary fans (Gillespie 2005). After all, further research should investigate the power relations between the corporate media and fandom today.

As our main research method is netnography, we did not meet our informants in person, but depended on their postings on the online forum for data gathering. We also acknowledge that while this paper paid attention to fan activities such as gift exchange or popular cultural capital sharing, it left out an aspect of fans' emotion and labour. Such a labour can be expressed in various forms—individual and community labour, both immaterial and material spanning across social, creative, affective and emotional labour practices. In relation to this question, it would be worthwhile to study what implications the Girls' Generation's images in the *Gee* music video project in relation to existing Asian women stereotypes. Further, the method of netnography in this paper examined its audiences as homogenous. What needs to be further examined is an inquiry into modalities of fan practices in relation to the differences in terms of nationality, ethnicity, class and gender. Like most ethnographic research, we focused on a small number of subjects in this study. As such, while generalisation from this study might be called into question, we tried to demonstrate interpretive subtlety and nuanced cultural understanding that are strengths of ethnography. All in all, more empirical research is required on the processes of participation and empowerment of fandom, and its interaction and tension with the ongoing commercialisation and corporatisation in the online universe.

References

Alexa. (2012). YouTube.com. Accessed 17 June 2012 on http://www.alexa.com/siteinfo/youtube.com.

Anderson, B. (1984). *Imagined Communities*. London: Verso.

Barker, C. (2004). *The Sage Dictionary of Cultural Studies*. London: Sage.

Baym, N. K. (1998). "Talking About Soaps: Communicative Practices in a Computer-Mediated Fan Culture." In C. Harris and A. Alexander, eds. *Theorizing Fandom: Fans, Subcultures and Identity*. pp. 111-129. New Jersey: Hampton Press.

Bourdieu, P. (1993). "The Production of Belief: Contribution to an Economy of Symbolic Goods." In R. Johnson, ed. *The Field of Cultural Production: Essays on Art and Literature*. New York: Columbia University Press.

Brouwers, J. (2008). "YouTube vs. O-Tube: Negotiating a YouTube Identity." *Culture of Arts, Science and Technology* 1(1), 107-120.

Burgess, J. and Green, J. (2009). *YouTube: Online Video and participatory Culture*. Malden: Polity.

Fiske, J. (1989). *Understanding Popular Culture*. London: Unwin Hyman.

_________ (1992). "The Cultural Economy of Fandom." In L. A. Lewis, ed. *The Adoring*

Audience: Fan Culture and Popular Media. pp. 30-49. London: Routledge.

Frankel, M. S. and Siang, S. (1999). "Ethical and Legal Aspects of Human Subjects Research on the Internet." Report of a Workshop. 10-11 June. Washington, DC. Accessed on 29 August 2012 from http://www.aaas.org/spp/sfrl/projects/intres/report.pdf.

Giesler, M. and Pohlman, M. (2003). "The Anthropology of File Sharing: Consuming Napster as a Gift." *Advances in Consumer Research* 30, 273-279.

Gillespie, M. (2005). *Media Audiences*. London: Open University Press.

Gray, J. (2006). *Watching with the Simpsons: Television, Parody and Intertextuality*. London: Routledge.

Grossman, L. (2006). Time's Person of the Year: You. *Time* (13 Dec). Accessed on 20 Jan 2011 from http://www.time.com/time/magazine/article/0,9171,1569514,00.html.

Hogart, R. (1992). *The Uses of Literacy*. New York: Penguin.

Hwang, Y. (황용희) (2009). "Girls Generation Fever in Thailand: *Gee*, the number one for six weeks in a row" (23 March). Accessed on 29 Dec 2010 from http://news.kukinews.com/article/view.asp?page=1&gCode=ent&arcid=1237831198&cp=nv.

Jeong, G. (2011a). "Every Nine-Member of Girls' Generation is Beyonce." *The Joong-Ang Daily* (16 January). Accessed 6 February 2011 on http://article.joinsmsn.com/news/article/article.asp?total_id=4932745&cloc=olink|article|default.

_________ (2011b). "K-Pop Music videos on YouTube, viewed for more than 800 million time in 229 countries." *The Joong-Ang Daily* (16 January). Accessed on 6 February 2011 from http://pds.joinsmsn.com/news/component/htmlphoto_mmdata/201101/17/htm_20110117005404c000c010-002.GIF.

Jupp, V. (2006). *The Sage Dictionary of Social Research Methods*. London: Sage.

Kim, H. (김현록) (2009). *New History: Girls Generation's Gee, No. One for Nine Weeks in a Row* (13 March). Accessed on 29 December 2010 from http://star.mt.co.kr/view/stview.php?no=2009031318410269666&type=1&outlink=1.

King, S. (1996). "Researching Internet Communities: Proposed Ethical Guidelines for the Reporting of Results." *The Information Society* 12, 119-128.

Ko, K. (2010). "YG, Checking Real-Time Responses through YouTube." *NewsEn* (27 October). Accessed on 6 February 2011 from http://www.newsen.com/news_view.php?uid=201009150923491001.

Kozinets, R. V. (2006). "Click to Connect: Netnography and Tribal Advertising." *Journal of Advertising Research*, September, 279-288.

_________ (1997). "I Want to Believe': A Netnography of the X-Philes' Subculture of Consumption." *Advances in Consumer Research* 24, 470-475.

Mauss, M. (1924). "Essai sur le Don, Forme Archaïque de L'Échange." *Année Sociologique*, n.s., 1, 30-186.

McMillan, D. W. and Chavis, D. M. (1986). "Sense of Community: A Definition and Theory." *Journal of Community Psychology, 14*(1), 6-23.

Sandlin, J. A. (2007). "Netnography as a Consumer Education Research Tool." *International Journal of Consumer Studies* 31, 288-294.

Serres, M. (1980). *Le Parasite*. Paris, France: Grasset.

Shim, D. (2007). "Korean Wave and Korean Women Television Viewers in Singapore." *Asian Journal of Women's Studies* 13(2), 63-82.

SM Town Official YouTube Channel (2012). http://www.youtube.com/sment.

Son, H. (2010). "Research on the Analog Emotional Communication Appeared in Digital Media Design." *Journal of Korea Contents Association* 10(11), 146-153.

Thornton, N. (2010). "YouTube: Transnational Fandom and Mexican Divas." *Transnational Cinemas* 1(1), 53-67.

Index

A

B

C

R

- Shirlena Huang
  싱가포르국립대학교(National University of Singapore) 지리학과 교수

- Mike Hayes
  태국 마히돈대학교(Mahidol University) 인권학프로그램 교수

- 이상국(李相國)
  서강대학교 동아연구소 교수

동아시아의 초국가적 이슈와 관리체제 값 22,000원

2012년 11월 15일 1판 1쇄

저 자	Shirlena Huang · Mike Hayes · 이상국
발 행 인	임 삼 규
발 행 처	**지 문 당**
주 소	413-756 경기도 파주시 광인사길 85(본사) 110-360 서울시 종로구 돈화문로 82(서울사무소)
등 록	1997. 12. 30. 제406-2003-000038호
영 업 부	(02)743-3192~3 팩스(02)742-4657
전자우편	sale@jimoon.co.kr
편 집 부	(02)743-3096 팩스(02)743-0227
전자우편	edit@jimoon.co.kr
홈페이지	www.jimoon.co.kr

ISBN 978-89-6297-151-4